The Human Race

Also by Terence Dixon (with Tony Buzan) THE EVOLVING BRAIN

The Human Race

Terence Dixon & Martin Lucas

INTRODUCTION BY DESMOND MORRIS

THAMES METHUEN · LONDON

To Alex and Hilary

First published 1982 in Great Britain
by Methuen London Ltd
11 New Fetter Lane, London EC4P 4EE
in association with
Thames Television International Ltd
149 Tottenham Court Road, London WIP 9LL

ISBN 0 423 00430 1

Filmset by Northumberland Press Ltd,
Gateshead, Tyne and Wear
Printed in Great Britain
by Fakenham Press Limited, Fakenham, Norfolk

Contents

Acknowledgements

No book of this kind can be written without the help, cooperation and hard work of many experts. Over three years, in addition to the considerable benefit of working with Desmond Morris, we consulted dozens of different academic authorities and specialist sources in five continents. Here we give them all general thanks and refer readers to the bibliography so that they may follow up ideas in the fullest contexts. Also, we worked in the field with people of many cultures – the Balinese in Indonesia, the Samburu in Kenya, the Yapese in the South Pacific; we travelled to India, Japan and the more familiar cultures of Europe and North America. We enjoyed direct experience of people with widely diverse ways of life – hunters, farmers, factory workers, sportsmen, police, artists and priests, to name but a few. This exposure to such different systems, ideas, attitudes and beliefs was invaluable.

This book must speak for itself, however, and what it says is also the result of the dedication of many other experts – experts in the field of making television programmes. The other producers, Graeme Duckham and Peter Tiffin and the researchers Gloria Cooper, Jill Fullerton-Smith, Deborah Gaunt and Thelma Rumsey worked long and hard at the delicate task of assembling complex ideas and presenting them in an accessible way. To get this information to the screen we were fortunate to have the considerable technical expertise of Raymond Sieman (Camera); Brian Rendle (Sound); Christopher Uttley (Assistant Camera); Rex Phillips, Kris Kalinski (Assistant Sound); Bill Minto, Nino La Femina (Electricians); Freddie Slade (Dubbing). In the cutting rooms we were ably supported by Trevor Waite, Ray Ball, Dan Carter and Terry Pantling (Film Editors) and Bernard Cooper, Ann Leno, Robert Mann and Malcolm Newman (Assistants). Jenny Holt kept an eagle eye on the thousands of feet of film material that flowed through, and Ian Kestle's artwork for the titles and graphics was outstanding. The organisational reins of this galloping undertaking were firmly held by our production secretary, Amanda Lowe, and the Production Assistants Sally Barnsley and Alison Ryan. In particular, we must thank Deborah Gaunt in her other role as picture researcher for the book, Nicholas Jones of Thames Publishing for his tireless dedication to the book; and Ian Martin, our Departmental Controller at Thames, for his unswerving intellectual, practical and moral support for the whole project.

Terence Dixon
Martin Lucas
London
January 1982

Introduction

Being human means belonging to the most successful animal species that has ever lived. *The Human Race* is a celebration of that success story. But being successful involves special kinds of problems and dangers. Instead of hiding in our shells, like tortoises, we have stuck our necks out in so many directions that some of them were bound to be chopped off. Building our civilisations has cost us dearly in human suffering and stress, and we are still a long way from knowing how to handle our enhanced status. But we are miraculously resilient. No sooner do we create a new problem for ourselves, than we set about solving it and, in so doing, drive ourselves relentlessly on to a new level of achievement.

For some, the onward rush is too rapid. Instead of speeding to the Moon, they would prefer to pause, and sit and watch the sunset. This is understandable, for we have hardly evolved at all since the days of being simple, tribal, hunters. Despite our libraries and our computers, our machines and our technology, the body of modern man remains much as it was back in the Stone Age. His brain, too. But that brain was endowed with an insatiable curiosity and a fierce intelligence. Originally it acquired its complexity as part of a need for bleak survival. Gradually, very gradually, as its inventions accumulated, the business of keeping alive became easier and easier. Eventually, it thrust mankind through the survival barrier and into a new world where there was surplus energy and surplus time. We used this energy and this time to explore and to build.

We explored the external environment and spread across the face of the globe. We explored the internal environment and developed concepts and ideas. We built settlements and machines, and we built languages and societies. If we did pause for a while, the sunset soon became boring. The brain-power that had carried us on could not be switched off. The thinking energy within us was part of our animal nature, and we were saddled with it. Our occasional longing for the simple past could be no more than a fleeting nostalgia, quickly engulfed by our burning urge to investigate new possibilities.

Every one of our basic animal qualities was exploited and expanded. Our caves became cathedrals, our grunts became poems, our yelps became symphonies, our small superstitions became great religions, and our real hunts for prey became symbolic hunts for ideals. From small tribal beginnings grew costume and architecture, language and humour, art and science, politics and law, sport and commerce. And as each of these new trends gained momentum, the glories of their achievements increasingly masked the animal drives underlying them. Instead of being proud of our animal origins, we became ashamed of them and even denied them. Instead of risen apes, we saw ourselves as fallen angels.

Some years ago when, as a device to remind us of our humble origins, I referred to us as 'Naked Apes', there was an outcry. I was accused of stressing the beastliness of man and of ignoring his loftier attainments. Since I have great respect for animals, I found this criticism rather odd. And among the subjects I wrote about in *The Naked Ape* were mankind's loving behaviour, his parental care, his feeding patterns, his play and his curiosity. If these are beastly properties, then I am happy to be a beast. Nevertheless, it is true that in that book I stressed those aspects of human behaviour in which we remain similar to other animals. I largely ignored those ways in which we have amplified our basic animal qualities and gloriously extended them. It is the aim of this new study, *The Human Race*, to concentrate on precisely those developments. While doing so, however, the underlying animal drives that urge on our civilised pursuits and shape them in so many ways, will never be forgotten. There is nothing we do today, not one single act, that is not somehow influenced by our primate ancestry. Every cultural flower has grown from an animal seed, and has strong animal roots holding it firmly in place. It is the task of *The Human Race*, while examining the rich blooming of civilisation, repeatedly to remind all of us of those powerful roots.

★   ★   ★

It is often the presenter of a major television series who writes the book expanding the ideas that he has put forward on the screen. The fact that *The Human Race* has been written not by me, but by two of the series producers, may need a word of explanation.

One of the starting points for the series was my book *Manwatching*, in which I dealt with many of the topics discussed in the six programmes that make up *The Human Race*. In that book, I set out my ideas on such subjects as clothing, sport, religion, sex, aggression, art and parental care – all of which are among the aspects of human life discussed as central themes in *The Human Race*. For me to have written this new book would have involved a great deal of repetition. A solution would have been simply to re-issue *Manwatching*, but that would be unfair to the series, which goes far beyond *Manwatching* in many areas. We have therefore produced not one book but two, satisfying both demands. For those who have not read the original book, there is a special, shortened version called *The Pocket Guide to Manwatching*, which concentrates on those topics dealt with in the television series. Then there is this volume, which follows more closely the various programmes.

The major problem in planning the series was one of reduction.

How could we present the whole of, say, human art and religion in a single programme? If we used too many examples, the result would be visual indigestion. If we used too few examples, the picture presented would be inevitably biased and unrepresentative. This dilemma gave us our major challenge. Although ultimately it was necessary to limit the number of examples used for each topic, it was possible to obtain a kind of balance by careful selection. If there are regrets, they are not for what was filmed, but for what could not be filmed – unless, of course, the series had been extended from a total of six hours to one of sixty hours.

Although expanding the programmes, this book naturally faces the same problem. A great deal of the human story has of necessity been omitted. If this were not so, the work you are holding would be a vast encyclopedia. But in each chapter there are sufficiently diverse examples to give at least a sketch of the major aspects of human life we have investigated.

Desmond Morris
Oxford
January 1982

Colour Illustrations

Singular Success

All animals are equal but some are more equal than others.
— George Orwell: *Animal Farm*

Orwell, for his satirical purposes, was parodying Abraham Lincoln's Gettysburg Address of 1863 ('... a new nation ... dedicated to the proposition that all men are created equal ...'). But one animal on Earth is significantly 'more equal' than all the others. All species are, by definition, unique, but there is one species whose uniqueness is so dramatic that it transcends simple definition and puts it quite clearly into a class of its own. That species is *Homo sapiens*, the human race.

This is not to deny that we share characteristics with all the other animals on Earth. All living creatures share a similar chemistry in their basic cellular structures, and an ultimate dependence on sunlight for energy. We share many more complex functions with other species too: we breathe, mate, protect our young and live in communities.

Yet, and this is the theme of our book, the human race is *different*. No other animal builds cathedrals, plays football, tells jokes, gets married, has prisons, writes symphonies, elects presidents or goes to the Moon; nor do they have anything remotely resembling what we would recognise as a moral code; nor do they endeavour to explain their own existence as part of some complex order, or record their own histories. If they did record their histories, most would be works of infinite boredom – 'migrated again', 'foraged for food', or whatever limited range of activity was involved, would recur forever. Having evolved, *Homo sapiens* is the only animal which has developed more than the most basic responses to changing environments. It makes sense to talk about 'primitive' *man*, our 'Agricultural Revolution', and our 'Age of Enlightenment', because our behaviour and its codes change in time as we create cultures, which are themselves subject to constant change. It makes no sense to talk about a 'primitive' *gorilla*. Gorilla behaviour is as primitive or sophisticated as it ever has been.

We have inherited many characteristics from an evolutionary past going back millions of years before *Homo sapiens* emerged. Even the difficult process of understanding language is related to this genetic inheritance: a child can learn words, but his or her capacity to make sense of phrases, to perceive links and breaks between individual spoken words, and to comprehend the meaning involved, seems to be, at some level, an inheritance rather than a pure process of learning. Of course, *what* and *how much* he or she comprehends will depend on a whole variety of factors, including the particular stage of language acquisition he or she is at. But this merely emphasises the complexity of each human being, and the infinitely more complex nature of his or her behaviour within society. We can no longer believe that human beings are born as a 'tabula rasa' – a blank sheet upon which each society will write its own story afresh. Each human child brings with it inherited biases to particular actions and behaviours, and a need for those sources of satisfaction which every culture must provide if it is to endure.

The Human Race is an attempt to track down what these inherited biases might be, and how they manifest themselves. It is concerned with finding themes and patterns, rather than presenting a complete descriptive survey. A comprehensive review of all the data on human activity would have to include all the books, television programmes, magazines and newspapers which have appeared and which continue to appear in their thousands.

Although human social organisation is enormously flexible, the same basic behaviours appear in every human society. We inherit powerful drives to make deep attachments to other individual human beings, and to respect and care for other members of the small human groups to which we give our loyalty. Every human culture must respect these drives. They are the source of all human co-operative achievement. Yet at the same time, these drives energise the terrible destructive wars of which only humans are capable, by unifying one group against the other.

We all belong to the same unique species, yet no two people, let alone two societies, are the same. This book seeks to explore those aspects of behaviour which separate us from other animals. At the same time, it looks for those common threads which weave through all the apparent diversity evident in individuals and societies, both today and throughout history.

Since human beings are so influenced by the demands of the local cultures which they have created, any attempt to reveal these common elements faces enormous difficulties. Superficially similar activities may be carrying out a quite different function from one society to another, and from one individual to another. It might seem obvious to assume that all human beings wear clothes simply as protection against the elements, but closer investigation reveals that in many cultures, clothes do not carry out this function at all. In many cultures, it is equally or more important that clothes reflect the status, sexuality or role of the wearer. On the other hand, apparently unrelated events may share a profound common basis. The unruly soccer fans at a British football match, exasperating to their elders, may far more closely and directly resemble African warriors, the elite of their tribe, than either of them might ever imagine.

Some activities which we usually disregard as peripheral can be revealed as having unrecognised functions vital to healthy human life. The many common elements which link all human sports, for example, are all clues to their common underlying structure. Human beings frequently engage in sports without material profit, or will even pay others to engage in them just so that they may watch. Human sports may tell us a great deal about the kinds of behaviour

Thousands of different human technologies produce the things seen here. The automobile and construction industries alone employ hundreds of them. The great modern city is the ultimate monument to our technological and associated social development. So dramatic and rapid has this development been, that for the last few thousand years the dominant element in the human environment has been other human beings.

evolved by our ancestors to suit the hunters' world in which they lived for so long.

Our need and ability to organise, order and manipulate the world direct us to create culture, the unique human world of symbol and meaning which is beyond any requirements of mere survival. These cultural worlds act, in their turn, upon us. It is impossible to consider what human beings would be like without language, without art or religion, or without technology. Slowly but surely, over hundreds of thousands of years of evolution, these aspects of our cultures have themselves played their own part in forging our species' uniqueness. They are now as much an essential part of us as our anatomy and physiology.

Yet, if all the history of genus *Homo* were to be expressed in terms of just one year, only a few days would separate us now from the long summer of our species' hunter–gatherer past – a summer in which the great majority of our interests, hopes and abilities were shaped, and then immortalised in the genes that are passed down to us. In our modern world, how important is this legacy? How far can human nature be understood in terms of this ancient inheritance? How far are we constrained, in our world of media and motorways, to enact patterns of behaviour laid down in evolutionary time? *The Human Race* examines such questions.

It has been said that for 98 per cent of human history, we have lived in small groups of hunter–gatherers. It seems likely that our modern behaviour reflects inherited biases towards the sort of activities which are intrinsic to such a life-style. In the fertile and well-stocked country in which this way of life evolved, it offered a satisfying and relatively comfortable life to our ancestors. Until game hunting was made illegal in Kenya in 1977, the Samburu people hunted buffalo in a way which gives us an idea of what hunting in fertile country may have been like for early man. After a preliminary planning session, a group of seven or eight men take up positions among the bushes on the edge of the dense woodlands in which the buffalo hide during the night. At dawn, as the buffalo emerge to graze, the men creep with great stealth to within a few yards of the quarry, and the leader finally spears it at close range. It is then cut up and taken home for a feast. The Samburu are pastoralists with a high-protein diet, and the meat obtained by hunting was not an important part of their food intake. Clearly they did not hunt purely to feed, but found hunting deeply satisfying in its own right. (See page 51.)

All human beings live in organised societies. Members of small-scale traditional societies, which live in close contact with the animals and crops on which they depend, often evolve complex and colourful practices and beliefs. This Balinese festival is an example (see pages 168–70). The form of traditions, art and religion in a society bears a logical relation to its way of life. As the circumstances and histories of no two societies are exactly alike, a multitude of rich and varied human expression has resulted.

The human urge to explore and achieve made it inevitable that we would take the prodigious leap beyond the planet itself. Indeed, our unique awareness of and interest in the cosmos has had a profound relationship with our progress. The discovery of laws of planetary motion, in the early seventeenth century, for example, enabled us to contemplate and use systems of logic and order quite outside the direct experience of our senses. Johannes Kepler (1571–1630), who with Galileo described these laws, was the first person to predict travel in space. This space walk by Edward White, 135 miles above the Earth during the Gemini 4 mission in 1965, was made possible only by our ingenuity in wrapping our bodies, and the steady development of 'technology', which started with simple tool use. (See opposite and page 207.)

Spectacular Inhabitants

Members of the human race are not naturally covered in armoured scales, thick fur or colourful plumage, as is most of the animal kingdom. The environment in which our species emerged, and the way of life it adopted, must have favoured our being naked.

There is no one generally held explanation as to why our distant ancestors lost their thick coat of hair. There may be no single reason, but a likely possibility is that as the early man-like creatures came to depend on the hunting–gathering way of life, rather than being herbivorous, they shed their heavy coat so as not to overheat as they chased prey over long distances. An exposed skin surface was advantageous back in those primeval days of strenuous hunting in hot climates, but now the vast majority of us have abandoned the naked condition, except in our most private moments. As our evolution continued and we developed our personal and cultural characteristics, uniquely human, we became the planet's most spectacular inhabitants, progressively adding several distinct layers between our naked skins and the outside world.

For millennia we have triple-wrapped our relatively puny bodies. Using plants and animals, and other raw materials from our environment, we have covered ourselves up: first in clothing, then in buildings, and finally in the structure of our settlements. Naked in a desert, two human beings would appear much alike to an observer. But cocoon them in their habitual triple wrapping and they could be as different as a prime minister in one of the world's great capitals is from a swine-herd in a mud-hut village.

Our time spent naked is so tiny in relation to the rest of our existence – and we are only naked by choice, significantly, in our most private moments – that nakedness is no longer the natural condition of our species. When the first contact was made with the Tasaday people of the Philippines, in 1971, they were found to be wearing simple loin-cloths and carrying-belts, although their technology was that of the Stone Age.

Nakedness is now so unnatural that it can evoke some of the most powerful human reactions when it does occur. To force a fellow human being to strip is the ultimate humiliation. It is a classic technique for interrogation or instilling terror. At another extreme, some people find the display of human nakedness disturbingly immoral, even pornographic. This is fortunate for those who choose to make a living exploiting the shock of ourselves as we really are, but, as we shall soon see, the mere removal of clothing is an unsubtle

This detail from an early sarcophagus in the Vatican museum depicts the biblical version of the origin of clothing.

and rather minor theme in the long and diverse history of wrapping ourselves up. What we are concerned with here is that very diversity, and the complexity with which we transform ourselves and then our surroundings.

The alchemists of the Middle Ages sought to transform lead into gold. But we are all in a sense alchemists of a much more dramatic kind. We take cotton, dye and silk and turn a human being into a king. We take wood and clay and metal and transform it into the house of God. Every aspect of our behaviour has its associated paraphernalia, trappings and settings, each with its own vivid and complicated meaning. Other animals may build nests and dens, but human building and clothing has, uniquely, far more significance than merely being functional.

Clothing

In the modern world, we are so conditioned to humans being clothed that the mere display of naked female breasts and legs can evoke powerful responses: eager interest from some males on the one hand, and bitter condemnation from self-styled guardians of morality on the other.

Let us begin with clothing, and consider its origin and development. Considering the widespread condemnation of so-called pornography, and the ancient biblical association between nakedness and the Fall, one might be forgiven – particularly in the Judao–Christian world – for believing that the fundamental reason for covering up was modesty. But the evidence refutes this. The earliest known garment is on the Venus of Lespugue (named after the site of its discovery in France). It is a narrow skirt or apron which hangs *below* the buttocks on the rear of the figure. Exactly what the nature and

The Venus of Lespugue, about 27,000 years old (Upper Paleolithic or Late Stone Age), is one of a number of small figurines, found widely scattered in Europe.

function of the garment was, is unknown. Very little is known at all about these Stone Age figurines, fashioned in Europe about 20,000 years ago. The obviously female ones are held to be fertility figures and this, the only one with clothing, appears to be wearing twisted strands of wool or flax. But it is hardly a modesty garment. The fig leaf is not the original article of clothing.

The latest anthropological work indicates that the function of the earliest clothing was to carry objects. In primeval times, our hunter–gatherer ancestors must have had to travel over considerable distances. For the male hunters, carrying would have been much easier if they were wearing simple belts or animal skins into which weapons and tools could be tucked or from which they could be hung. For the female gatherers, more elaborate carrying devices would have been necessary. Not only would collected food have to be transported back to the settlement, but if they were to carry the babies, females would require bags or slings.

The further potential of plant materials and animal skins would hardly have gone unnoticed, so another function of early clothing, providing comfort and protection, would have developed almost simultaneously. It seems likely that the genitals were the first to benefit from this protection. They would be particularly vulnerable in the wild undergrowth. As the human race multiplied and spread out from the warm lands in which it evolved, it covered up more and more to maintain body warmth.

Today, we still dress to maintain warmth, and to carry objects in our clothes. Interestingly, most males still carry things on their person, as if they are still hunters who need to keep their arms free,

These young Nuer females from the Southern Sudan (*left*) are certainly not naked, but in their culture it is appropriate to display their genitals in this way, rather than cover them up. The number of bands of beads indicates the wealth of their fathers, and therefore their value as potential wives. A similar disinterest in modesty is displayed by the males of the nearby Dinka people (*right*).

The Human Race

The sumptuary Laws of Edward III (1327–77) required that: 'No bright under the estate of Lord, esquire or gentleman, nor any other person, shall wear any shoes or boots having pikes or points exceeding the length of 2 inches, under forfeiture of 40 pence, and every shoe-maker who shall make pikes for shoes or boots beyond the length stated in this statute shall forfeit for every offence the sume of 40 pence.'

while females tend to have a separate bag for carrying, as if they are still food-gatherers. But these two functions of clothing are now only two of many potent uses to which we put our clothing.

Dressing is something we each do between twenty and thirty thousand times during our lives. But just because it is so common-place, we tend to overlook the significance of clothing types. This was not always the case. A few hundred years ago a gentleman could be fined or imprisoned if his doublet was of the inappropriate length for his status, or if his shoe point did not conform exactly to that of his rank. Even today, there are rigid rules in some societies. It is still taboo for Indian females to display their legs.

Paradoxically, we are simultaneously obsessed with novelty and tradition, and although we use clothing to define and display our membership of a particular group, the rules for what is acceptable dress for that group may change. In affluent societies, this results in 'fashions' (and we should remember this if we think that Western society is free of such rigid rules as the Indian ones). By changing their clothing style frequently, but more or less simultaneously, members of a group both satisfy their desire for novelty, and obey the rules, so demonstrating their membership of the group.

This idea of fashion in clothing is the modern form of a desire to play about with the human shape which is older than one might think. The existence of the cave decorations illustrated shows just how long we have experimented with the human form.

An artist of some 25,000 years ago, painting on the walls of Spanish caves, played around with the basic human shape just as different cultures sub-sequently came to do. These diagrams show the patterns, re-sketched for clarity.

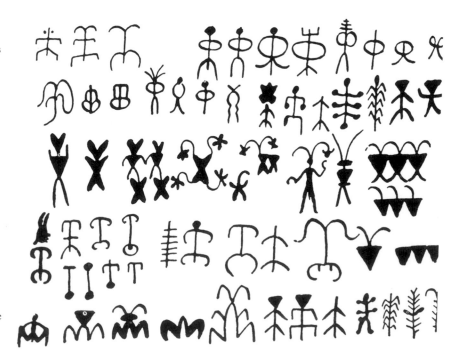

A casual observer from another planet, naively assuming that perhaps clothes were designed to *fit* the body rather than to *disguise* it, could be forgiven for believing that, from time to time, for example, only males had legs, only females had legs, nobody had legs, all females had one huge breast, or that no females had breasts. Certainly, he would think that *Homo sapiens* came in some very varied shapes.

As fashions change, an independent observer might think...

...nobody had legs...   ...only males had legs...   ...only females had legs...   ...females had one huge breast...
...or no breast at all.

How did it all begin? Once the genitals were covered up for comfort and protection, there was a potential to adjust and organise the body's sexual signals. The tremendous power of the visual stimulation of our bodies could be controlled. There is enormous variety in sexual signalling. From the simple and obvious displays, like the penis sheaths of the New Hebrides, or the genital emphasis of female Dinka, to the complex subtleties of modern jeans, *all* clothing transmits a powerful sexual message, even when not immediately apparent.

The garments of the female on page 35 (top left), for example, obscure the breasts and genitals from view, yet at the same time they send out a clear signal saying, 'I am feminine.' This ambivalent, double message is important in the complex social world of modern times, where we are surrounded by strangers every day. What her clothes are saying is: 'I have breasts, but *you* cannot look at them. I *have* female genitals, but they are not for *you* unless I so choose.' She does not deny her gender, but she makes it clear that her sexuality is strictly limited in its availability. If she took a more extreme position, the balance of her clothing signals would shift. If she were a nun, her garments would become free-flowing and enveloping, concealing as much as possible her female contours; if she were a prostitute, she would emphasise the lines of her breasts and hips more strongly.

So a female displaying herself can transform her body in a number of different ways. Usually, in Western societies, she exaggerates the exposure of one patch of skin and conceals the rest. She may expose her legs and cover her shoulders, or cover her legs and wear a low-cut dress that exposes her cleavage, or the main area of exposure may be her back. If she revealed too many areas of bare skin at the same time, she would send out signals that were too blatant, too crude, making her seem so easily available as to be sexually indiscriminate, and therefore less attractive as a potential loving companion.

Far from modestly covering up the genitals, this New Guinea penis gourd is a vivid illustration of the very opposite intention.

Some females may claim that there is no sexual element in the way they dress, but there always is, even if they are not conscious of how it works. High-heeled shoes, for instance, elongate the legs, which makes them seem more sexually adult. Pre-sexual girls have legs proportionally shorter to their total height. The tilting of the feet caused by high heels emphasises the protrusion of the already larger female buttocks. Breasts are frequently lifted to exaggerate their hemispherical shape, and therefore makes them seem both larger and younger. The lips and cheeks may be reddened to mimic the physiological state of sexual arousal.

At different times, in many cultures, men too have indulged in very blatant gender emphasis. They still do. However, historians of fashion have observed that there is a particular persistent element in female clothing which is absent in the male. Grace Vicary, an American academic who has written a great deal about the matter, argues that *restrictiveness* is the most important feature which makes female clothing feminine. Vicary points out that almost every part of the female anatomy has at some time or another been severely restricted. Footbinding, hobble skirts, corsets, and the vision-limiting headgear of Arab women are extreme examples.

The effect of tight corsets on the female body (1: lungs, 2: liver, 3: stomach, 4: large intestine, 5: small intestine, 6: bladder). All this would presumably have been impossible had nature connected the lower five ribs to the breastbone.

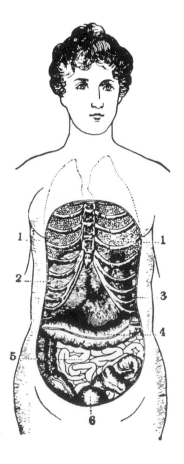
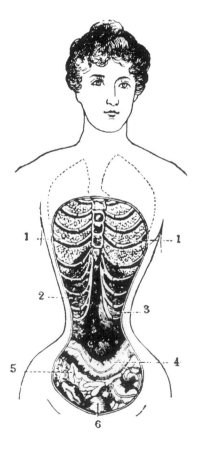

Since female emancipation in the West, this restrictiveness, implying subordination to males, had declined, but it has by no means disappeared. Business suits of the 1950s and '60s have tight skirts which still restrain movement. They are hardly the ideal outfit in which to compete with a predatory male. Even in clothing which apparently allows as much leg movement as the male, the retention of high-heeled shoes severely limits the action of walking (as well as permanently damaging the feet).

Today's more casual dress may appear to have reduced restrictiveness in female clothing, but even heavy boots often have feminine high heels. Nor are apparently 'unisex' clothes truly so. The originally male jeans are now specially cut for the female form. The ubiquitous modern jeans have become perhaps the most overt gender emphasis in modern society. The genital area, although covered, is clearly delineated. The vital anatomical differences between male and female are vividly displayed.

The mirror image, so to speak, of the 'helpless' female is the 'super-powerful' male. Today this is mostly subtle – jackets with lightly padded shoulders, a slight heel to increase height, and so on. But if a male particularly needs to display power – if he is a policeman, for example – then his body can be virtually transformed. Height can be exaggerated with protective headgear. Thick and heavy clothing makes the body look broader and stronger. Boots appear to enhance the power of the legs. Further, an important aspect of uniforms is the display of group membership. The message is no longer 'I am an individual', but 'I am a cog in a powerful wheel, and when you deal with me you deal with my whole organisation.' Uniforms are immediately identifiable beacons of power and authority.

Part of the function of most police uniforms is to display super-masculinity which enhances the exercise of power and control.

When someone embodies super-human authority, it is hardly surprising that his clothing should echo that super-status very clearly. No matter how much religious teachings stress the importance of humility in all things, a successful priesthood has always displayed proud and impressive vestments of one kind or another – clothing which clearly demonstrated their dominant status within the hierarchy of worshippers. What is more, by wearing a style of costume that is a relic of a bygone age, the clergy add the authority of time to their status.

The mitre was not always the exclusive headgear of bishops. In the early Middle Ages other figures in authority such as judges and mayors also wore them (*right*).

The implication is that the expensively dressed man has more sex appeal. Such images as this, where the male is displayed almost as a trophy, are frequently used to sell male clothing (*far right*).

Policemen and bishops are exceptional males and their clothing display reflects this just as vividly as an elaborate tribal head-dress. *All* men display their status with their clothes. With only a very few exceptions, the aim is to display as high a status as possible. Both human sexes look for more than merely physical attraction in a long-term mate. We instinctively look at the parent potential as well. Will this man be able to provide for our children? Will this woman be a successful mother? It is hardly surprising, therefore, that a substantial element of male sexual signalling through clothing should emphasise wealth, position, power, and high status generally. In the developed world today, this mostly means the conventional suit and tie, or something very similar. In other societies it could be a head-dress or a particular garment. Nevertheless, some interesting variations occur.

Some males, particularly in the contemporary West, consider themselves of such high status that they hardly need to display it with their clothing. Many people in the currently fashionable work areas of the entertainment industry or the media are cases in point.

They may appear in very casual clothes, even clean versions of what a manual labourer might wear. There are two aspects of this that are worth noting. First, it is extremely likely that a subtle but important signal will override the apparent message of the casual dress. Extremely expensive shoes or a costly wrist watch will say, 'I have such high status that I don't need to wear clothes to prove it. But just in case there is the slightest doubt, you have only to imagine what this detail cost.' Secondly, this inverted status display is most likely to occur where the high status is conveyed in ways other than with clothing. Rock stars, for example, have famous faces and do not need a wrapping to proclaim their celebrity. A movie director is so self-evidently dominant on the set that any kind of power clothing would be simply superfluous.

The majority of us, however, are anonymous to strangers, and to most or many of the people we have to deal with in our daily lives. Therefore, we use our clothing to display as accurately as possible who and what we think we are. Now that conventions, let alone laws, about clothing are virtually non-existent, and now that technology is so sophisticated and communication so efficient, we have a superbly exploitable potential for rapid change. We mentioned 'fashion' earlier. Being 'in fashion' means discarding clothes not because they are worn out, but simply because new clothes spell affluence. The greater the affluence, the more rapid the fashion cycle becomes. Changes of style are made almost arbitrarily, to emphasise newness. The result is often perversely bizarre, but no matter how odd the wearers may look, they manage to enhance their social status with their highly specialised clothing signals. Clothing transmits a double signal. Here there is both individuality – signalled by the particular garment chosen from the wide fashionable array, and group membership – signalled by the wearing of something considered 'in' during the current season.

Buildings
The second layer of our triple wrapping, the next achievement of that brilliant human alchemy, affects not the body itself, but its immediate environment. Layer two is in the form of containers which we design with even more energy and imagination than our clothing. They can even be mobile. Sometimes, outside our clothes, we wear an additional suit of expensive metal, perhaps as elaborate as a Rolls Royce or a Ferrari; you might call it a suit of display armour.

However, more importantly, our true second wrapping is of a more substantial and immovable kind. Our buildings, like our garments, provide not only comfort and protection from the elements, but also offer the same opportunity for symbolism. Just as the mitre and the robes make the bishop dominant over the faithful by making him seem much taller and broader than he really is, so the cathedral building itself proclaims the dominance of the

Almighty over the lives of the worshippers, by being much taller and broader than any ordinary dwelling. If this is God's house, then the deity must indeed be a giant force.

The larger the building, the more impressive the intended statement of faith. One of the greatest gods worshipped in Western society today is money, and it follows that commercial buildings now tower even higher than those concerned with the ancient

Although it is not one of the tallest buildings in San Francisco (those in the financial district are much taller) the Catholic Cathedral is still a towering symbol.

religions. The time when the cathedral was the tallest building in the city has long passed. Where these new fiscal gods are celebrated, the ultimate competition appears to be to construct the tallest building in the world. In 1970, when the World Trade Center in New York was completed, it achieved the record with a height of 1,350 feet. It was not to remain the ultimate status symbol for long. Four years later, the Sears Building in Chicago took over, with a height of 1,454 feet. Of course, the world's loftiest inhabited building is not there merely to provide shelter, any more than the bishop's mitre is to keep out the rain.

Buildings, because of their size, complexity and relative longevity, have still more potential, beyond protection, and beyond mere status display. The human urge to create finds an outlet in buildings. This urge is very ancient indeed. Buildings initially provided protection but, like everything else in the human success story, soon had more elaborate purposes.

In the beginning it must have been difficult for our earliest ancestors after they had come down from the trees in primeval forests. How did they protect themselves from prowling night-time killers? They were puny creatures themselves, and the killers were powerful and with sharp claws and teeth. Fire had not yet been controlled. So how did they survive the dark night? Perhaps they climbed back into the trees again until dawn. Perhaps they huddled in groups to frighten the killers away with combined shouts and screams.

They may have retreated into the safety of the caves. Certainly, the idea of cave-dwelling prehistoric man is well established as the popular image of how we were before we became house-builders. It is not that simple. Although there is evidence of cave dwelling as much as 300,000 years ago, the popular image of the caveman comes from our ideas of the inhabitants of Europe 25,000 to 30,000 years ago, the time of the Ice Age, and of the earliest known cave paintings. But what about the million or more years before that? In many places, there were no caves available. From fossil evidence, we know we certainly did not restrict ourselves to cave-rich areas. In fact, it looks as though we were builders from the earliest days of the human story. The oldest known evidence of building is in the much investigated fossil site in the Olduvai Gorge in Tanzania and is 1,800,000 years old. It appears to have been the foundation ring of a circular shelter. We know no more than that, but it is startling evidence of the great antiquity of the human urge to build.

In Africa today, Bushmen still build simple lean-to shelters, and this is probably the way it all began, countless years before we started to hide ourselves away in caves. Cave-dwelling may well be only a local specialisation, resorted to where natural shelters were available ready-made. The idea that the little round huts, so common as primitive dwellings all over the world, originated as imitations of our primeval caves, is little more than a wild guess. Round huts

Samburu women construct-
ing a traditional hut in
Northern Kenya.

were much more likely to have started out as tree branches, leant
up against one another like the ribs of an umbrella, and then covered
over with animal skins or foliage. Even apes make beds for themselves
at night, pulling in the branches all around them, so it was hardly
a giant step for early humans to construct little tents for themselves.

Tent-like structures are still popular with many cultures today,
and it is from structures like these that the first solid dwellings were
no doubt developed. As they became more elaborate and grew in
size, they became the centres for family life and the places where
possessions could be kept. They became *home*, the heart of the human
territory. From wood and skins and leaves, round huts progressed
to become stronger, more permanent, and often stonebuilt structures. But although it gained in strength, this form of construction
was still an awkward shape for combining with other structures.

This difficulty was overcome with the major human development
of the cube, or box-shape. By making the sides of the house
rectangular, and then covering the four walls with a roof, it was
possible to place them next to one another, and join them up with
doorways. The *room* had been invented, and the multi-unit dwelling.

Nearly ten thousand years ago, this method of building was already leading to the construction of clusters of rectangular buildings that together made up the first complex human settlements, such as Jericho in Jordan and Catal Hüyük in Turkey. We are the inheritors of that ancient invention, and for the vast majority of us it remains the basis of our domestic dwellings, our houses and apartments.

The remains of Catal Hüyük, in what is now southern central Turkey, shows one of the earliest examples of the crucial development of cube-shaped buildings. Artifacts from 6,500 BC have been discovered, and some archeologists suggest that the city itself may date back to 8,300 BC, making it arguably the oldest known city. Inexplicably, it was abandoned about 5,600 BC.

Modern architecture is capable, of course, of changing all this, of making our dwelling units any size or shape we desire, and yet we have stuck to the ancient pattern, one that has been around now for at least ten thousand years.

The Dymaxion house, pioneered by Buckminster Fuller since 1927, is cheap to build and efficient to run. The relative lack of success of this revolutionary concept seems to indicate an over-riding human love affair with the box-shape.

No matter how successful we are, our houses still contain many ancient features. Around the house itself there is an outer perimeter – the symbolic boundary of our primeval home base, often guarded now by a 'defensive' barrier, such as a fence, a wall or a hedge. Inside is the garden, where we may still grow a few edible plants, even if we are in a part of the world where our food is entirely supplied by systematic farming.

Our sociability and interdependence are now more wide-ranging than ever before, so many people are allowed to intrude into this outer section of the home territory, to bring things to our door – letters, papers, household goods, and so on. Occasionally, they may enter the first of the truly private areas – the hallway, actually inside the solid boundary of the home itself. But beyond the hallway there are still more boundaries, going deeper and deeper into the privacy of the dwelling. These are delineated room by room, each one becoming slightly less available to outsiders. Guests are allowed to enter the general living room, and closer friends may take a step further, into the eating quarters. But, up the stairs, or somewhere more inaccessible, are the bedrooms and bathrooms, the most private rooms of all. The bedrooms are the places where we, the owners of the territory, feel most secure. This is where we retreat, like any animal to its lair, whenever we are at our most vulnerable: sleeping, sick, mating, bathing, or naked for some other reason.

With great wealth, we still obey the same basic biological rules, and structure our homes in much the same pattern, even if we tend to decorate them with much greater care and fill them with more lavish and expensive belongings. Los Angeles, for example, with its movie stars, recording industry and television moguls, has the world's largest concentration of millionaires. But even in very affluent districts such as Beverly Hills, Bel Air, Malibu and Brentwood, the same basic pattern exists. The private habitat may be more elaborate, but if we are rich, we do not build ourselves vast rooms a hundred feet high and a hundred feet long. Instead we choose to live in houses with *more* of the same kind of small room; a little bigger perhaps, but not much. Human needs are very fundamental.

California is a good example of an environment which provides interesting opportunities to satisfy all our fundamental needs. The climate and topography are favourable, and some of the most attractive dwellings have utilised this in a special way, mixing up the indoor and outdoor spaces to provide a more varied home environment. Rooms and 'garden areas' are mixed up.

Sally Woodbridge, who has written several academic books on West Coast dwellings, has made a study of Californian 'Garden of Eden' housing. She has a theory as to why this particular exploitation of a relatively small piece of land was so successful. She has observed in talking to owners of such houses that although they may spend relatively little time in the 'natural habitat', outdoor, part of their dwelling, the time that they do spend there is disproportionately important to them. She attributes this to some powerful 'biological clock that speaks to some instinct rather than to actual facts'.

It is almost as if the house has once again become a little encampment, with shelters and open spaces, but with a rather more elaborate, sophisticated design than any Bushman would ever know. If you have enough money in California or southern Europe or Australia, where climate and topography suit, you can turn your personal home into something approaching a small primeval settlement. Perhaps that is why so many people consider places such as California to be a kind of Garden of Eden. Unfortunately most of us do not live like this.

The third layer
Most of our dwellings are 'wrapped', or surrounded, by not an idyllic natural habitat, but a most unnatural one. The third layer of our triple wrapping is perhaps the most significant of all. This outer layer is the perimeter of our settlement or home-base. Sometimes it is a real physical barrier like thorn bushes, a moat or a city wall, sometimes it is a boundary line on a map. Whichever, it wraps around us psychologically, to give us a sense of safety and security when we are inside it, in the very heart of our tribal group.

This third layer is alchemy at the grandest level: the taking of hundreds of elements from the natural environment and using them to create an entirely new environment on a gigantic scale. The crucial change in human existence which enabled this massive shift from simple settlement to super-city came about ten thousand years ago with the Agricultural Revolution.

As farming improved the efficiency of feeding to the point where there was, for the first time, a regular food *surplus*, human specialisation could begin. Before, *everyone* had to be involved in the business of getting food – just like other animals, which often spend almost their entire waking lives searching for food or eating it. Farming meant that mankind could develop special trades, and whole areas of human activity could flourish and grow.

As villages increased in size, their design changed. The huts and buildings became grouped in special ways, with important central spaces and meeting places: the design is basically the same all over the world. There was never anything regular or geometric about these small settlements. They grew almost organically, as if they were some kind of plants or cluster of bushes. Wherever you approach such a village, or small town, you know your relative whereabouts, even if the actual town is unfamiliar, by the unique combinations of changing landmarks. These alter with each step you take. You gain a rich sense of being in a community. When this pattern is converted by unimaginative planners or architects into a geometrically perfect grid, all this reassurance is lost, and the settlement dweller finds himself miserably deprived of his natural tribal setting, in some soul-less suburb or over-planned new town.

That is why so many country-starved people of the 'developed world' today dream of owning a small cottage in a tiny village, where they can enjoy once more their ancient tribal feelings, of belonging to a small, irregularly placed, territorial cluster of dwellings.

The city as a stimulus

Of course, against this urge to escape to the simpler, smaller settlements of the past must be put man's equally powerful urge to invent and explore new sensations, and to build bigger and better structures – not for living in but for a whole variety of specialised needs and endeavours. Every aspect of our behaviour has its staggering and abiding physical monuments: our work, our sports, our art, our music, our religion and our politics. Each has its towering shrines and temples. We may hanker after the trees and hedgerows, the lakes and streams, as if we are seeking the lost Garden of Eden, but if that is really what we want, all the time, then we have been

The density of modern urban life. Shoppers in the Ginza district of Tokyo.

Female clothing can send out dramatically different signals: modest but alluring (*above left*), completely non-sexual (*above right*), or pseudo-masculine (*below left*). The display of as much of the body as seen in the photograph *below right* is acceptable for a professional model at work, but in less flamboyant circumstances it would be too blatant. Also, it is one thing to appreciate a photograph – but quite another to deal in the flesh with someone dressed like this.

Modern Western-style body decoration (*above*) is naturally limited to parts of the body that are visible, and is predominantly female. Among the Samburu of Kenya, by contrast, the male warriors make up their faces (*above right*), while the females colour their breasts with red ochre, as can be seen on page 110. Only unmarried Samburu women paint their faces.

Sixteenth-century watercolours of East Coast American Indians by John White (*right*).

The traditional clothing display of this Mekeo leader in Papua New Guinea clearly signals his high status.

A view (*above*) of the internal courtyard in a typical house by developer Joseph Eichler in Sunnyvale, California. Outdoors and indoors merge (see page 33)

The Algerian mudbrick village (*above right*) illustrates the natural irregularity of small settlements (see page 33).

Wooden houses in downtown San Francisco (*below*) are part of a varied topography. By contrast, downtown Los Angeles (*right*) may look glamorous at night, but imagine this endless stretch of indistinguishable suburbs in daylight (see page 41).

singularly unsuccessful at attaining it. In reality we have con-
centrated ever-larger populations in the densely packed super-
settlements we call cities. We have transformed our natural habitat
into a vast sea of hard, straight surfaces, with stone and metal and
concrete and brick. We have trapped ourselves, not in lovingly
tended personal territories, but more in little boxes, little cages in
a huge menagerie, where we, our own captives, must live cheek by
jowl with total strangers.

We are not biologically equipped to live in such a way, in populations that go so far beyond the natural tribal level where everyone
knows everyone else by name and no one is lonely. It simply is not
possible for us to know, personally, the thousands who live with us
in the great urban sprawls. They, of course, do not know us, so they
may, in certain circumstances, treat us as if we belonged to a foreign
species – sometimes, a prey species to be attacked or robbed without
compunction.

So a city must have its compensations, or it would never survive.
People would simply leave it and return to smaller settlements. The
positive side of the city is that, with all its specialisations, it is a
wonderful place for stimulation and opportunity. During the past
ten thousand years of surpluses, trading, and, above all, specialisations, a unique richness of human cultural interaction has been
possible. The modern city – appropriately enough, since it is
physically our largest and most spectacular creation – reveals a great
deal about us and our paradoxes. The primeval hunting urges to
strive and to achieve occasionally conflict with more recent cultural
adaptations, which re-direct those urges to drive us to seek more
and more novelty and stimulation. But now we have cities, we cannot
go back, for we know and value what they have to offer.

So, on one hand we have created cities of hopeful dreams, on the
other, ghettoes of bitter disappointments. What can be done to
reconcile these two apparently inevitable but fiercely contradictory
elements of the modern urban world? The fault lies not so much
with the design of the buildings themselves, but the sheer size of
the city. Man the primeval hunter, turned man the worker, is still
a tribal animal, but he is now living in a super-tribe. As the numbers
grew and the cities expanded, they were fulfilling the super-stimulus
function, but to accommodate the people they either went upwards
in high impersonal blocks, or outwards in sprawling, centreless
suburbs. In both cases, a sense of local identity was lost.

Biologically, the ideal city would be one in which a compact,
central area provided all the super-stimulation and excitement that
our inventive genius requires, with a ring around it of separate and
distinct living centres: small complete towns with their own smaller
centres, with enough space for a full family life, and with small local
industries. Then, perhaps, the population could have the best of
both worlds.

At the moment, almost every big city has the two, stimulus and home-territory, mixed up together, with commuter chaos, alienation, stress and crime. Buildings are such long-lasting objects. It takes an age to change things, even when it is clear what must be done. In the meantime, each great city has to face the problem its overgrown bulk has created.

Los Angeles is an excellent example of the problem. It just spread out in all directions, laying concrete over orange groves with hardly any focal points at all. It is possible to drive for over twenty miles in almost any direction through seemingly endless, almost featureless vistas. Section after section merges together in a stream of low-rise concrete boxes. Two-thirds of the entire city space is devoted to the automobile, one-third in freeways and roads, one-third in car-parks.

Some of the freeways are exciting and spectacular, and of course, they are essential to the life of Los Angeles, because cities have always been unconsciously constructed according to how long it takes a human being to cross them. To be a definable entity at all, the super-stimulus part of the city must be crossable in about one hour. Cities grew in parallel with the speed of transport, so they have been, at appropriate times, either walking size or horse-drawn size. Los Angeles is perhaps the only great city of the world that is automobile size. It developed recently enough to accommodate itself to non-animal, private transport. But the motor car has been with us infinitely less than the blink of an eye in evolutionary time – the Model T Ford began mass production in 1907 – and is now seriously threatened. The car is a very mixed and questioned blessing, and with hindsight we can see the dangers of building an environment which is almost totally dependent on it.

So, even in California where the climate and so many of the special natural features are agreeable to the human race in one sense, the human race in the other sense – the race to transform and interfere – can lead to enormous problems. But just as Los Angeles can serve as a warning, so the other great city of the Golden State, San Francisco, can provide a more optimistic lesson. Excluding the wealthy, the star-struck and those who have no choice, there is a strong preference for San Francisco over Los Angeles as a place to live – or even as a place to visit. Why should this be? The two are both large cities: Los Angeles has 6,700,000 people, San Francisco 3,150,000. The reasons are accidental but important.

San Francisco, the senior West Coast city, grew up accidentally, little by little. Los Angeles was more of a boom-town explosion, thanks to the success of its motion picture industry. It spread like a forest fire along the coast. In 1880, the population of San Francisco was 234,000, compared to 11,000 in Los Angeles. By 1930, Los Angeles was twice the size of San Francisco, with 1,238,000 to 634,000. Although both cities have their excitements and their good qualities, San Francisco seems, from a biological point of view, to win on two main points: scale and layout.

Downtown Los Angeles: a
seemingly endless urban
sprawl.

Downtown San Francisco: more landmarks. You know where you are.

Unlike Los Angeles, San Francisco grew up before the advent of the internal combustion engine, and therefore has a very different scale. The city clearly dominates the motor car, with feet and cable cars almost as important as means of transport. This results in a more human scale for the city centre, one that can be grasped by the human animal as it moves about inside the downtown region.

The layout, the topography, is also important. San Francisco is loaded with landmarks and special local features, so that wherever you are, you *know* where you are, just by glancing at the horizon. The city is very hilly, giving characteristic changing angles and slopes as you move about. The Bay provides not just a water's edge, but a uniquely distinctive water's edge, full of easy-to-remember detail.

The topography of San Francisco gives it a double advantage over Los Angeles. Not only does it provide the city with its unique shape but it also, because of the surrounding areas of water, isolates the suburbs from the main city centre. This means that instead of growing outwards as a great, characterless sprawl, they were forced to develop as separate entities with their own social centres and their own local characteristics. Sausalito, Marin County, Berkeley, Menlow Park, Oakland, and the rest each had to become its own separate community, but at the same time had access to the city centre, the place for the great social excitements: theatres, museums, stadia, great shopping stores, restaurants. The inhabitant, whilst living in an attractive local community, can also enjoy the big city whirl. Unlike so many modern citizens, he can have it both ways.

Surveys we made and analysed reinforce the biological theory and the general reputations of the two great cities. The figure for people 'very satisfied' with their city was twice as high in San Francisco as it was in Los Angeles. The rate of dissatisfaction was over five times higher in Los Angeles. If these percentages apply to the population as a whole, then over two million Los Angeleans out of today's population of seven are unhappy with their city. Citizens in many of the other great centres of population around the globe feel much the same way, but we and they should remember that the motor cars, fossil fuels, concrete boxes and all the technological wonders that are part of urban life are neither good nor bad *in themselves*.

The city-dweller has to balance the crowding, pollution and high cost (oil-rich Arabs are the most likely buyers of some expensive London houses) against the stimulation and opportunity that the concentration of people and resources provide.

The danger of our ingenuity
The unbearably high density of human bodies in such cities is at the root of the problem. An increasingly high number of people are beginning to feel that they are living not so much in the freedom of a technological Garden of Eden, as in a teeming, restrictive Human Zoo.

We can blame the Agricultural Revolution, the Industrial Revolution, the planners, or the gods, for removing us from the Garden of Eden, from the biological inheritance of a million years in the open air. We are *all* responsible. The human race is relentless, inventive and dynamic. We think and talk and act and interfere with everything, and we breed with ferocious efficiency. Human alchemy has transformed the environment until what we have made of it begins to dominate us.

In the end, our resilience and ingenuity must also help us to find solutions to the problems we have created for ourselves. We will find ways to beat the problems. We already do it in a thousand small ways: the apartment dwellers, tending their indoor plants or their tiny window boxes of flowers, put back into their world a little symbolic reminder of the wild vegetation that once surrounded them; the joggers in the streets run again, like hunters on the chase; the children playing in the park rediscover the natural elements of earth and sand. Each in his own way keeps in touch, however symbolically, with his ancient inheritance.

No matter how far down the road the human race takes us towards a brave new world, we are still breathing, eating, sleeping, copulating, living primates, highly evolved mammals whose giant brain is at once our towering strength and our dangerous weakness. Curiosity may have killed the cat, but it has been the making of the human race, and it is our greatest single attribute. It has also forced us to walk a tightrope, one which gets higher and higher with each startling new discovery. To slip now could be lethal, possibly for the whole species, but our biological inheritance has endowed us with a wonderful sense of balance. The way we use this inheritance, combined with our startling ingenuity, is the subject of this book.

CHAPTER 3

Masked Hunters

Hunters or killers?

The concept of 'Man the Hunter' has attracted criticism recently. Some people have felt that the idea of *Homo sapiens* as 'killer apes' is somehow derogatory, yet to deny it is misleading when we study our own behaviour. It has been argued that in an apparently violent modern world too much emphasis has been placed on our species' hunting inheritance, as if it condoned forms of violence other than the killing of prey for food.

Kalahari Bushmen;
1980 Olympics.

While it is certainly true that our species has always been opportunistic – quite prepared to scavenge already-predated meat, to raid nests for eggs or fledglings, to capture easy prey such as crustaceans and so on – the overwhelming evidence is that for more than 98 per cent of its entire existence so far, *Homo sapiens* has relied on energetic hunting as a basic survival strategy. We make a mistake if we ignore this evidence, for it is a key to a great deal of our behaviour. Today, we are not hunters 'red in tooth and claw', but we are certainly masked hunters, symbolic hunters.

We must avoid a confusion. We are 'killer apes' in that we kill to eat. We still do, even if remotely. Our roast beef does not commit suicide. But it does not follow that we are biologically programmed to be savage beasts, innately destined to roam about indiscriminately killing each other. Human aggression is discussed in Chapter 5, so it is appropriate here to consider other evidence about the nature and importance of our long hunting past.

From Tanzania, there is evidence of bipedalism between three and four million years ago. This distinctively proto-human two-

The bleeding pit in an abattoir. Most of us have become so unaccustomed to this aspect of meat-eating that we find such sights distressing.

The huntsman and his dog (*above*): an association thousands of years old.

An Australian spear fisherman (*below*) with his prey caught off the Great Barrier Reef (see page 52).

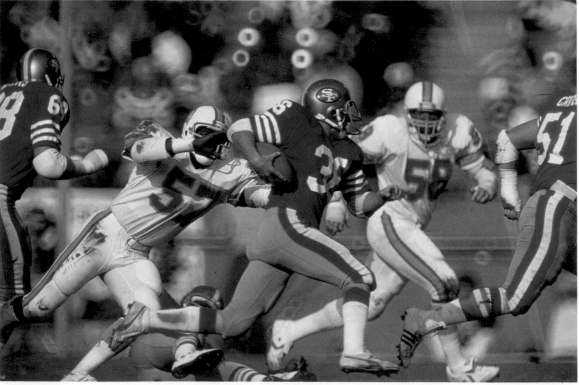

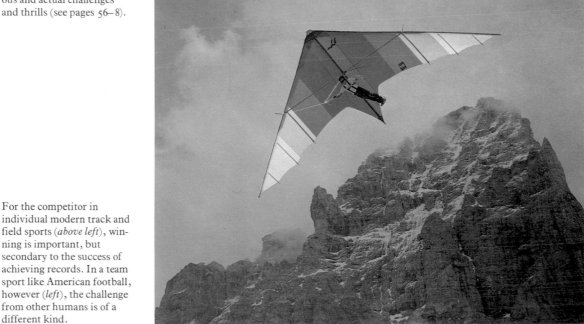

The increasing interest in elaborate danger sports (*above*, *right* and *overleaf*), among both spectators and participants, is the result of television, increasing affluence and leisure. Such sports provide both vicarious and actual challenges and thrills (see pages 56–8).

For the competitor in individual modern track and field sports (*above left*), winning is important, but secondary to the success of achieving records. In a team sport like American football, however (*left*), the challenge from other humans is of a different kind.

legged stance and gait is unique in the whole class of mammals. More than two million years ago, according to fossil records, our pre-human ancestor *Australopithecus africanus* had stone tools and was eating meat. By one and a half million years ago, our own genus *Homo* was well established, with a large brain. All these ancient developments in the evolutionary story cannot be separated from the behaviour that must have been associated with them. Bipedalism itself, for example, had a multiplicity of behavioural advantages. It facilitated better all-round vision and faster travel over longer distances, and it freed the hands for tool use and carrying. It also causes unique anatomical difficulties in giving birth, so that babies have to be born in a characteristically underdeveloped condition. The human brain, for example, is only a third of its full-grown size at birth. This in turn necessitates the long period of parental care and teaching. As our ancestors came to depend more and more on learning to achieve success, there was an evolutionary pressure to increase learning capacity – intelligence.

By more than a million years ago, then, we have ancestors highly adapted to exploit their environment, with weapons, tools, and the large brains which developed in parallel with hunting. It is important to remember that human hunting is a very complex behaviour, infinitely more complicated than the vegetarian or scavenging patterns that preceded it. Human hunting involves planning, communication, co-operation, co-ordination, and systems of distribution, all of which required considerable intelligence. Again, in this indivisible process, adding meat to a vegetarian diet was in itself a spur to further development. Meat is rich in protein and fats; it can be dried and stored against hard times. A very little of it can supply the same amount of food value as a great deal of fruit and vegetables, which are time-consuming to gather and eat. So the hunting way of life allowed more time to explore and be curious.

The evidence of contemporary observation is significant as well. We know that agriculture and the consequent rush to the civilisation and population levels that we have today is an extremely recent development in our species' long history. Therefore, what we are today must be the result of *millions* rather than *thousands* of years of evolution. If we look at ourselves, what do we see? A species with a hunger for achievement, a love of thrill and risk, a physiological need for strenuous exercise, and an athletic, muscular anatomy, as different from the foraging monkeys as the eagle is from the scavenging buzzard. We just could not be as we are – physically or mentally – if we had evolved as passive scavengers.

Sports

Human sports are an essential clue as well. Although individuals may choose not to participate, there is scarcely any civilisation that is without a developed interest in some activities that could broadly be considered sports. The more complicated the culture, the more

Some of the seven thousand participants in the 1981 London Marathon. This is but one example of the recent awareness of our biological need for physical exertion. The New York Marathon of the same year attracted fourteen thousand.

complicated and various the range of sporting behaviour, of symbolic, masked, hunting.

For some, even in the developed world, the ancient hunting pattern itself is kept alive, in the form of blood sports. Even though the killing of prey in this way is no longer a matter of survival, it is retained as a lethal pastime, the animal victims such as grouse or pheasant often being eaten as luxury foods. All over the world, millions of amply nourished people – three million in Britain alone – enjoy 'hunting' for fish, although most anglers would not describe it in this way. Sports fishers will often use the lightest tackle to prolong the struggle of the fish or set off into the deep sea to find larger, more difficult prey. Certain fish can be caught with ease and certainty by using as bait a fragment of a gland from another fish. But this is so seriously frowned upon as 'unsporting' that it is hardly ever done. Clearly, a personal sense of mastery, a delight in exercising the skills of the hunter, is more important than the food that is obtained in this way. Many anglers even hunt inedible prey, as do all fox hunters, who list all kinds of ecological excuses for enjoying the exhilaration of the chase and the excitement of the kill.

The rapid urban growth which followed the Agricultural Revolution might have frustrated the sporting instincts of the new city-dwellers, but the ancient Romans avoided the problem nearly two thousand years ago, with a device which is still very much with us today. The great Colosseum brought the hunt to the people by confining it in an arena. The arena not only compressed the hunting field, but also intensified the activity itself. Five thousand wild beasts, imported from many parts of the world, were slaughtered on the Colosseum's opening day.

There were also *human* victims in that great amphitheatre. When considering this, however, remember that the Romans were a dominant race with rigid hierarchies. The lowest levels in their *own* hierarchies were scarcely considered human, and rebellious outsiders were regarded as a legitimate prey species. The hunting down of Christian prey in the arena not only intimidated that group, but also reinforced to the audience the power and control of the rulers.

The climax of the primeval hunt was always group celebration, with praise and admiration for the victorious hunters. The hunters were always a minority in the tribe, but everybody shared in the event at the end. As the hunts became more symbolic, they were incomplete without spectators to share in the triumph of the winners.

There are still parts of the world where systematic killing of animals for sport is quite widespread, from cock fighting to bull fighting. For most human beings, however, this is as distasteful as the direct killing of animals for food has become. Modern societies now employ specialist farmers and slaughterers to do their food killing, but retain vigorous, fast moving or even dangerous sports involving animals, often related to the work of the area, like the Calgary Stampede, celebrating the tough, rumbustious life-style of

the cowboys, or the Grasmere Games in Britain, reflecting the farming life-style of the Lake District.

Animal sports are important, but are by no means the predominant part of the picture. The origin of those track and field sports which now have their ultimate exposition in the Olympic Games is more closely linked to the *human* behaviour forged during the long hunting period.

The earliest sporting 'meetings' (as they are still often called) were probably ritualised competitive celebrations or re-enactments of important everyday skills, used to add spice and interest to routine gatherings. Present day events such as Calgary and Grassmere contain such elements, and even at the Olympic Games, the number of aiming, throwing, running – that is to say, specific *hunting* – activities is overwhelming.

The difference now is that the hunting has become totally symbolic; today's masked hunters find human competition more demanding and satisfying than competition involving only animals. Some sports contain a strong element of the symbolic kill. These combat sports, from wrestling, boxing and the martial arts to more

Copies of this early-twentieth-century re-construction, by the contemporary archeologist Professor Nispi-Lane, of the Flavian Colosseum were sold as souvenirs to tourists. The original caption read 'The great hunt of the wild beasts.'

The Human Race

The fell race, highlight of
the annual games at Gras-
mere, in the northern English county of Cumbria.
It takes about nine minutes
to struggle to the top of the
fell, and a mere three to
hurtle down again.

Calgary Stampede

abstract versions such as tennis, are certainly ritualised fighting, but
there is much more to them than that. Even the most violent combat
sports have stringent *rules*, designed to prevent serious injury, and
a referee of some kind to see that the rules are observed. We should
never overlook the fact that the objective is 'victory', rather than
the 'destruction of the opponent'. Yet sport is the only widely
admired and valued area of human activity which is solely based on
success at the expense of others.

The terminology is often quite specific. Soccer – and chess –
players 'attack' or 'defend'; cricket has its 'strike' bowlers and its
'leg traps'. When V. J. Armitraj lost to Jimmy Connors during a
recent Wimbledon tennis tournament, his defeat was blamed by the
commentators on his lack of 'killer instinct'.

For poets, painters, engineers or architects, the attainment of goals
is inherently unsullied in this way. That is why most sports have a
massive compensating factor built in: the ideal of sportsmanship.
Being a good sport, or playing the game, is a necessary paradox.
Because sport has such a powerful negative element in it, there
is a universal convention whereby the victor honours the defeated
opponent.

Before and after bouts of
ritualised fighting, judo
players bow solemnly to
emphasise that their
relationship is one of mutual
respect rather than personal
antagonism.

For over a hundred years
wooden staves have
replaced swords in the
Samurai-based Martial Art
of Kendo. Today, swords
are used only privately and
without the approval of
the Japanese Government.

Since positive striving for success is the predominant aspect, just competing against a fellow human being is often not challenging enough. Many sports involve competition not merely against rival athletes, but against the absolute elements of time and distance. In many cases, the winner of an event may not be in doubt; the contest is between the athlete's own body and the all-important record book. The whole apparatus of international competition and highly publicised records enables a competitor in a single race to take on not just a few opponents but, in effect, the entire world.

The need for risk

Sport has always embraced sophisticated human technology and used it to provide new challenges and new absolutes to take on. Only human beings can race each other at more than 150 miles per hour. Although motor racing is little more than a mechanised version of one element of the hunt, the chase, it embodies such a high risk factor that it captivates many of today's masked hunters. Death is one opponent we will never ultimately outrun. The certainty of eventual death is uniquely human knowledge, so we enjoy seeing death-defying exploits and even narrow escapes. We love to breathe a sigh of relief as we watch a fellow member of the human race challenging our greatest enemy.

Lloyds of London regard a Formula I driver as the highest risk in the life insurance business, at more than five times the average. A premium for a driver would be twice that of a mountaineer or intrepid explorer, and nearly three times that of a skydiver.

In an interview, racing driver Jackie Stewart described the experience of risk-taking, and perhaps explains why human beings *need* an element of risk, which they can often achieve sufficiently merely by watching others:

'I think what happens to a man when he drives a racing car is what happens when anybody gets very excited doing anything: adrenalin pumps. The fluid rushes through your system and gives you a tremendous tingling feeling. I think when a man is so high adrenalin-wise, things are so close in his senses. This is a very unique thing to motor racing. That's what it does to me. I see things very clearly. I see people very clearly. At the speed I'm doing, I can still pick out individual photographers or somebody moving the wrong way or an umbrella going up in the grandstand. You may see five thousand people in a grandstand, and suddenly one raises an umbrella. If things like that are being seen at speeds of, say, a hundred and fifty or sixty miles per hour, there is something odd with the man's system.'

Perhaps if risk-taking sharpens the clarity of our vision, this is because, during our evolutionary development, we became tuned into a high-risk way of life. A human existence that is too snug and secure is too tame for our nature. Too much safety dulls the human mind. Perhaps the human race just has to keep racing, if it is to respond fully to its animal heritage.

For a long time, most high-risk sports were much more for the participant than the spectator. It was hard to see the conquest of a mountain, or the whole of a long downhill ski race. Now, thanks to media coverage, they are very popular with the modern sports fan. The ultimate arena has become the domestic television set.

There is, however, a category of sports which is the most popular of all. Significantly, it is the most complicated. It seems that nothing is as rewarding or interesting to us as the interlocking of two opposing *teams*.

Team games of all kinds demonstrate how much more stylised and elaborate than its ancient origin masked hunting has become. The contests are designed specifically so that the participants are actually prevented from achieving their objectives by organised groups of opponents. They can even be thrown to the ground. The players not only have to display bravery, athletic prowess, throwing or aiming skills and the ability to vanquish opponents. In the process of the game they have also to obey many stringent and seemingly illogical rules which make their task even more complicated. We have mentioned rules intended to prevent injury. These are different. Soccer players may not pass the ball to a colleague who is behind the opposing defence. Rugby players have to pass the ball backwards. Basketball players cannot move without bouncing the ball. . . .

The way that these difficulties are overcome is, of course, through co-operation between players on the same side. This is what makes the modern team game, however abstract or complex, so satisfying, so symbolically in touch with our evolutionary heritage. Many successful predators hunt in packs, relying on mutual co-operation, flexibility and clever strategies, even more than on their essential athleticism. Some people today enjoy these largely mental aspects of the old hunting pattern in their own right, preferring indoor intellectual sports such as chess or bridge. But the most popular sport in the contemporary world is soccer – the perfect analogue to the primeval hunt. Here, rich in symbol and ritual, are all the vital ingredients; the planning, the strategy, the unpredictability, the running, the aiming, the goal, and the ecstatic celebration. Here is the all-male hunting pack in full cry.

Work

Top soccer stars are public heroes in the 146 countries where the game is played, because the mass of spectators in the real or electronic arenas can share in their vigorous life-style as the ultimate pseudo-hunters. Although they are called 'players', they are in fact professionals. Football is their everyday job of work, but most of us do not think of it as such because it seems so dramatic and fulfilling. Very often we think of work as a boring necessity, the opposite of

The annual Shrovetide 'football' game, which has been played at Ashbourne, in Derbyshire, for centuries. Over two days, the 'uppers' from one end of the town grapple with the 'downers' from the other. As in many early versions of football, the teams' object is to be in possession of the ball when a common goal is reached. Today, it would be chaotic if such unregulated games were frequent and widespread, so the modern descendant has complex rules to make the contest more stylised and formal.

Constable's 'The Haywain' (1821) and Lowry's 'The Lake' (1951) are expressive interpretations of life before and after the Industrial Revolution.

Most British coastal resorts – such as Skegness – owe their expansion to the explosion of annual holidays which accompanied the Industrial Revolution. The poster was issued by the Great Northern Railway *c.* 1920. Now, travel horizons have widened. In these days of jet travel and packaged tours, it seems, ironically, that 'you've made it' when you can afford to take your vacation in a place of almost primeval beauty, unspoiled by millennia of civilisation. That is the message of the advertisement (*bottom*).

Pink sands at North Beach, Harbour Island.

For the past ten years, perhaps, it was Greece. Or Spain, France, Italy.

Now, this year, give yourself the trip you've earned. The one you've been working for. The one you'll remember all your life.

The Bahamas. A place like nowhere else on earth.

Bask in Nassau's cool, colonial history. Rub shoulders with the high rollers in Freeport's casinos, nightclubs and restaurants.

Lose yourself in the tranquillity of our 700 beautiful Family Islands, with exotic names like Bimini, Crooked Island and Exuma Cays.

Wind-surfing, sailing, sub-aqua. Beautiful things to buy. Sumptuous places to stay. Fly by one of the four scheduled direct flights that leave London every week, or via anywhere in the USA.

The fabulous Bahamas. From only £400 for a fortnight. When you arrive, you'll know you've arrived.

BAHAMAS
It's better in The Bahamas

THE BAHAMAS. YOU'LL NEVER WANT TO LEAVE.

To: Bahamas Tourist Office, 23 Old Bond Street, London W1X 4PQ.
Telephone: 01-629 5238.
Please send me your information pack on holidays in The Bahamas.

Name _____

Address _____

_____ Post Code _____

sport, because most of our jobs do lack the essential elements of a modern masked hunt.

In some cases in industrial societies, the nature of work, with its endless repetition and goal-less, arbitrary work periods, is the exact opposite of the nature of sport. The inveterate human need remains, the need to achieve goals actually or vicariously. The apparently unique human ability to enjoy things vicariously, to get satisfaction by watching others do what we would like to do, is the very foundation of sport's widespread popularity, as many a bored worker/ passionate soccer fan will testify.

Although spectator sport provides a lot of stimulation, just because it is vicarious for all except the players, it can never be quite sufficient. What we actually do still matters.

The best work is that which is not thought of as such at all. It is not only in sport that we can see similarity between our heroes' work and hunting. Just as we can enjoy chess or bridge because they have some of the vital non-physical components of hunting, so we can see in certain people's jobs the same kind of achievement as hunts provide.

Writers and artists, for example, achieve discernible goals; they also have trophies to display and share with tribes. Entertainers, who, with sports personalities, form the most popular group of heroes in the public eye, are a fascinating example. Not only do they act out important, interesting or amusing matters for us to enjoy vicariously, but they actually hunt us, their audience. After a successful show, expressions such as, 'I killed them', 'We knocked them in the aisles', and 'I had them in the palm of my hand' indicate the power struggle that has been going on. Audiences are notoriously difficult to please but, if the masked hunter / entertainer is successful, they succumb. The prey reward the hunter with laughter or applause. The favourite of the modern movie mogul, the blockbuster, borrows its name from a demolition bomb.

The salesman hunts his order down, planning the strategy with his colleagues, dealing cleverly and flexibly with his potential customer until the coveted prize, the order, is won. The stockmarket also has an appropriate vocabulary, with 'bull' and 'bear' markets, and the persistent hope of 'making a killing'.

An important feature of satisfying work is not the activity itself, but the fact that sought-after goals are achieved. Many of us do hard, boring, dirty labour, in our own houses or gardens, without thinking of it as 'work' in the derogatory sense. Many a car factory worker will count the hours until he finishes 'work', only to spend a great deal of his leisure time engaged in much the same activity on his own hot-rod.

Another factor, of course, is working for oneself, achieving one's *own* objectives as opposed to being an employee. When the Industrial Revolution required the agricultural labourer to become the factory worker, a massive social change was necessary. The eighteenth-

Nowadays, in industrial societies, short-term pastimes seem to mimic our work (see page 54). In Japan, there are arcades of pachinko machines. The modern automatic machine requires little or no skill, but it is descended from a single-ball machine which required a great deal of skill to play. The maximum prize is a token worth about £36 ($70) which can be exchanged for goods such as cigarettes and chocolates. The average player buys 300 balls at a time, costing about £3 ($6). This can keep him or her in action for about half an hour.

century agricultural labourer, like vast numbers of people in the developing world today who live directly off the land, hardly had an ideal life. But they had relationships with diurnal and seasonal rhythms and small communities which are a very important part of our evolutionary heritage. The rise of mass production and the consequent conurbations eliminated even those vestiges of the hunting–gathering pattern.

How society influences us to accept 'work'
Special techniques were developed to convince people that a grotesquely unnatural behaviour was, after all, a proper thing to do. It was not just coincidence that this period, the start of the Industrial Revolution, was the heyday of the Victorian moralist. Throughout human history, rulers have enhanced their supremacy with moral authority. Only four hundred years ago, English monarchs claimed to hold their thrones by Divine Right. So it is not surprising to find the power of the pulpit in support of the first industrial rulers.

Birkenhead, in the industrial North of England:

'He that will not live by toil,
Has no right on English soil.'
— Charles Kingsley

'But 'till we are built like angels,
With hammer and chisel and pen,
We will work for ourselves and a woman
for ever and ever, Amen.'
— Rudyard Kipling

The more tedious and inhuman the work became, the more powerful the moral message had to be. The puritan work ethic was quite successful, and to a lesser extent still is, but other techniques were necessary. Holy days became holidays, and new service industries grew up to counteract the dulling effects of industry itself. In Britain, for example, great urban pleasure grounds abounded, packed with thrilling mechanical rides, shooting galleries and coconut shies. Previously sleepy seaside towns were galvanised into rapid growth to accommodate the mass of employee–workers escaping from factories, albeit only once a year.

Even today, the annual vacation is of tremendous importance to most people. For the great majority, it is an opportunity to briefly relive an almost primeval existence. The most attractive resorts are typically 'unspoiled' by urbanisation and industrialisation, places where holiday-makers run about, swim and play in a natural setting, perhaps for the first time since the previous year.

One of the most successful techniques for encouraging employees to accept their work can be observed today in one of the most successful industrialised countries, Japan.

By the end of the Victorian era, industrial workers flocked to fairs and pleasure grounds which promised a variety of mechanical thrills. The word 'thrill' is derived from the Old English *thirlan*, meaning to pierce or to hurl (as with a spear or lance).

Kenjiro Tomita is in his mid-thirties. He began working in the Technics electronics factory when he left school at 15. He is foreman of line 9, a group of twenty-five workers. His group, like all the others, has a 'QC' circle (from the English language expression 'Quality Control') which meets to discuss ideas for improvements to the products, which are then passed upwards to middle management. He lived in a company house for four years, but is now buying his own through the company's mortgage scheme which offers advantageous interest rates. His leisure time is mostly spent in the company's recreation centre with his wife and daughter, or playing rugby and baseball for company teams.

Japanese society has several characteristics which make it easier for the skilful industrial managers to exploit the commercial potential of mass production. Each Japanese is born and grows up in a rigid double world, a world which divides absolutely into *uchi* and *soto*. The word *uchi* means the automatic and largely unchanging inner circle of each Japanese's life. Into his or her *uchi* comes family, school mates, and finally fellow workers. The outer world of *soto* contains more or less everybody else. The separation of *uchi* and *soto* is rigid, but not totally inflexible. In-laws, for example, move from *soto* to *uchi* when a marriage takes place. Mergers and business associations can widen the *uchi* of the workplace.

This traditional loyalty structure means that workers very rarely change jobs, and that the employing company takes on a pseudo-parental role. By and large, Japanese industry provides almost everything for the worker, outside the factory as well as inside it. Housing, leisure pursuits and financial assistance for the employees are as much the business of the company as its manufacturing and trading.

Just before eight each morning, Japanese radio broadcasts rhythmical repetitive music for a few minutes. All over the country, workers congregate, factory by factory, office by office, to do limbering-up exercises together. From the directors to the cleaners, most employees take part even though it is never compulsory. Group physical activity of this kind is healthy not only for the individual but also for the corporate bodies. It reinforces the sense of common identity and purpose.

Japanese management, building on the foundation of these strong traditions, has been very successful in reconciling the fundamental contradictions of mass production and individual satisfaction. The 'Magic Number' theory suggests that there are numerical 'rules' relating the size of groups and the orientation of individuals within them. An integrated, interdependent group with a common purpose diminishes its efficiency as its size increases beyond twenty or twenty-five people. Voluntary social groups such as the unit of family and friends tend to have up to a hundred members. In broader communities, the optimum cohesive size extends to some five hundred. That appears to be the number that an individual with a normal modern life-style can personally know, use, and generally cope with. It should, for example, be the maximum size of a school, since only up to that size can a headteacher know *all* the pupils. Huge corporations employing thousands of people in an impersonal artificial setting clearly have a problem.

The typical Japanese solution to this problem is to divide the large work force into small operational units. Not surprisingly, the size of the average basic unit is about twenty-five people. These groups have a kind of super *uchi*, and a special pride in their own part of the production process. They share a definable, obtainable goal. They can be a successful, co-operative pack.

The success of Japanese industry and the nation's relatively high standard of living is recognised world-wide. There are, however, negative aspects of this very success. The powerful group loyalty, though very efficient, does risk a reduction in the general level of human individuality and rebellious creativity. The routine of industrial activity, despite the presence of all-important objectives, brings with it the danger of making *too* much of life, outside work, a matter of routine. The highly popular Japanese game of pachinko, for example, in which over a hundred chromium balls a minute clatter through a kind of passive, automatic pin-ball machine, is played in circumstances more resembling those of the workbench than the playground. It requires almost no skill, and the outlay on the game is many times the value of the prizes won.

Japan is a small country which, because of its trade-created wealth, can support a large population. Overcrowding is commonplace, and the space for leisure facilities, in particular, is limited. There are computerised golf machines with which a round of eighteen holes can be played without moving from the console. Tennis courts are perched high on the roofs of skyscrapers. There are even small artificial ponds in the centre of Tokyo, where massed anglers sit for hours hooking out the same group of fish, which are replaced in the water after each catch. There is something unsettling about this parody of the great hunting inheritance.

Each culture has its own circumstances, however, and problems with the legacy of mass production are found in all modern industrial societies. A fundamental difficulty with the Western systems is that the goal of the labour – the finished product – is so remote and the size of the assembly lines so large. The only satisfaction for vast numbers of employees is not some direct form of personal achievement but the indirect reward of symbolic tokens we call money.

Money and materialism

Except in the perception of some pathological individuals, money is of no real use or value until exchanged for goods or services. We are now completely removed from the natural, primeval system of effort and direct reward and find ourselves in a world of symbolic exchanges. This exchange system has led to the entirely new forms of social organisation, which are the basis of the modern cash- and credit-based economies of the world.

Almost every commodity has at some time been used as money: sea shells, salt, coral, chickens, horses and even people. Nails were being used as currency in Scotland as late as 1775. The use of symbolic tokens, however, has often created problems. When currency was introduced into ancient Greece, the peasants borrowed money to buy grain, instead of, as previously, borrowing grain itself. For the first time, what was borrowed and what was paid back could be different. The peasants thus forced up the 'price' of grain in times of poor harvest: in other words, they invented inflation. The Chinese used paper money for six centuries, but abandoned it in the fourteenth century because, again, it caused inflation.

The Romans were probably first to use a widespread monetary system. The word 'money' derives from the Latin *moneta*, after the goddess of the temple in Rome where their currency was coined. Nevertheless, the dominance of money in human affairs has not been continuous since. As Hugh Thomas says in *An Unfinished History of the World*: 'That era [the Roman Empire] was the only time before the sixteenth century when the use of money was so widespread as to make the shortage of it a serious inconvenience or even a misery for more than a minority of the people. Otherwise, the majority lived on their own produce, served their masters according to their status, and rarely saw a coin from one year's end to another.'

By the early nineteenth century, the mass production of goods by large labour forces created what must have seemed a perfect circle of commercial activity. Workers receive money for producing goods, which enables them to buy other goods. More goods produced in the system give more money earned to buy more goods. This circle of materialism, the pursuit of goods as an end in itself, has important in-built limitations, ignored for too long, but now forcing our attention.

In the first place it depends on large groups of people living in large communities – much larger than the five hundred mentioned earlier. In small settlements, from hunter–gatherer groups to agricultural villages, each individual has an important role in a clearly defined social organisation. In cities and conurbations, our roles, our status and our place in the community are largely signalled in terms of commercial success, which in turn is best displayed in the form of expensive commodities. Materialism has become so much the basis of Western culture that large secondary industries, advertising and marketing goods, exist to reinforce it and encourage its growth.

Peter Marsh, who runs one of Europe's largest advertising agencies, explained in an interview how advertising adapts to what it perceives as people's aspirations and drives:

'Advertising holds up a mirror to life. It does not shape it. There's no persuasion involved except the statement. It's responding to people's needs.

'We found from research that certain people do not want to leap from one social group into another. They want to stay within their social group, but actually get to the top of it. They want to have central heating and double glazing, but within their council house. They want to be able to go to the working men's club every night of the week instead of just Saturday and Sunday. Products fall into that same category.'

Improved creature comforts and the undoubted attractions of the incredible range of available products are great assets, and enhance our lives in many ways. Peter Marsh continued:

'People decide what they want and then decide how they will get it. And indeed if a wife sees something that perhaps her neighbour's got that she would like and they can't afford it, maybe that's the motivation for the husband to get his promotion, work a bit harder, work three extra shifts, and that cannot be bad. There is this need in human nature to achieve and buy and provide.'

This view, however, ignores the fact that production and purchase of goods and services, however luxurious, can never satisfy all our dynamic human needs.

A second built-in limitation of materialism is that, for the circular system to survive, particularly in a commercial world where most money used is money borrowed, it has to transform itself from a simple circle into an ascending spiral. *More* new and better goods available all the time and *more* money in the system to buy them.

The dangers of materialism

For many people, the acquisition of goods is an end in itself. However, events have demonstrated that the slightest break in the spiral – lack of goods or lack of money to buy them – quickly disrupts the system. A way of life based on acquiring goods is not an innately stable system like hunting or subsistence agriculture. It is more like a spinning top; it must be *kept* spinning if it is not to fall down. So the system needs a constant demand for new things, so that money is constantly fed into the system. Therefore, the last thing it needs is goods that last forever. 'Built-in obsolescence' was the phrase coined to describe the fact that manufacturers prefer their products to deteriorate and thus need replacement. Apparently the technology exists to produce imperishable fabrics, everlasting light bulbs, rust-proof motor cars and so on. But we do not have them, or anything like them, because our system depends on an endless cycle of cash transactions which keep the ball rolling.

Riots, lootings and violent demonstrations have occurred in Britain, the United States and Europe when people, for whatever reason, have perceived themselves unable to get in on the materialism spiral. Impoverished ghettoes have experienced so-called 'racial' flare-ups. Periods of high unemployment which forcibly exclude large numbers of people from the spiral, when they have insufficient income, inevitably generate social unrest.

In the Communist bloc, the system is no less materialistic; it is just that the control of the wealth is centralised in the hands of the State, instead of being in the control of private corporations. Hence, a similar but distinct problem can erupt – lack of goods when the single, State-controlled source of supply fails, or prices them out of people's reach. Such difficulties were conspicuous in the events

In the summer of 1981, several of Britain's inner-city areas were the scene of fierce confrontations between police, looters and angry demonstrators. The Scarman Report, which was set up by the British Parliament to report on the events, concluded by quoting from an address by President Johnson which appears in the *US Report of the National Advisory Commission on Civil Disorders* (1968): 'The only genuine, long-range solution for what has happened lies in an attack – mounted at every level – upon the conditions that breed despair and violence. All of us know what those conditions are: ignorance, discrimination, slums, poverty, disease, not enough jobs.'

Polish workers queue for food in Krakow in April 1981.

in Poland in 1981, which culminated in the imposition of martial law and severe rationing.

City violence is not only a result of frustrated materialism; it is also a reaction against the unnatural suppression of our powerful, active, ancestral urges. If we are unable to express ourselves in a *con*structive way we may well do so in a *de*structive way. Both construction and destruction are creative acts. They *both* bring about changes, although one is positive and rewarding, the other negative and damaging.

Unemployment, robots and leisure

In particular, unemployment or serious underemployment can be individually depressing and nationally problematic. To be un-employed means not just exclusion from full participation in the system of materialism but, more seriously, separation from the mainstream activities of the social group. With welfare and the other social benefits of modern tax-paying civilisation, actual physical deprivation is properly rare. The main complaint of the unemployed would-be worker is not the absence of more elaborate or expensive possessions, but the dulling lack of a purpose, a feeling of inadequacy. This sense of failure is bound to be felt acutely by a member of a species whose evolutionary success has resulted from the increasing development of energy, inventiveness, creativeness and, more im-portantly, co-operation to obtain a shared objective.

Until now, the heavy industries have been a major employer, with employees at production lines in car factories, steel works and similar plants. As production is automated, this large area of employment is contracting. A job on a production line may not be entirely satisfy-ing intellectually and emotionally but it does fulfil part of that human need to feel wanted and valued.

Against this, we must remember, as we have seen, that employ-ment – in our contemporary sense – is a very recent human invention, which often makes very little use of the great drive and energy that has made our species so remarkable and successful. The introduction of robots may have made clear what was previously obvious, but unrecognised: any task which a robot can do is hardly an ideal occupation for a member of the human race. The replacement of men by machines has made us realise how mindless are some of the tasks our industrial way of life has made us perform.

Industrial technologists are exceedingly proud of automatic machines which can distinguish between, say, two bolts of different threads; great claims are made for equipment which can be programmed to finish and paint an uneven surface; a machine which can 'read' colour coding and thus perform robotic wiring-up is considered to be a marvel of our modern age. All of this induces a kind of anthropomorphic paranoia. Some 'hunter' members of the human race are in a state of panic because human ingenuity has devised machines which have a small percentage of the sensibility

Masked Hunters

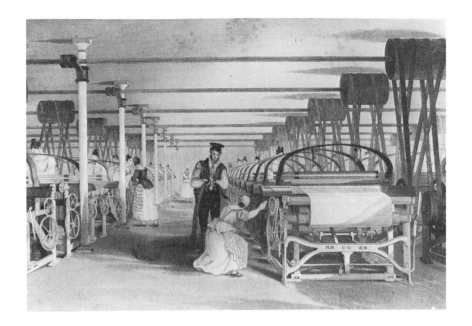

The shape of things past, present and to come. Power looms in a British textile factory c. 1840; a modern Brazilian equivalent needing minimal human supervision; and a totally automated synthetic yarn plant in South Carolina.

and intelligence of a two-year-old human baby. What the automation sciences have really revealed is that routine, repetitive tasks are, in terms of our proper technological inheritance, *beneath* our human dignity rather than an inherent part of it.

As a species, we do not actually regard success in material or employment terms alone. The basis of our admiration for certain groups and individuals is that their ways of life reflect those crucial elements of human behaviour which were forged in the hunting–gathering millennia. We admire people, in whatever sphere of activity, who achieve desirable goals; those who 'set their sights high', 'make a killing', or 'bring home the bacon'. We may *envy* wealthy people, but they are very seldom *admired* simply for their money. It follows, then, that there is no justification for defining failure in material or employment terms *alone*.

It is perhaps worth remembering that the glories of ancient Greece were generated by an elite who depended on slaves to do the routine labour. In our new robotic age, slaves will once again perform the boring menial tasks. But this time the slaves will not be degraded humans, but the technological products of our fertile inventiveness. Domestically, many of us already rely on robots to wash our clothes and our dishes, to answer our telephones, to wake us up in the morning, and to cook our food. This has already had the positive effect of liberating many females from time-consuming chores, and enabling them to develop other more rewarding pursuits both from the home and in the workplace. We already take it for granted that domestic robots will free us to spend more time with our children at weekends, or with our hobbies, for example. Yet we *fear* the robot at work.

There can be little doubt that the immediate future for our industrial societies will be a difficult period. Employers and employees face the task of changing habits and practices which have grown up over long periods, even hundreds of years. Yet these times are trivially short in terms of the evolution of our species; there is no biological necessity for our present way of living built into us by evolution. There *is* a biological need to set and achieve goals, and to make use of unique creative intelligence.

Automation, and the changes it will bring, are another challenge to our prodigious ingenuity. That ingenuity has existed and prospered for a great deal longer than the relatively recent concepts of 'work' and 'materialism' as we know them today.

The lessons
We cannot predict the future, but we can learn from the past. The Industrial Revolution, because it depended on huge labour forces, went hand in hand with a population explosion. It might just be that the *need* for less people will *result* in less people. It may be that the rise of the robot machine will operate almost as a breeding-limitation device, enabling a decline in our human populations to

a more appropriate global level (although as we will see in the last chapter population size is not the major threat to the world's continued survival). We could aim for a level at which, unlike ancient Greece, *every* human being can be part of the elite.

Three hundred years ago, 92 per cent of England's population was engaged in food production. Today the figure is 2 per cent. Yet, by and large, ever increasing populations have found ever increasing numbers of jobs to do. Two hundred years ago, there were about 6 million people employed in Britain. In 1980, it was 22 million. Only fifty years ago, it would have been impossible to predict the numbers of people now employed in advertising, television, telecommunications, computers, or the travel industry. It will be very surprising if the next fifty years do not bring about equally dramatic occupation-creating innovations.

We are coming to the end of what must be seen as a fairly brief historical period in which people were massed together in factories to do something called *work*. Most historical changes are painful; the change into the industrial society was painful at the time, but it brought with it the great benefits and freedoms of mass affluence as well as the boredom and dehumanisation. The challenge to us is to keep the benefits and lose the drawbacks. The hope for us is the same as it has been for every previous period of human history: each new generation has its own chance to study the past, to keep only the best of it, and to make a new start.

Golden Tongues

Human beings are intensely sociable. Although they can go for considerable periods without communicating with one another, most humans spend a large part of their waking time engaged either in talking or listening, or in the symbolic equivalents, writing and reading. Our desire to be sociable even extends to other species, particularly those like chimps and dolphins, which seem to share with us a general drive to make some sort of contact, either by direct body contact or by synchronisation of gaze or gesture.

Can animals talk?
Every species except ours seems to lack our ability for true speech, to produce and respond to that highly informative stream of sounds which somehow enables us to describe objects, debate ideas, and discuss the past and future as well as present events. Of course, species at all levels of the animal kingdom communicate, by specific means as varied as the pheromones ('smell signals') by which moths find a mate, and the trumpeting of elephants. The thing about speech is that the infinite variety of combinations of sound, and therefore of meaning, allows humans to communicate in a uniquely powerful way.

For a long time, human beings have hoped that the inability of animals to speak might simply reflect a lack of the vocal equipment to generate speech. A few years ago a number of studies began to indicate that this might perhaps be the case, when, in the United States, a number of apes, notably the chimpanzee called Washoe, were taught some of the hand signals commonly used by deaf people. Washoe was said to have acquired more than fifty deaf language signs. She was taught by physically moulding her hands into something like the appropriate shapes. Subsequently both Washoe and a number of her successors produced several of these shapes in what appeared to be conversational situations, and for a period it looked as if they might steadily acquire enough of a sign vocabulary to be able to engage in real conversation with their trainers. As research and analysis proceeded, however, earlier hopes began to look over-optimistic. The apes usually showed little interest in producing statements that went much beyond the 'Washoe want orange' level, and they showed little ability to vary the order of signs deliberately, or to assemble signs in the longer sequences typical of human language. Finally, detailed analysis by some sceptical observers of the interactions between trainer and subject suggested to them that actually the apes were responding to tiny reinforcing signals in the face and manner of the trainer, and more or less blindly producing the signs required. This kind of process was first demonstrated many years ago in the training of 'mathematical' horses and dogs, who appeared in music hall performances doing simple sums and counting. They were asked to stamp a hoof, or bark the number of times the answer was, which they apparently could do. In fact, they would stop at the correct number by responding to the tiny movements of relief that their human observers made when they reached that right number. A similar explanation has been offered for the apparent ability of dolphins to respond to a variety of signals from human beings. Nevertheless, many researchers reject this explanation and claim that what the apes can do is actually a kind of primitive talking and the debate continues among the academics as to whether these animals really are 'talking' or not.

Body language
We will return to the astonishing complexity of speech, but let us now look at the general ability to respond to tiny body movements which is shared by a number of species and is itself a highly efficient channel for communicating moment-to-moment feelings.

Dr Roger S. Fouts, of the University of Oklahoma in America, is the present guardian of Washoe. He is convinced that apes can purposively communicate signs. Here he exchanges signals with one of the new generation of 'talking' apes, Moja.

The body language of children often differs from that of adults. This boy holds his arms in a way typical of small children but rarely seen in adults.

Human beings are supremely sensitive to this kind of communication. Children begin to move in rhythm with the body movements of adults addressing them sometime between the ages of two and six weeks, and a high degree of synchronicity of small body movements can be observed in all human beings when they are in conversation with one another.

Maintaining rapport with other human beings relies particularly heavily on what is called body language: all the non-verbal signals which human beings send to one another, and which communicate a great deal about their perception of a social situation – sometimes whether they want to show how they feel, or not.

It has been calculated that, as a species, we have a repertoire available to us of more than one hundred separate distinguishable facial expressions, gestures and movements, which would make us, even without our ability for speech, the most voluminous communicators

Humans, even very young children, can convey a great deal of information about their feelings by subtle variations of facial expression.

in the animal world. It is now recognised that the process of maintaining a conversation has at least as many body language elements as it has verbal exchanges, and these are produced with such subtlety and balance that the process has been compared to an elaborate dance, of which all human beings are capable, but few are aware.

The human face is uniquely expressive. Eye movement, for example, has a crucial role in regulating the rhythm of human conversation. Typically, eye contact is held between people about one third of the time that they are talking together. The more friendly they are, the more often they look at one another. Often a speaker will signal his intention to speak by looking away from the other person, and then continuing to look away while speaking, but where someone perceives himself as of higher status than the person he addresses, he will often make and break eye contact first, and then

It has been said that 80 per cent of the communication that takes place in a conversation takes place non-verbally. Information is conveyed about our dominance or submission to others, about our like or dislike of the person we are with, and about our degree of involvement in the situation.

refuse to make it again with the other person. In a new and strange social situation, whether it is a tribal festival or a cocktail party, people will often exaggerate these behaviours so as to send clear signals to people who do not know them well.

These initial encounters proceed through a well documented and orderly ritual of exchange. The eyebrows are often lifted to communicate amiable and receptive feelings, and some hand or arm gesture is often made, a salute or a handshake, to indicate involvement. Most typical of all will be the broad smile, the human gesture of recognition of the other as a fellow social being.

The human smile is universal, as is perhaps the pout, the snarl, the sneer and the human faces of alarm and distress. The smile is first observed in human babies as early as four or five weeks old, and can at first be induced by any human face, or indeed by any stimulus that broadly resembles a face. Not until the child is four or five months old is the smile reserved for the mother, and sometimes other close relatives.

However, all these signals, even the ubiquitous smile, are directly modified in expression and frequency by the particular expectation and traditions of the culture to which their user belongs.

The human smile has an enormous power to generate friendly feelings in human beings, and this is reflected in the early age at which children produce it.

Although these children come from Britain and Papua respectively, the facial gestures indicating their distress are virtually identical.

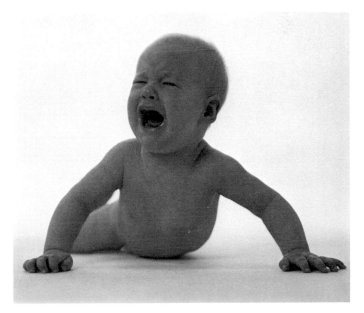

In Japan, for example, the smile is used in a great many situations where it would not be considered appropriate in Western culture. This is not so much because the Japanese are endlessly good-natured, but because holding a smile tends to inhibit the actions of many of the other facial muscles, effectively creating a mask. This is an important characteristic in a society which is unusually private about expressing emotion. This need for privacy is also reflected in the widespread Japanese practice of repressing the eyebrow flash that is found in many other societies during first meetings. Communicating position in the social hierarchy, however, is far more important to the Japanese than it is, for example, in Western society. The Japanese are more expected to indicate relative status in everyday life, by the controlled use of eye contacts, proximity and head bowing, than almost any other contemporary culture.

Visitors to Japan are often surprised by the widespread incidence of mutual bowing, which takes place when people meet. The depth of the bow subtly indicates the degree of respect felt for the person who receives it.

Even within one particular culture, the expected body language of one group will vary from that of another. In Western society, for example, women are usually expected to hold themselves quite differently from men, and to smile more often. Some feminist researchers have argued, however, that many of the expected body signals of women in our culture are in fact deferential signals, and that in a more liberated society, women would be able to stand and move in a more assertive way. Certainly the body language of an individual does not only send messages to others, it also sends them back to its initiator. If a particular culture demands that its members move and hold themselves in certain ways, these postures and movements will remind individuals of what is expected of them in that culture. Their clothes often confirm and reinforce these expectations, and it is interesting to think about the messages to their wearers which are built into the various costumes worn by men and women as discussed in Chapter 2.

Our ability to respond continuously to fine changes in the body language of others depends ultimately on the human ability to make very fine discriminations and to process a great amount of information. This is most dramatically exemplified by verbal language.

Verbal language
A sociable human being uses about thirty thousand words a day, about six hundred million in a lifetime; and each one of these words is actually a complex sequence of sounds and pauses, containing far more of both than we are usually aware of. The near miracle of our capacity to generate these messages is perhaps rivalled only by the enormous job the average human being does in understanding them. No other animal on earth begins to approach our sheer physical ability to handle the complex information content of language, quite apart from the abstractness and richness and meaning that is conveyed. The exercise of human language exploits an ability, unique to human beings, to remember and predict sequences. We make what are in effect finely calculated gambles on the probability of the order of sounds and pauses to be expected in words.

A similar scanning technique is used by the brain to grasp the meaning of whole sentences. The unconscious ease with which we usually do this is only revealed to us when we try to follow rapid speech in a language which we know, but we are not totally fluent in. All normal languages carry much more spare information than is strictly necessary to convey a message just so as to assist in this process of scanning, and this maintains comprehensibility in all kinds of situations. When people are very familiar with a language, they can understand it even when it is heavily accented, slurred, distorted, or even when large amounts of each word have been removed.

This robustness of human speech is exploited in all those situations where human beings have to work in noisy surroundings. A particularly striking example of this is the American Stock Exchange in

New York, which is able to operate in an almost unbearable level of cacophonous din. A great deal of supplementary message exchange also goes on there using a hand-signal system. It first evolved during that period in the nineteenth century when the Exchange operated on the streets of New York, and the brokers had to communicate with the clerks in their offices above the street, without the benefit of telephones. The system still plays a valuable part in the business of the exchange, and it gives us a valuable starting point to consider what it is about human language which makes it so uniquely different from any animal communications, quite apart from the volume of information which it is able to convey.

Mastering the hand signal code is an essential part of every broker's skills in the American Stock Exchange. Brokers claim that it allows them to carry out 'the fastest deals on Earth'.

The sign system of the Stock Exchange consists of a repertoire of specialised gestures, which operate rather like mimed telegrams. These convey simple instructions to buy or sell, questions, and basic messages like 'Going to lunch'. Human beings have evolved simple gesture systems like this whenever noise or distance prevent them speaking to one another. They are all fascinating in their own right, and convey far more than the simple mood information of body language. Even so, such a system can only convey a very limited number of messages, because each signal cannot be altered so as to vary or extend its meaning. The significance of this restriction is shown up if the Stock Exchange code is compared to the sign languages used by the deaf.

Deaf sign languages
Deaf people all over the world have refined and developed sign systems of great complexity. These are now often passed on directly

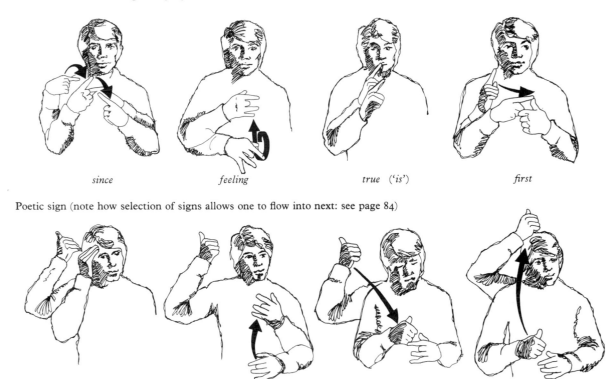

since   *feeling*   *true* ('is')   *first*

Poetic sign (note how selection of signs allows one to flow into next: see page 84)

because   *feeling*   *itself*   *foremost*

from deaf parents to their children (deaf or not), as well as being taught deliberately to the newly deaf. Until recently it was assumed that, of necessity, such a system must be inferior to spoken speech, if only because it seemed to lack the complex grammatical rules which govern spoken and written speech, and which give it its vast range of expression. More careful investigation, however, has revealed that, among the deaf, the meaning of signs is changed by subtle variations in the movements which make up the performance. These movements are themselves systematically organised according to what are, in effect, grammatical rules. The grammatical rules of deaf sign language depend very little on word order or additional qualifying signs, and it was probably this lack of equivalence with spoken language which led many observers to under-assess its richness. As if to confirm the depth and range of expression actually available to deaf sign language users, there now exist a number of deaf poets. These artists creatively distort and alter the expression of signs, or select them from the deaf sign vocabulary of other countries, so as to produce an aesthetic experience only available to those fluent in sign language. If, as several researchers believe, deaf sign language is as complex and expressive as spoken language, the clear implica-

Every deaf sign language is different, but in all cases a sign consists of a hand shape (sometimes using both hands), a relationship between the two hands, an orientation of the hands, a place of articulation with respect to the body, and movement. All these components come together simultaneously, which makes sign language very concise – i.e. there is a lot of information in a sign/ movement – as well as subtle and expressive. American researchers, Ursula Bellugi (of the Salk Biological Institute) and Edward Klima (Professor of Linguistics at the University of California at San Diego) believe that research into sign language may ultimately reveal the fundamental characteristics of all human language systems.

Deaf poet Joe Castronovo
has aroused tremendous
interest among the deaf
community in the United
States with his vivid and
expressive poems. These
pictures are taken from his
poem 'Aurora Borealis'. By
definition, the sentences
of poem do not trans-
late into spoken English,
because so much meaning is
captured in one sign/move-
ment, but an approximate
translation reads:
  'Nordic fingers
  Dream to Birth
  Sunken Garden flowers
  Now, Yang to Ying.'
This is accomplished with
one complex flowing
gesture.

tion is that human language-using ability goes much deeper than our ability merely to make speech. It reflects an ability to assign meanings to *any* series of signals or words, or indeed any kind of discrete events, and then to generate enormous numbers of complex messages by re-grouping or changing these elements according to agreed systems of rules. These rules, usually known as grammar, may be agreed between human language users, but only the very simplest rules can be described.

Grammar, rules and order

It has been estimated that there are at least one thousand basic grammatical rules in English, and another thousand or so special and complex rules, but no one is quite sure. The 'grammar' we learn at school is only a very shallow representation of all the subtle and complex rules of true human language. These rules give human language users an enormous range of potential messages to exchange.

It has been calculated that it would take about ten million million years – one thousand times the age of the universe – for one person to utter all the theoretically available twenty-word sentences in the English language. Many of these would be entirely *new* messages, enabling human beings to create and describe completely unprecedented ideas, plans, and techniques. The immediate biological effect of this is that human beings do not have to inherit a specific set of instincts or behaviour patterns, in order to organise their behaviour. Patterns of behaviour can be *devised* and debated. Human beings are the only species with such a choice of behaviour, the only truly political animal.

Learning language

How do we ever achieve such a complex skill? Acquisition of language by humans does not depend just on the application of intelligence and human learning ability. It is a part of an inherited human development programme, but it has to take place in an existing community of speakers.

Human children are widely addressed by adults from their earliest days in 'baby talk', the over-stressing of rhythm and pitch which is found all over the world. It sounds remarkably similar, from one culture to another. This apparently casual activity actually plays a crucial part in the child's orientation to language and, during this period, it seems that children are gaining some idea of the range and complexity of the 'phonemes' or basic word elements which their mother language contains. The words of all languages are based on re-combinations of a fairly limited number of phonemes. There are about forty-five in English, but languages can operate quite effectively with far fewer. Hawaiian has only thirteen phonemes, yet the language is as complex and far ranging as any other.

By the age of about one year, children are making specific gestures to objects typical of the action they see associated with them; they will raise their hand to their mouth when shown a cup, for example, and they are beginning to produce words. Some observers believe that the making of such gestures resembles an early stage in the development of primeval human speech, and it is striking that these gestures are made by the child even in the absence of other people. It may represent part of the process by which children first grasp the idea that separate objects exist.

Up to the age of eighteen months or so, a child may have a larger repertoire of gestures than it does of words, but with further development, the gesture repertoire quickly declines. The acquisition of a vocabulary is not directly related to intelligence, and there is wide variation in the rate. One survey of middle-class twenty-month-old children, for example, found children who had learned only six words, and others with three hundred and fifty words. All were of normal intelligence.

Vocabulary increases rapidly with age, so that the average five-year-old will probably have a repertoire of about two thousand words, and be able to understand at least twice as many. More significantly, children begin to combine words into two- and three-word sentences as early as the age of two, and these sentences rapidly increase in

Human children inherit a tremendous drive to extend their language-using abilities. This can be readily harnessed to the acquisition of reading. Although children can learn the general notion of what books are from a very early age, few children can learn actually to read before the age of about four.

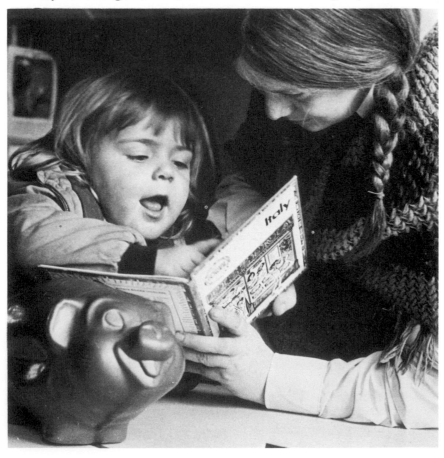

length and complexity so that by the age of five the child is fairly fluent with most of the basic thousand or so grammatical rules of English, for example. This is an enormous accomplishment, yet it is achieved without conscious effort by all normal human children, and it requires no conscious teaching on the part of adults. Indeed, the process by which small children acquire language is very resistant to any modification or interference. It proceeds in a predictable order, according to its own timetable, and is virtually impossible to stop. It is not a trial-and-error process of trying to copy adult language, and, as they mature, children creatively adopt various strategies to create their own early grammatical rules. In English, for example, they often go through a period of putting '-ed' at the end of all verbs to indicate the past tense. Early grammatical rules like these contain 'errors', compared with adult grammar, but these 'errors' are not altered by adult correction. In its own time, quite unconsciously, the child will adopt more sophisticated rules, finally matching its language with that of the adult community.

Children all over the world, at early stages of development, create the same kind of early grammatical rules, and it seems very likely that the specific characteristics of each particular human language are elaborations of this basic and inherited human rule-making ability. It follows that learning to speak is no great problem to human children, since the languages they acquire are built upon foundations of a grammar-making ability that they already possess. Far from language being a problem for them, children have a powerful drive to master a complex language even under a handicap as considerable as deafness.

Possession of a true human language enables its user to describe complicated relationships of space and time between abstract objects, and to do so quickly and with a great economy of words. We do not know whether our ability to generate and comprehend grammatical language follows from our general human intelligence, or has a crucial role in developing it, but it certainly underlies humans' enormously flexible yet stable social behaviour.

Language as an aid to survival
The key to understanding the origins of language is recognising the commitment of our earliest ancestors to a life based on close small-group co-operation. Because of their relative weakness and vulnerability, the members of the earliest human groups were highly dependent on one another for protection and support. Their common survival depended on all the members of the group conforming to its rules. The survival potential of the group would increase if its members' intelligence and flexibility increased, because they would have a larger range of behaviour to deal with new problems and opportunities. Unfortunately, increasing the flexibility of individuals in a group also increases the chances of individual assertiveness, and thus *dis*organisation of the group. This paradox can be

resolved if intelligent individuals share a common language which makes them highly responsive to one another.

Our social groups are as securely unified by our acceptance of the agreed rules of grammar and the meanings that our language conveys, as those of our simple primate relatives are by their inherited patterns of social behaviour. The crucial difference lies in the potential for free and flexible action that language leaves us.

The earliest languages were probably barely grammatical, involving far more gestures and facial signs, as well as vocal signals, than we are now familiar with. Even so, their immediate effect was not only to increase the complexity of the message that could be exchanged between group members, but also to deepen their intimacy with one another.

Like many other hunter–gatherer cultures, the Bushmen of Namibia spend most of their free time chatting to one another. They have a vast repertoire of songs and stories, which are a vital part of daily life.

The value of language in maintaining intimate human contact cannot be over-emphasised, and even now, a great deal of the language exchange that goes on between humans has little function other than to remind them of their common membership of the same group, and their acceptance in it. This small talk has been called 'grooming talk', since it can be compared to the mutual grooming that goes on between members of several co-operative primate species. More dramatically, early language allowed humans to extend and develop group activities more complex and various than those available to any other species. For example, groups of hunters could agree to return to a home base, they could plan their hunt and then could quickly modify it as new circumstances dictated.

How culture develops language and vice versa
They could also pass on new techniques and experiences in the forms of stories and traditions. From these developed the uniquely human

attribute of *culture*, that accumulated repertoire of information, beliefs and traditions that distinguishes one group from another. Language ensures its transfer from one generation to another. Since the earliest writing we have is only about six thousand years old, it is impossible to say when complex cultures first developed, but a number of observers believe that it was 50,000 to 100,000 years ago. It is from that period that we find the first evidence of art, complex rituals and finely crafted tools.

Once language had appeared, it is quite likely that the development of grammatical ability proceeded quite quickly. Once humans began to divide into different groups whose prosperity depended on the maintenance and development of specific cultures, passed on through language, then the pressure of the environment was no longer on individuals, but upon the society of which they were members. A society whose members could articulate their traditions, techniques and plans more effectively had immediately better chances of survival than one which could not. Within each social group, there would be powerful pressures towards individuals having increased language ability.

The linguistic species we became had little difficulty in generating highly grammatical languages with great power to manipulate symbols. All modern languages exhibit this creative and manipulative power. Though there are cultures which are technologically more primitive than Western ones, there are *no* grammatically primitive languages, and though there are enormous differences, all human languages have much in common. They all distinguish, for example, between nouns and verbs.

They are not, however, equally complex; the very old languages spoken in primitive communities tend to have more complicated grammatical rules. This makes them sound more elaborate and long-winded than the modern streamlined languages, and harder to learn, but they are often vividly descriptive.

Where they represent well-established societies, the older languages directly and clearly reflect the interests of their users. The cattle-keeping people of East Africa, for example, impressed the earliest white explorers with their astonishing ability to recognise and identify a particular cow out of their vast herds. An analysis of their language has since shown that the name of each cow is a list of small words, sometimes called 'bovemes', which together specify items like colour, coat pattern, horn shape, and temperament. The range of adjectives is also very large; there are, for example, more than twenty separate words for shades of brown. These characteristics reflect the speakers' intense interest in cattle. Of course, they have no words for describing the parts of motor cars or aeroplanes.

To an extent far deeper than we usually recognise, all human languages embody the accumulated wisdom and beliefs of the groups which evolved them, reflecting the fact that for humans, it is *cultures* which evolve and survive and perish, not just groups of individuals.

It is not surprising, therefore, that although all humans inherit a common language-using ability, there are still more than three thousand separate languages current in the world today, and there probably have been tens of thousands.

Different languages do not develop purely because of geographical isolation. Just the opposite may be the case. One group in close proximity to another may develop a separate language in order to exclude that other group, which may be a competitor for resources. There were until recently, for example, several hundred languages crowded into the New Guinea Highlands. A specific language effectively excludes non-members of the home group, and give successful cultures continuity through space and time, rather as genes convey the characteristics which distinguish one specific species from another.

This relationship between the identity of a culture and its language is keenly felt by members of the culture who are loyal to it, and who gain their sense of self-worth from it. Groups which feel their cultural identity is threatened, like the Welsh Nationalists or the Basque Separatists, will fight to maintain and extend the use of their own language. When a culture loses its own unique language, it loses most of its identity as a separate group, and this can happen quite suddenly.

An example is the Mohawk Indians, who still live in upper New York State on the St Lawrence river. A substantial proportion of the adults still speak Mohawk fluently. However, the richness of Mohawk is not sufficient to keep it alive. Its preoccupation with the natural world and a tribal system which has almost completely

As one culture subordinates another, it usually swamps its language and customs. Language can therefore be a vivid symbol of independence and authority to the submerged culture. These demonstrators were protesting about the use of English on public signs in Wales.

disappeared seems increasingly irrelevant to many young Mohawks, and this is reflected in the fact that, according to the Mohawks, out of the six thousand or so now living together around the US–Canadian border, only about a *dozen* of the children under twelve now speak the language fluently.

Adults still enjoy the language's long-winded, detailed and metaphorical resonances. It clearly reflects the way the Mohawks saw themselves in relation to the world around them, and how they organised their tribal life. Mohawk Chief Tom Porter explained to us: 'Every time we have ceremonies, which is throughout the year, our elders always tell us never to lose our Mohawk language. Our language was given to us by the creator, the maker of the whole world, and our language, they say, is the language that came out of this Mother Earth right here, and out of these trees you see growing all over and the birds that's in this area. All these elements contributed to our Mohawk language. My grandma, who passed away last couple years ago, she said, and I believe it's true, "Mohawk language, when you're telling a story, looks like you're watching a great big colour TV, and then when you hear story in English language it looks like a twelve-inch TV black and white." That's the difference, she says, and it's true because I heard many stories in Mohawk when I was growing up.

'To give you a sort of an example of what I'm talking about – take this shirt that I have on. We say in English, "You have a red shirt on." Well, OK. That's just a red shirt, but in Mohawk we say, "On-ne-kwen-ta-ra ni-wa-so-ko-to na-ak-kia-ta-wa." That means that "red" isn't just red. It means "blood that runs in my veins".

'And so I'm saying, "The shirt that you have on is the colour of blood." See? Very descriptive. Connected with living things. When we say "green", the colour green, we *can't* just say "green". We have to say "O-hon-te ni-wa-so-ko-to o-hon-te". That's what we call the grass that grows all over this Mother Earth. Her coat. And so when we say somebody has on a green jacket, we have to say that the jacket is "the colour of the grass". And in many other ways it's connected with all of the forces of the universe, with life.

'We call this earth right here our Mother Earth because she grows things – makes things grow to support life and us. So we call her "E-sta-en". It means in Mohawk "Mother Earth", and our own mother from which we were born, we call "E-sta-en", and her sisters we also call "E-sta-en" which means "mother" as well. So that's the way we look at it.

'Now then also in our beliefs, by our elders' instructions to us, we call "the thunder that comes from the west", "rak-sota", which means, in my language, "grandfather", and my mother's father, my father's father, and all men of that age, whether related to me or not, we call "rak-sota" too. But the *first* grandfather is the thunder, and all the human beings are the second. We are of secondary importance. We also say "a-son-te-ne-kawa ka-ra-twa" which means "moon", or "the night-time sun", our grandmother; she is the *first* grandmother. My mother's mother and my father's mother are the next grandmothers in line of importance.

'We call the sun "kio-ke-ne-kwa ni-wa-so-ko-to ka-ra-kwa". It means, "The sun is our eldest brother and his duty is to watch over us." It's to warm the day, to energise all life of the Earth, to make life go and continue on. That's all in our language. We believe that we people are not the boss. We are not the commanders of the rivers, the wind, the thunder. We are not the commanders of Mother Earth. We are only at the mercy of the elements, of the rivers, lakes and oceans, of the sun and the wind, and of the birds and the animals. We are way down on the list, we are dependent on them.

'In most people of the world it's the other way around. They think that the human being is the boss of all life, but in our language it's very distinct. Because our language came from all these elements of which I am talking to you about, there's no way that we can have the relationships that we've always had for hundreds and hundreds of years in the English language. Our elders told us we can't continue any more ceremonies if there was nobody to speak our language anymore, because English just doesn't make a relationship, a bond, like our language has done for many hundreds of years. Our songs, our dances, our ceremonies and everything, even how we relate to our mothers and our fathers and uncles and cousins, it's all specially described in the language that we have. We must keep our language. If we lose it, then I might as well jump in the river. That's how important it is to me.'

A similar collapse is occurring in many Indian languages in North America, which only a hundred years ago enjoyed more than two thousand indigenous languages. Most of these are now gone, and some now reside only in the brains of one or two very old people. In a sense this was inevitable. A language is a dynamic entity, constantly changing to fit new circumstances. Although the Mohawks, like many other minority groups, may continue to fight to preserve their language, it will inevitably become a dead language, learned only as an academic exercise, unless the way of life that it evolved to fit could be resuscitated in some way. The process of linguistic colonisation proceeds dramatically, matching the increasing similarity of our ways of life everywhere.

About a dozen languages now dominate the earth. Chinese is spoken by about seven hundred million people, which makes it far and away the most common. Spoken English has only about three hundred million speakers, but is more widely distributed, and has the advantage of being a world commercial language. It is closely followed by Hindi–Urdu and Russian, each with about two hundred million speakers.

Dialects

Humans increasingly live in large urban communities dominated by a single language, but within these single-language communities there are considerable variations of pronunciation, or even of agreed grammatical rules. The way each one of us speaks is one of our most individual and revealing characteristics to other fluent speakers of the same language. This is particularly the case in Great Britain, where a dialect specifies the speaker's origins and educational background to a fine degree. People may have learned, as children, to speak in a way they dislike as adults. It is quite common for such people to modify their speech so as to reflect their new adult status. They may maintain this new speech style at all times, or simply switch into it when, for example, meeting important people or talking to them on the telephone. This 'code switching' is particularly prevalent when people who feel a sense of comfort and identity when using their own original dialect, and so retain it, come also to believe that it restricts their effectiveness in wider social life. It is a very common technique among urban black people in the US, reflecting the separate lives and opportunities of the black, compared to the more economically powerful white community.

The dialect spoken by many American blacks differs in several ways from so-called 'standard English', reflecting its origins in the English first spoken by black slaves. The extent to which black English is simply a variant of a southern US dialect, or a unique dialect generated from the contact between the African languages of the slaves and the English of their masters, is still being argued by the linguistic analysts. It is also an emotive issue among black

Although people of different colours mingle closely in public life in the United States, they maintain largely separate cultural traditions; this is reflected in their differing use of language.

Americans, because many of them feel that it is crucial that blacks should respect and admire the African origins of their dialect. From the perspective of this chapter, however, either point of origin is equally admirable, since modern black English demonstrates one of the most moving and optimistic characteristics of our human language ability.

It is likely that the first slaves used a 'pidgin' English, since they were learning a new language as adults. Pidgin uses only the simplest grammatical rules. It may have been either a degraded form of English, or a simplified mix of their own languages with English. But human beings cannot continue to use a pidgin language as their first or only language. The inherent drive to linguistic complexity and to a more extensive and detailed range of reference ensured that within one or two generations, the descendants of black slaves were using a fully grammatical dialect variation of English.

The dialect of modern black English is distinguished from standard English by its more streamlined grammar. There are fewer inflections. For example, speakers can use un-inflected plurals ('five girl') or possessive ('a boy hat'), and it has some special uses of words, such as the use of the word 'be' to represent a continuous state of affairs ('He's coming but he ain't be coming' means, 'He's coming now but he doesn't *usually* come'). These characteristics don't in any way weaken the descriptive or referential power of black English;

rather, they reflect the functions which black English carries out for its speakers. Black English is not faulty standard English, but a variation suited to local needs.

If there is a sense in which there is one single black community in the US, it is a community which is particularly skilled in, and impressed by, *verbal* dexterity and fluency in real-life face-to-face situations, rather than by *written* language. This applies not only to a concern with live songs, poems and stories, but to an interest in the opportunities that language offers for social manipulation. In the ghettoes of many American cities, this becomes particularly crucial among poorer blacks, who may have to exploit their linguistic skill and wits as their only resource. In the ghetto, blacks take a great pride in their ability to maintain a brisk and pungent repartee, and to manipulate the cadences and rhythms of speech. Coming from the lips of a fluent and inventive speaker, black English can have an enormous vitality and metaphorical power. It has to be heard to be fully appreciated.

So important is linguistic style and its application to the ghetto blacks that they even have classifications for rhetorical situations. In New York, where we recorded these activities, the expression 'ranking' is generally used to describe the activity of putting other people in their place by coming up with a colourful vituperation which the other cannot cap or match. It is carried on between young

This gang leader maintains his authority over his Hispanic and Negro followers by his fluent command of language. His everyday speech is a constant flow of aphorisms, rhymes and obscenities.

men who know each other well, and involves treading a narrow line between admired riposte and dangerous insult. 'Jiving' is the more detached activity of coping with, or attempting to manipulate, authority, often whites.

'Rapping' is the effective general presentation of the self in speech. It is particularly striking when it involves the presentation of previously prepared rhymes and phrases, designed to seduce a young woman. Here is an example, as spoken by 'Father Divine', leader of a mixed-race group in Brooklyn:

Hey! What Baby!
I never see you standing there
Looking all.
With all that red on.
Looking like you're red hot!
What a baby! Mother of soul!
Walkin' like a Hip
And shining like gold.
All you've gotta give me
Is a little bit of time
So I can rap to you an' express my mind.
I got diamonds on my fingers
And gold around my wrist.
But I'd rather have your name on my telephone list.

I could rap to you while you listen to me
And I'll blow your mind quite viciously.
With your hair like a cloud
That rests in the sky
And your eyes like semi-precious stones,
Your lips are the thickness of deep moist soil
And your tongue like the waves of the sea.
Your breasts are like a cluster of grapes
And your belly like the sound of the sea.
But your thighs are the work of Nature's greatest creation
Created for the purpose of delivering
My nation!

Black English is not a degraded version of English. The ways in which it is different from standard English are orderly and consistent. Even so, many blacks in America are confused about their attitude to the style of speaking which they have inherited. On one hand, it gives them identity and solidarity with other members of their community. On the other, many of them sincerely believe that it is a primitive way of speaking, full of grammatical mistakes. The most happy outcome we might expect is that over the years, the dilemma will resolve as elements of black English continue to enter standard English, and vice versa. The process by which our ancestors recognised and grasped the most vivid and effective forms of language still operates in us now, particularly as these vivid forms can manipulate and motivate people, and this will undoubtedly maintain the penetration of black English into standard English.

Our ability to communicate is a powerful reminder of our common humanity.

The power of a language to move people emotionally or change their beliefs is one of its most important characteristics. Language has always been a means by which groups of people can be motivated and co-ordinated.

Speech as a motivator

We discussed earlier the idea that facility in language might be 'selected for' in the evolutionary sense, as the best communicators would make the most successful tribes, best able to co-operate in groups. We are therefore probably the descendants of those groups which contained the most persuasive speakers and the most receptive listeners. As societies evolved to create more rigid systems of social organisation, the direct and immediate link between rhetorical and persuasive ability and personal authority was often weakened, but in those many societies which do have some form of council or debating arena, linguistic ability is still closely related to social influence. In complex Western societies, the skills of persuasion are exploited in various professions and activities, but also enjoyed as activities in their own right, as in debating societies. These have little function other than to allow individuals to exercise and demonstrate their powers of verbal manipulation, but the skills they exercise play a vital part in the political processes which rule Western lives.

At certain times, in disputes or at rallies or conferences, the ability of one person to motivate and co-ordinate many becomes crucial, and presents an avenue to political power.

The English Speaking Union was founded in 1918 'to promote understanding between English speaking peoples'. It has branches all over the English-speaking world. One of its main activities is promoting the activity of debating. A major debate takes place once a month at the headquarters in Charles Street in London.

An analysis of the techniques of effective and persuasive public speakers shows that their power lies not so much in what they say, as in the way it is said. Effective public speakers often deliver their speeches in a rhythmic cadence which both emphasises a line and gets the listener ready for the next one. Winston Churchill was a master of this technique, and often wrote out his speeches in a verse form, so as to remind himself of these rhythms, such as:

We shall not fail
or falter.
We shall not weaken
or tire.
Neither the sudden shock of battle,
nor the long drawn trials of vigilence and exertion,
will wear us down.
Give us the tools ...
And we will finish the job!

Winston Churchill, 9 February 1941

Many of Winston Churchill's most striking speeches were recorded by the BBC. They still have a considerable power to move listeners, long after the events to which they related have passed into history.

It was this sort of preparation, perhaps, which prompted fellow politician F. E. Smith to remark, 'Winston has devoted the best years of his life to preparing his impromptu speeches.'

The use of rhythm is often assisted by alliteration or by the repetition of a single line. President John F. Kennedy, in his famous 'Ich bin ein Berliner' speech in 1963, uses the line 'Let them come to Berlin' again and again with increasing frequency. Martin Luther

King, in his beautiful oration at the Lincoln Memorial, Washington on 28 August 1963, uses 'Let freedom reign' like this:

Let freedom reign
from the mighty mountains of New York.
Let freedom reign
from the Alleghanies of Pennsylvania.
Let freedom reign
from the snow-capped Rockies of Colorado.
Let freedom reign
from the curvacious slopes of California.
But not only that.
Let freedom reign
from the stormy mountains of Georgia.
Let freedom reign
from the Lookout Mountain of Tennessee.
Let freedom reign
from every hill and molehill of Mississippi,
from every mountainside.
Let freedom reign.

As well as being a major force in the Black Civil Rights Movement in the USA of the 1960s, Martin Luther King Jr was a commanding public speaker. He combined the rhetorical traditions of the gospel church with a piercing political analysis of black exploitation.

In all these, and many other cases, highly evocative phrases like, 'Give us the tools and we will finish the job,' and 'Let them come to Berlin,' are used to evoke powerful feelings and exploit them. The paradox of the effective political speech is that it combines perhaps the most basic properties of language, the non-linguistic properties of rhythm and cadence, with its most abstract ability to evoke powerful and wide-ranging symbols.

Naming and stereotyping
The influence of language over human behaviour can scarcely be overstated. When, as a species, we acquired symbolic language, we left the limiting world of stimulus and immediate response forever. We classify objects and to assign names to them. We then respond to these names, not to the realities they represent. Black people in America, for example, can be called 'nigger' by a fellow black, but not by a white. This is perfectly rational behaviour, since in one case the name evokes a closeness and common identity which is beyond insult, and on the other, it is a derogatory and prejudiced labelling of one stranger by another.

Stereotyping, the way in which we can misuse the classifying power of language to oversimplify our responses to other human beings, and to lend dignity to our fears and prejudices, is a common source of human misery. When other people become classified as objects through the symbolic power of language, which seems to happen extremely easily, much of our human restraint disappears. The unique ability which language gives humans to empathise, that is, to place themselves in one another's place, which is the basis of our shared human consciousness, can evaporate. The power of language to create malevolent witches, conspiring Jews and moronic negroes has played a decisive part in the excesses of human aggression. By the manipulation of stereotypes, dictators can cajole their subjects into behaviour more dreadful than we can discover in any other animal. Yet our behaviour can never be entirely determined by authority, for the very language which allows manipulation also allows us to theorise, argue and debate. So new views of situations are produced, and lead to social change, whether by reform or revolution.

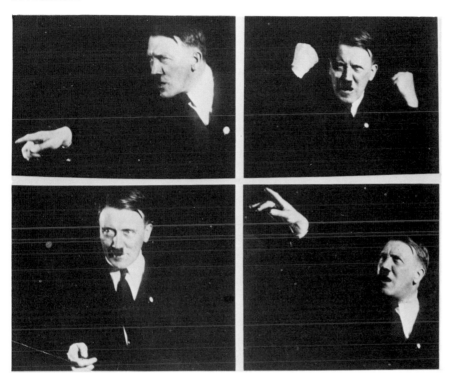

Humour and laughter

Another means by which we demonstrate our frustrations with the society we live in is by making them the object of our sense of humour. This is an important force in social change, which is often ignored. Being amused is a condition with which we are all familiar, but which is very difficult to describe. It is intensely personal, and yet publicly signalled by laughter. All normal human beings can laugh, and laughing appears in children as early as one or two months old. Laughter results from an involuntary pattern of tensed chest muscles, followed by a rapid inhalation and exhalation of breath. It is almost certainly a mechanism which releases tension. An apparently similar activity is seen in chimpanzees and some other primates. Humans very often laugh together, and, as every comedian knows and research has confirmed, people laugh louder and more frequently when those around them are doing so. Laughing almost certainly represents a genetically inherited human expression of common agreement and relief, and certainly for most people a good laugh is welcome and worth seeking out for the easing of tension which it provides.

In Great Britain and the United States, adults play a game with children called 'This little piggy goes to market'. It exemplifies the way in which parents shock children in a safe setting, so as to make them laugh.

Human adults enjoy evoking laughter in their tiny children, and this is done with remarkable consistency across the world. They make mock attacks on their children, tickling them, menacing them, or mock-biting them. They sometimes lift and shake them, or even throw them in the air and catch them again. Like the exaggerated contours of baby talk, this activity is directly evoked as a consequence of the parents' interest in the child, and has no conscious motivation. Its effect is to subject young children to mild stress in a secure setting.

This stress is finely calculated by the parent, and the production of a laugh signals that the child has successfully coped with mild feelings of fear and insecurity. This accustoms the child to the kind of shocks and fears which are inherent in human life, and which every member of the species, initially so highly dependent, must eventually learn to cope with. This element, shock in what is recognised as safe circumstances, is a universal characteristic of situations in which human beings laugh. The only exception to this is when human beings laugh in order to define a situation as essentially safe when they are not quite sure that it is – for example, people trapped together in a lift will, after a while, make jokes about their predicament. This has the effect both of reducing the tension and of redefining a group of strangers as a group with a common problem.

As children grow up, situations which make them laugh become more complex, but the underlying factors – some tension, fear, or even shock, in secure, and thus bearable, circumstances – continue. It is disturbing for small children to witness violence, both because it directly frightens them, and because their own aggressive feelings have often to be repressed. Yet children enjoy Punch and Judy shows and the knockabout routines of clowns and *Tom and Jerry* cartoons, because although violence occurs, it does so in a safe and bearable setting, without real damage.

Our verbal fluency allows us to extend our sense of humour into situations we have not experienced ourselves – in those little stories we call 'jokes'. As a species, our experience is most firmly shaped and controlled by verbal symbols. So much so that we are made anxious or shocked if these symbols turn out not to mean what we expect. But when this is done in a playful way, as in jokes, this is satisfying and amusing, and indeed we seem to search out this satisfaction. As children gain more control over the symbols of language, they are increasingly amused by riddles and puns which playfully distort and alter the meaning of words and phrases, so that for a while they can safely lose control of them. As we grow older, simple manipulation of word meaning loses much of its power to surprise and amuse us, but not if it is combined with assaults on the rationality on which our personal security depends, or on the social rules and conventions on which our society depends. Interfering with these may be shocking, either because it directly threatens our grasp on reality, or because it arouses fears of retribution for broken taboos.

Jokes and taboos

A comedian like Benny Hill has a vast enthusiastic following largely because of his skill in manipulating conventional and respectable public speech so that it evokes references which are normally considered illicit and reprehensible. Take this sketch as an example. Benny is playing a French boy:

BENNY: I vas. I vas noticing zees girl.
HENRY: Noticing?

BENNY: I think she vas Elsie.
HENRY: Elsie who?
BENNY: No *Elsie*; very *helsie*.
HENRY: Healthy!
BENNY: Yes. All the ladies vas helsie because you see they all had big happy tits.
HENRY: They had what?
BENNY: Big happy tits.
HENRY: Oh! Big *appetites*! Did you speak to them?
BENNY: No, I didn't want to cockroach upon their privacies.
HENRY: No, *en*croach. You didn't want to *en*croach.
BENNY: Oh yes! I must always use the feminine 'hen', not the masculine 'cock'!

The popular British comedian Benny Hill has developed cheerful vulgarity and sexual innuendo to a fine comic art.

The conventions of social life which our language ability has allowed us to devise and maintain are so pervasive and various that they provide an enormous range of situations in which humorous symbolic manipulations can be made. It would be impossible to try to classify and define them here. Exactly what will make people laugh will vary constantly, if only because those playful attacks on the security which a given individual enjoys vary with time and circumstances. This makes any rigid classification of humour difficult and unrewarding, if not futile. However, attacks upon social conventions only make people laugh if these conventions are both unpopular and perceived as not totally powerful or necessary. For example, Billy Connolly asks: 'What do an ostrich, a pelican and the Tax Office have in common?' The answer: 'They can all stick their bills up their arse!'

The topics about which jokes are made provide a map of areas of tension in a society, and show us where its members can perceive change or the necessity for change. There are very few jokes about incest, for example, since that is a fundamental restriction in all societies. To contemplate breaking the incest taboo is too deeply disturbing. But anyone in Western Europe is familiar with jokes about mothers-in-law or wives, although such jokes decline in frequency as the real restricting power of marriage and relatives declines in society.

Contemporary jokes are more often about issues like war, crime, or racial dispute than they are about the sexual repressions typical of earlier times. Charlie Williams, a black comedian, tells a story about entering a strange restaurant: 'The waitress says, "Excuse me, young man, but we don't serve darkies." I say, "That's all right, I don't eat them!"'

As we observe who shares our sense of humour, we can identify how widespread our own sentiments are. Laughing has functions for the group as well as for the individual in the release of tension. Bob Hope triggers a response from a very broad section of Americans when he says: 'I'm not surprised to find out there was bugging in Washington. The last time I was there I asked the hotel operator for the number of the FBI, and she said, "Just speak up, honey – they'll hear you!"'

Jokes as bonds
People who laugh together, or at one another's jokes, feel drawn together. Their feelings are synchronised. Laughter both evokes and depends on feelings of warmth and rapport.

To be successful, a good comedian must have an intuitive grasp of all the subtle signals which represent a warm and secure relationship with his listeners. A successful comedian is likable. To Western audiences, the mischievous grin of a Benny Hill, the Glaswegian cackle of a Billy Connolly, or the lightning repartee of a Bob Hope are all in some sense attractive. However, successful comedians must

Laughing is such a pleasure
that audiences will pay a
considerable amount to
enjoy it.

With his multi-coloured
suits and his 'little blue
book', the British comedian
Max Miller became enor-
mously popular between
the wars as 'the Cheeky
Chappie'. He was the last,
and probably the greatest,
of the music hall comedians.
He died in 1963 aged 68,
but is still remembered with
great affection.

also radiate a sense of danger. A number of perceptive observers have recalled that Britain's most successful between-the-wars comedian, Max Miller, was able to produce a delicious thrill of nervous anticipation in his audiences, as he walked out on to the music hall stage. This frisson was produced by a routine which modern audiences would find merely risqué.

Humour as a means of change

The power that humour gives humans to safely contemplate rejecting the rules and conventions which order their lives, without being overwhelmed by anxiety, means that, whether they know it or not, many comedians are actual agents of social change. Their jokes often help a useful reassessment of social conventions. Where they attack the coercive and punishing power of oppressive government, jokes can weaken the forces of repression, or reflect dissatisfaction. In all totalitarian states there is a continuous underground exchange of disrespectful witticisms. For brief moments at least, the people enjoying the jokes can cut their masters down to size. Their laughter is a gesture of defiance and personal freedom.

Of themselves, jokes and the laughter they produce do not have an automatically redeeming moral value. Members of any group of people who feel they cannot express their hostile feelings outright will make up and appreciate jokes about the object of their frustration or resentment. Racialists, for example, make racial jokes. Jokes can be just as cruel and vicious and moronic as the people who enjoy them. Jokes can be put to the service of repressive forces, to discipline minority groups or to remind the majority of their superiority.

Humour is fundamental

Despite the reservations above, most of us would agree that, in some way which we cannot fully articulate, joke making and a sense of humour are almost always a valuable and ultimately liberating force in the human temperament. Although making jokes may not be a profoundly creative activity, the ability to playfully manipulate meaning, upon which our sense of humour depends, is a vital and enduring part of being human. We suspect that our sense of humour may reflect an ancient and inherited wisdom of our species more profound even than our linguistic ability. It is wisdom that can detect and often destroy the absurdities to which we can be led by the power of symbols.

Our sense of humour can even help us to bear anxieties which cannot be escaped. The possibility of failure, fear, pain and the certainty of death are real to us as they are to no other animal, because our language allows us to move in imagination through space and time to a point where our most precious security, our own existence, will be denied. Without a sense of humour, it would be difficult for us to live with all the knowledge and responsibility that our clever brains and golden tongues have given us.

Passionate Survivors

We often think of our emotions as a potentially disruptive force in our lives, perhaps in conflict with our rational and intellectual abilities. Many people think of them as representing the lower or more animal side of our natures, as opposed to the more spiritual, higher aspects of the human personality. This reflects a distinction first made by the founders of the early Christian church, which still pervades our thinking, and which makes a sharp distinction between man and animals.

Is violence innate?
Until comparatively recently, most people in the advanced European cultures assumed that the lives of most animals were governed by raw emotions like greed, lust and a general willingness to attack and eat one another. Films set in the African jungle, made only thirty or forty years ago, depict brave white hunters, forever having to shoot charging gorillas, elephants, rhinos, leopards and lions, all determined to kill humans when they were not already busily engaged in trying to kill each other.

During the late nineteenth century, Charles Darwin's insight, that the process of evolution depended upon the 'survival of the fittest', was widely misunderstood as the explanation of some natural law by which all wild animals were engaged in a constant battle to survive. What Darwin really meant was that the animals most likely to survive are those which can most effectively exploit the opportunities offered by a particular habitat, but this was lost to popular consciousness.

As the general idea that humans had evolved from a simpler species spread, coinciding with the discovery of various simple tools and paintings of great antiquity in caves in France and Spain, the ideal of a brutal creature, the 'caveman', entered Western mythology. It is this kind of creature, endlessly squabbling and fighting over food and women, which is represented in films like *One Million Years BC*. It is widely believed that only as these creatures evolved to the greater intelligence and creativity of true humans, were they able to create stable systems of law and order. These were uniquely human institutions which protected us from the aggressive inheritance of our lower, more animal, nature. However, as the new science of ethology developed – the study of the natural behaviour of animals in their own particular habitats – it slowly became clear that animals in the wild actually led well-ordered lives which could

The Yanamamo (*left*) subsist by gardening in the dense forest on the borders of Venezuela and Brazil. Contacts with civilisation are erratic, and it is believed that there are still many Yanamami who have had no contact with white people. They practise unremitting warfare between villages, stealing women and children from one another. No fully convincing explanation for the ferocity of their way of life has yet been suggested. The Samburu of Kenya, on the other hand (see pages 120–23), rarely actually use violence, although they are a warrior society. Usually, the threat they offer to potential attackers is sufficient to prevent actual fighting, even though their warriors, the Morans (*below*), have to defend a territory of more than ten thousand square miles against raids on cattle.

In the Rift Valley in Northern Kenya, volcanic activity
warms springs and rivers,
helping to maintain dense
populations of small fish.
These Turkana boys (*right*)
stun the fish by jumping
into the water, and then
grab them with hands and
teeth. The aquatic theory of
human origin (see page 114)
stresses the possibility that
activities like these directed
the very earliest proto-
humans into hunting as a
strategy for survival, despite
their inadequate physical
equipment. By contrast, the
great mammalian predators
(for example, *far right*) had
evolved formidable
apparatus with which to kill
their prey (see page 113).

Although they are not
allowed to marry until their
age-set is disbanded (pages
120–23), Samburu Morans
have frequent affairs with
young girls – more romantic
than sexual. If a pregnancy
should result, it is termi-
nated by older women forcing the girl to drink fer-
mented cow dung. Here the
Morans and girls assemble
for one of their frequent
dance sessions. Everyone
shown here is wearing
normal everyday dress.

involve complex and sophisticated patterns of social co-operation. It was true that predators would stalk and kill their prey, but in disputes with one another, over mates or territory, it was discovered that animals depended almost entirely on *displays* of threatening behaviour to maintain order.

Where actual fighting does take place, for example between members of a wolf pack, the victor is instinctively restrained from continuing to attack his opponent once that opponent has indicated, by offering his throat to be bitten, that he is defeated. As more evidence of similar procedures was gathered, it appeared for a while that human beings were the only species which could actually kill its own members. This is still broadly true, although exceptions have been found. Confined animals, particularly those under stress, will attack each other or themselves, and even quite liberal confinement presents problems. Those apparently gentle species, like deer and doves, who normally settle their disputes by the loser running away, are, in captivity, obliged to continue to dispute until one is killed or badly injured. For a long time, one of the orang-utangs at Chester Zoo was confined in a separate cage because he had 'wilfully murdered' members of his own family. The real explanation for his

Since the discovery of human remains in caves in Western Europe, the brutish 'cave man' has entered modern mythology.

behaviour was that in the wild, orang-utangs are monogamous, and the young normally move away to set up their own pairs on reaching sexual maturity. Confined to the same cage, this orang-utang's sons became invaders of his small territory. His attacks would normally have driven them away, but in this case it wasn't possible for them to leave, and the attacks continued until they died from their injuries. Early observations of the behaviour of baboons, far more sociable creatures, made at Baboon Hill in London Zoo in the 1930s by Sir Solly Zuckermann, reported that continuous bitter fighting was normal amongst baboons, but this was quite wrong. The aggression levels within the baboon pack were at pathological levels because of the sheer number of baboons confined together, and later observations of baboons in the wild showed them to be far more affable.

More curious examples have been found. Under certain circumstances, male lions will kill the offspring of other lions. The evolutionary logic of this activity is apparently that the killing lion is ensuring that its own genes, rather than those of a competing male, will be more likely to survive. The food provided by the ethologist Jane Goodall to attract the chimpanzees she studied also attracted baboons. She and others have reported that on some occasions chimpanzees would attack and eat young baboons, with whom they normally shared the food.

It is the rarity of such events, however, that makes them noteworthy. Despite these anomalies, the overall picture we now have of the natural world is that, under normal circumstances, very little actual violence occurs apart from the killing of prey. Certainly, no other species but man regularly disputes on the large and vicious scale of human war. No other species tortures its victims with the deliberate intention of inflicting pain, and no other species engages in murder to accomplish its wants.

If war and murder reflect an animal inheritance from the past then the human ancestor must be an unusually aggressive one. In the early 1960s, an idea spread, originated by the archeologist Raymond Dart, and popularised by an ex-scriptwriter Robert Ardrey in his book *African Genesis*, that humans were perhaps descended, not very far, from an unusually selfish and aggressive killer ape. In a sense, this ostensibly new theory was simply restating the traditional authoritarian belief that humans are essentially selfish and aggressive, but the apparent authority that these pseudo-biological conjectures gave to it worried many people, and has made them wary of any speculation about inherited aggressive tendencies in human beings. The current fashion is to hold that all aggressive expression is the result of social learning.

Violent and peaceful peoples

Certainly the degree to which the human potential for aggression appears varies widely in different cultures. At one extreme, groups like the Yanamamo people, hunter farmers of the Venezuelan jungle, fight unceasingly both between tribes and amongst themselves. One anthropologist remarked to us: 'You can tell when it's just a mild argument, because they only use the blunt side of the axe.' Yanamamo men and women are constantly bruised and scarred by disputes, and virtually no Yanamamo man dies of any cause other than violence. On the other hand there are societies like the Semai of Malaya who have strict taboos against any kind of aggression.

Culture clearly has a large effect on the expression of human aggression, but this does not mean that we cannot find some common pattern in the situations in which aggressiveness appears in different human societies.

Before we can do this, however, we have to map out the inherited tendencies to particular kinds of social behaviour which appear in all human groups. They are not the inheritance of some killer ape. Underlying the apparently arbitrary and contradictory range of human social behaviour, there is an essential and sensible programme of responses. It evolved to deal with circumstances under which almost none of us now lives.

To understand the sources of our social behaviour, we have to try to picture a time, several million years ago, when our essential human-ness began to emerge. Our ancestors made a commitment to hunting and gathering in groups.

Evolutionary selection for hunting
Hunting species typically develop in both agility and intelligence in order to be better able to catch their prey. Even more striking is the way they develop strength and natural weapons – teeth and claws – to kill their prey, and a ferocious drive to do so. Humans, however, did not evolve the strength, weapons and ferocity of the great predators. We remained relatively puny and defenceless, but committed ourselves instead to a style of co-operative pack hunting and foraging, which depended on flexibility, intelligence, and subtle and detailed communications for its success.

How can we account for this apparently incongruous survival strategy? It seems likely that it was first adopted in a less demanding form, and in a more secure environment than the competitive grasslands in which human beings hunted for such a large part of their history. We can not say with certainty what these early environments might have been, but one possibility is that humans are descended from those proto-human species which spent a period, some millions of evolutionary years, on the sea shore, or beside rivers and lakes. During this time, they might have extended their general collecting activities into catching crustaceans and small fish. The flexibility with which modern monkeys can adopt effective strategies to exploit unusual food sources is well established, and there is no reason to believe that our ancestors were any less opportunistic.

It is well established that as a species moves from one habitat to another, the range of its behaviour, and indeed often its brain size relative to body size, increases. Group co-operation would be useful in these early hunting activities, and even the ability to crack stubborn shells with stones might become important. Skills like this would provide the basis of the more effective hunting activities of later, true, human beings.

The aquatic theory
The general proposition that there is an aquatic period in man's past was first put forward by Sir Alister Hardy, the zoologist and oceanologist, in a talk intended for the members of the British Sub-Aqua Club at Brighton. It aroused such interest that he went on to expand on it in an article in *New Scientist* in 1960. He proposed that humans might have adopted this semi-aquatic life during the period before the appearance of the early hominid *Australopithecus* on the plains of Ethiopia and Tanzania. There is a period of about five million years for which there is no fossil evidence at all.

Hardy argued that a period of aquatic existence could also account for the first adoption by humans of their upright stance, for their loss of body hair and the patterning of that which is left, and the fact that among all primates, only humans have a layer of subcutaneous fat.

Since then a number of other equally plausible explanations have been offered for these various characteristics and the theory is still considered extremely speculative, having no firm fossil evidence to support it. Nevertheless, there is no fossil evidence which specifically rejects it, and it is an entertaining and exciting idea which rightly continues to be debated.

Intelligent hunting and individual bonds
In any case, whatever the initial reasons for this early human commitment to intelligence and group hunting, it was to have many positive implications. When we moved into the grasslands, intelligence, and the ability to communicate effectively that went with it, meant that pack members could split up, carry out different tasks, and then meet up again to pool resources. Females could spend more time with the young, confident that food would be brought back to them. Humans were able to maintain a home base. They were the first and only primates ever to do so.

This complicated social organisation proved to be enormously flexible and effective across a wide range of conditions. At its core lay, and still lies, a human drive to social solidarity, commitment and loyalty to other members of the small home group. This commitment was not just to the group in general, but to specific individuals. The first stable groups, of parents, children, elders and hunters, depended on specific bonds between individuals.

Bonding, rewards and sex
Almost every interaction between individual humans has been

modified to provide rewards for the sociable human being. These rewards provide the basis for one-to-one bonds.

Human beings find physical contact deeply satisfying. This is specially important for young human children. Dr René Spitz made a pioneering study, in the 1940s, of 91 children born orphans and placed in a foundling home. They were well cared for physically, but received no personal handling or affection. By the time they were two years old, their intelligence was at 45 per cent of normal children, and they were depressed and apathetic. Most 'could not sit, stand, walk or talk', and several of them simply wasted away and died.

One result of not having thick protective fur is that we are enormously sensitive to skin contact. Human beings touch each other a great deal and get great satisfaction from it. This is most clearly evident in the bond between mother and child. All human mothers like holding babies, and human babies like and need to be held. This is reflected in the urgency with which a human child reacts to separation from its parents, after the age of about eight months.

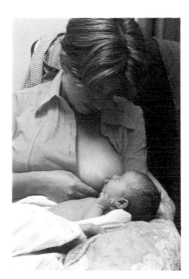

The flexible, complicated and subtle creature, a mature human being, can be produced only after a long period of detailed and loving care. The length of time during which a human child can be held and controlled is greatly extended by the fact that human children grow so slowly. Although there is no strict physiological reason why a one-year-old child should not be six feet high, a human being of such size and strength with a one-year-old's intellectual and emotional development would be enormously disruptive, so the growth process is carefully paced.

Adult males, no doubt, returned to the primeval home base in order to enjoy physical contact with their children. But an even more powerful reward was provided by sex. Unlike almost any other animal, we mate and breed at any time of the year. Human beings are far more sexually active than other animals, and less intermittent in their sexual activity.

Although times change, the urge to make pair-bonds appears clearly in every generation of human beings, all over the world.

Other animals are not particularly sexually interested in each other most of the time. Sex can therefore provide only a weak social link. In many species, all nearby males are highly motivated to copulate with a female throughout the brief period when she is ovulating and therefore sexually receptive.

This is likely to ensure fertilisation, but can be socially disruptive. One effect of the frequent inseminations of the human female, who was *always* potentially receptive, was that fertilisation was very likely to occur, yet without stresses on group solidarity which can result from a short and active breeding season. Instead of all males being aroused by one female at a specific time, each human female aroused a specific human male almost all the time. The development of the female orgasm, which may well be unique to humans, meant that each male provided a constantly rewarding stimulation to the female.

The rewards that humans gain from sex are genuinely broader and deeper than those gained by other species. The sensitivity of our skin, our creativity and ingenuity, all mean that sex is rewarding over a range of senses. This rich sexual heritage provides the basis for human 'pair-bonding', the development of mutual ties of loyalty and affection between adult couples. Pair-bonding is the biological basis of the human family.

Family bonds

Over time, all the members of a human family, not only loving couples, demonstrate a process known as attachment, the deep satisfaction that human beings feel in the presence of *certain* others. This may parallel the romantic affection which we usually call 'love', but it is far more fundamental. Attachment probably represents a real physiological process. Tests on business men away from home for a length of time showed a dramatic decrease in stress hormone levels while they were making a long-distance phone call to a wife or child. A similar mechanism may underlie the phenomenon in which prisoners of war often write letters home even when they know there is no possibility at all of them ever being posted. It may also help to explain why so many of the cards and letters we send each other often need say no more than 'Wish you were here'.

Even a couple of hours observing the behaviour of people in an airport departure lounge will reveal how much our cool, technological and apparently anonymous society actually rests on a vast network of attachments. The prospect of even a brief physical parting will bring real grief and disturbance to perfectly stable and normal human beings.

Although the powerful bonding that we can still see between parents and children, and between mates, makes biological sense, it is more difficult to account for the widely observed and dramatic bonds of loyalty which often occur within groups of men, particularly younger men. Since it can serve no reproductive function, it has been argued that this kind of bonding is simply a cultural phenomenon. But it occurs under such a variety of social conditions that it may actually be the remnants of the bonding between members of the same male hunting pack.

Men are physically different from women in ways quite separate from their reproductive differences. Men are bigger and stronger, and have better hand-to-eye co-ordination. Women, since they are adapted to producing a child with a head as wide as its body at birth, have a pelvic structure which makes running slightly more

Humans gain enormous
satisfaction from close
personal relationships.

difficult for them. Clues like this confirm to many observers that
in earlier times hunting was indeed a mainly male job, and that
women tended to remain at the home base. Since human hunting
would depend on close and detailed co-operation, a specifically male
bond would have a considerable advantage to a hunting group.

Early human character
The picture we thus begin to build up of our earliest human
ancestor is that of a rather sexy, affectionate and loyal creature.
When this creature went hunting, did different, more violent facets
of its temperament have to appear? We believe not, because to say
that the earliest humans were hunters is not to say that they evolved
the mentality of killer predators. The success of the earliest human
groups depended on a balance between a stable social system, and

a flexible and opportunistic food-finding strategy. This strategy has left its hallmark on the human psyche; our unique blend of curiosity, inventiveness, stability, and, most of all, intelligence. Undoubtedly in our foraging, we did kill animals, since they were a valuable and central source of food, but we do not need to conclude that this would require some innate human drive to kill. Far more typical of the human race is the pleasure of successfully exercising a finely discriminatory skill, of meeting and beating a challenge, and of receiving the acclaim of one's fellows. These were all probably much more fundamental components of the human hunting strategy than a mere lust for blood. This assessment applies to both sexes; although our physical structure may suggest some specialisation, between men and women, for different tasks, this does not imply a rigid division of skills. Resourcefulness, intelligence and creativity are, and always have been, evenly distributed across both genders. For the way of life we have described to work effectively for the earliest humans, there is no need at all to propose any kind of aggressive tendencies in them.

The modern Kalahari Desert !Kung Bushmen, perhaps the last hunters left in the world whose social organisation resembles in any way the kind of groups we are describing, have very low levels of personal aggression. Almost all important disputes are solved by the groups of people splitting up. There is every reason to suppose that our primal ancestors behaved in a very similar way. It seems most likely that the aggressive potential of human beings is not greatly different from that of most other species.

By this we mean that aggression occurs largely as a reaction to frustrating or threatening circumstances, and is most often shown in *threat* behaviour.

Aggression in modern humans
It is biologically far more effective for a species if its members simply threaten each other during disputes, rather than kill or seriously injure each other. As if to confirm this, human children observed in disputes which come to blows usually display a weak overarm blow, which is not much more than the extension of a threat gesture, the raised arm.

Observation of adult fist-fights, as they occur in real life as opposed to Hollywood films, reveals that the same ineffective movement turns up consistently, and then usually only after an extended period of threats, red faces and pushing. There is no reason to suppose that our primal ancestors were any more disposed to hurt one another seriously than we are.

How then can we reconcile this comparatively idyllic life with our present dismal realities of divorce, prostitution, murder, torture and war?

The inherited fundamentals of our nature have not changed. The period when all humans lived in small foraging groups cannot be much more than 50,000 to 100,000 years past, which is far too short a period for any major genetic, evolutionary change. What has changed dramatically, particularly in the last few hundred years, is our environment and the way we live in it.

Cultural and biological relationships

After a period of relative stability of hundreds of thousands of years, humans made a fairly abrupt leap into the complex systems of beliefs, values and traditions called culture. This move was probably precipitated by the development of true symbolic languages. From this time on, humans finally stopped living in a world of purely biological reality, and were committed to living in a world of cultural reality. Their experiences and decisions were heavily influenced by the symbolic meanings which each culture gives to the world and its events. The original patterns of bonding were still there – they cannot be repressed – but they now became formalised. The bonding between a man and a woman was formalised into a marriage, marked by some form of public ritual. The biological links between grandparents, aunts, uncles, cousins, and all the other relations in the same group, were formalised into the idea of kinship, with various privileges and responsibilities.

The Samburu

With the development of agriculture about 10,000 years ago, these kinship benefits and duties became increasingly important as a means to organise all the various jobs and duties that go with maintaining a stable agricultural community. Property also comes with farming cultures, and kinship provides a means of allocating property peacefully in societies with no money. The Samburu people of northern Kenya are a good example. They still live in a way which may show us many of the processes by which the earliest farming cultures harnessed ancient biological bonds so as to maintain a stable culture. The Samburu are distributed across about ten thousand square miles of high grassland near the East African Rift Valley, where they keep cattle. They carry out little or no tillage and are content to live largely on milk and meat for long periods. Each man has several wives, who live with him in a group of huts to which grazing cattle return each night to be milked. These little groups of huts, each with an enclosing brush fence, are evenly scattered across the grassland. There is no division of land, and there are no large units of organisation or central authority. A man's security and status are ensured by the ownership of cattle, so each man naturally wants as many as possible. With cattle, he can buy wives – wives who will give him boys to tend his cattle, and girls to be traded off in marriage for even more. Men are owners. They bleed the cattle, they kill them, and they gamble the money that selling an occasional steer to other tribes brings. Women do all the real work. In a real sense, the women are property too.

The ancient pair bond is used to provide a stable point around which to organise the distribution of resources. A wife's role is far removed from that of the equal and complementary participant in the primeval human group. This domination is emphasised by female circumcision, which is traditionally done just before marriage, and is a pointed and painful reminder that the woman is the least powerful unit of the entire social structure. When she does marry, she will be barely into puberty, but her husband will probably be at least in his thirties, and perhaps even older. He will have chosen her on the basis of her family status rather than because of any emotional attachment.

Yet even this life provides her with some of the attachments all human beings must have. She is attached to her children and the other wives of her husband, and perhaps even to her husband. If you watch the group of fifty or so married women who will be singing and dancing together at a wedding, laughing at each other's stories of husbands' incompetence and children's successes, it is clear that even their comparatively dismal life has its pleasures.

The Samburu preserve the autonomy of each little family group, yet they are still unified as one people, with a common system of defence, and common values. There are no serious disputes between those little groups. This stability is ensured by the allocation of cattle amongst families through marriage, but also involves an ingenious use of the bonding drive among young men. At puberty, a young Samburu male leaves his family to be circumcised and initiated into the 'age set', which is a group of all the young males of a given age range, whatever their clan or district, all across Samburu territory. He is then known as a moran, a warrior. He will remain so for ten or even fifteen years, until his age set is ended, and all its members become elders, finally free to marry and begin their own families.

The official duties of the morans are herding cattle, protecting the boundaries of Samburu territory, and generally acting as an unpaid militia. In reality, most of their time is spent together, hunting and feasting, decorating themselves, singing songs and generally having a good time. Their main function is to *display* Samburu military potential rather than to *actually fight* battles. Samburu society has a powerful respect for the force of the male group bond, and the moran system effectively harnesses this energy, loyalty and assertiveness, whilst still providing a powerful reminder, in the initiation, of the power of the adult society, which the warriors help to maintain.

It has been suggested that the widespread practice of initiation by circumcision, which literally draws a sharp line between childhood and adulthood, is an extremely ancient method of binding the young to a larger society. Before initiation rituals, each generation in the primeval group could have redistributed themselves according to new loyalties and attractions, and so begin new groups. The Samburu do not deny that new attractions develop between young people. Morans engage in frequent dances with young girls, and in romantic affairs, sometimes even with elders' wives, but they are not allowed to marry until their age set ends and the powerful old-boy network, which will cut across local and family loyalties, has built up among them.

Meanwhile the old men are free to accumulate wives and cattle, so the system is elegantly maintained, in a very stable way. It is so stable, in fact, that the Samburu have so far resisted all efforts by both the colonial and present Kenyan governments to change their way of life.

The Samburu give us a number of valuable pointers as to how the inherited biases of social behaviour can be exploited and extended by a farming society. All Samburu share common values, deeply rooted in common practices and a common relation to their resources of food and wealth. They have a powerful sense of shared identity, and everyone knows almost everyone else. This ensures a stable and orderly public life. Any Samburu can stroll through the dark anywhere in Samburu country confident that the only possible source of danger might be one of the few remaining wild animals. The price of this stability is the permanent and restrictive influence of the whole society on the life choices of each of its individual members. This applies particularly clearly to women. Their weakness is underlined by the dreadful female circumcision, which is quite different in operation and intent from that practised on boys. Where boys lose their foreskin in circumstances which allow them to display their bravery, and thus qualify to become more powerful in the society, women are virtually castrated. Even so, many young married women have to be beaten by their new husbands till they settle to their humble role.

There are, indeed, some other violent elements in Samburu life. Samburu *do* kill people. The morans kill strangers, if they can, who attempt to steal their cattle. Their sharp spears can always transform the futile overarm blow of early man into a killing thrust. The morans do this without any compunction, because they believe that the nearby tribes are not fully human. Other tribes do not wear the right body decorations; they do not practise circumcision; they do not even speak a proper language like Samburu. To the Samburu, raiders are not a people, so much as a problem – except that they provide a useful opportunity for the young Samburu to display their courage and daring, and thus remind all Samburu that they are one people, with a common property, their territory. In this way, the deeply laid and powerful patterns of biological *restraint* on human aggression are over-ruled by the cultural distinction between the morans' human identity, and the identity of their enemies.

On the other hand, the kinds of problems which we have to take for granted in our so-called developed societies, like child abuse, theft, rape and murder, can be said to scarcely exist inside Samburu society. By and large, Samburu society exploits the bonds and ties of our biological inheritance, successfully, producing a stable and effective society.

For a very long time, almost all human societies were organised in a very similar way, according to the obligations of kinship and tribal loyalty. But Samburu society is now an anachronism. The Samburu have not changed because their society has in it many

A Samburu bride leaves her father's *manyatta* (homestead) for the last time, to walk behind her husband to her new home. As members of the same clan may not marry, this is often a journey of several miles.

self-limiting elements. For example, a man can accumulate cattle, but not the land they feed on. He has to share good seasons and bad seasons alike with his poorer neighbours. If he accumulates a great many cattle, then they will be more likely to die in the next drought.

Technology and central control
Some societies, in a process which began only some 6,000 years ago, gained a more direct control of their sources of energy, water and land, and they created technologies to exploit them. They began to develop central control of resources, and central groups of dwellings, cities.

Over the last few thousand years, there has emerged a succession of centrally organised city-states and empires. The 'tribe' became extended to the 'super-tribe'. Many aspects of our social lives today reflect those experienced by ancient Roman and Egyptian urban dwellers. The only real difference lies in the sheer *scale* of our modern settlements, and in the technological sophistication which supports them. The latter takes us far away from any natural link with the resources on which we depend.

In these large urban societies, resources and duties are no longer allocated by age, sex and kinship. Instead they are allocated in a highly complicated and flexible way, by the distribution of money. Our social lives are now shaped around the way in which we acquire money and the way in which it is spent. A line is drawn between the public life of the mass, controlled by the law and its agents, and the private, intimate life of the family. Members of our modern, urban communities share some vague sense of common identity, but in public they are individually anonymous. Other human beings can even become an environment, within which people who are intimately acquainted move together, like fish through water.

In stable conditions, sub-communities will exist, even within these large urban settlements. The inhabitants of a group of streets around a factory will come to know one another on a face-to-face basis over several generations. The extended family – parents, grandparents, uncles, aunts – which emerges will create a stable network which surrounds each individual, not only with security, but also with the possibility of censure. This is essentially similar to the checks and balances built into the Samburu community. This was the typical organisation of rural life in Britain and other Western countries for hundreds of years.

In times of rapid change, these smaller community groups are often broken up. They were, for example, during the rapid and chaotic changes of the Industrial Revolution. It is no coincidence that early nineteenth-century Britain is distinguished by its high levels of criminal activity, public disorder, prostitution and child abuse. During this same period, however, the organisation of social life in the modern city gradually took the more stable form we now take for granted: large and flexible groups of small independent family units, which constantly change as families break up or move on, reflecting changes in the employment and interests of their members.

Modern societies
For those in the developed world, the small family is no longer a crucial element in the distribution of resources, as it is among the Samburu. It can, however, still provide a safe base from which its members can venture out into the hard public world of cash-flow and profit. When humans are unduly stressed by poverty, injustice, or simply the sheer enormity of coping with the complexities of urban life, the family may also be the point where these stresses come home to roost. The small family is the point at which human attachments are at their most intense. It is a place where feelings and fears are most openly stated. It can thus be one of the most dangerous places for a human being to be, both physically and emotionally. We react to pathological levels of stress, with pathological responses, like other species. During the long period of dependence of human children, there is ample time to produce disturbed individuals. We now know very well that human children, expecting and needing several years of cuddling and close attention, react very poorly to

parental deprivation and abuse. Children have enormous resilience and potential for recovery, but this can be insufficient. If it is, the damage they receive can reappear as neuroses or delinquency, or perhaps slip out of sight to reappear years later as pathologically vicious aggression. That aggression can be extended and amplified by our human energy and ingenuity. Sadists, torturers, wife-beaters and child-abusers all began their careers as wide-eyed and trusting tots.

Although we have only a very general notion of the kind of secure and loving conditions which help to produce secure and loving adults, it is clear that a great deal of emotional damage is done to young children in our society generally through casual ignorance. We do not often have much confidence in the instinctive biases and interests of little children; we have scant respect for their enormous need for personal confidence and authority. Our society still largely adheres to a false ideology which maintains that human beings are naturally selfish and aggressive, and that they require intensive bring-

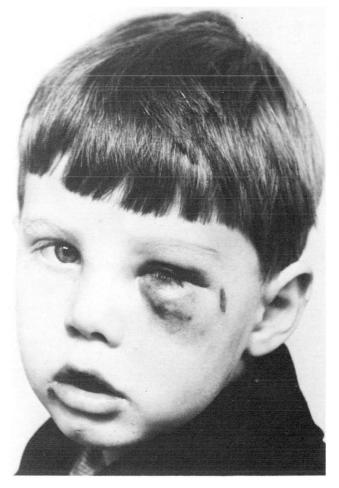

A great deal of the violence that occurs in modern Western society is directed towards children by their parents. The NSPCC estimate that in Britain in 1976, for example, 65 children (up to the age of 15) were killed, 759 were seriously injured, and 4,323 moderately injured. Bruising to the head and face is the commonest type of injury.

ing up or 'training'. Young parents who themselves come from families with only one or two children are particularly liable to this. These parents have lost the natural opportunity to learn how to care for children which comes from watching how younger brothers and sisters are looked after.

If we look at the behaviour of hunter–gatherer parents towards their children, we see that they regard their children as precious gifts, and, by our standards, spoil them outrageously. The parents also exhibit what many members of developed societies would regard as a ludicrous amount of serious respect for the needs and beliefs of young children. It is easy for us to argue that in our high-powered and sophisticated society, it is necessary for children to 'learn their place' and accustom themselves to the burdens of hard work and personal discipline on which our society depends. This is not true. Even if it were, the descriptions by many anthropologists of the relaxed, amiable and peaceful lives of the remaining hunter–gatherers suggests that we may often ask our children to pay too high a price for the benefits of civilisation.

Sexual liberation

In the modern Western world, the larger society can now provide almost all the services that more primitive societies could organise only through a network of kinship obligations. In these circumstances, the pair-bond and the sexual activity that go with it become less important as a source of stable organisation, and our sexuality can become completely detached from its original connection with the breeding-pair bond. Freed from the restrictions of the more traditional society, the sexual arena can become a site for the exercise of human ingenuity and enterprise. Our powerful ability to symbolise means that we can obtain sexual stimulation by extremely attenuated references to actual sexual situations. We can be stimulated by films, pictures, books and even conversations. The anonymous city can offer casual sexual intercourse quite apart from emotional commitment by either party. Sexuality can become a commodity for exploitation like any other (usually the sale of sexual activity by women to men).

The economic superiority of a male client over a female prostitute is only a special example, however, of the more general situation of women in most of the urban societies which have evolved from the early agricultural ones. Until comparatively recently, the pattern by which men were paid directly for their work, while women had to depend on their husbands for support, was widespread. But the situation is rapidly changing. More than half of all British married women now have their own job, despite high general unemployment levels. As work comes to depend more and more on training and intellectual ability, and less on physical strength and endurance, a similar movement is found in other societies. This is giving women a new confidence and authority. One curious result of this new

Like other pastoralists, the Samburu are utterly dependent on their cattle (*opposite*) for survival. This is reflected in the way their language can specify details of each animal accurately and individually to a much greater extent, and with much greater economy, than English, for example, could do (see page 120).

The Samburu discuss all important community matters at a meeting called *Nkwana* of a local council of male elders (*opposite*). After a general preliminary ritual of blessing the land, the water and the cattle, each speaker stands up to deliver an oration, punctuated by emphatic blows on the ground with his staff. Listeners may not interrupt or speak unless they too take the floor. Meetings are frequent and sustained.

Although Western society is now more liberated, there is still strong sexual stereotyping (*right*). The stereotype of proper female posture involved defferential positions of arms, hands and legs. Soft and semi-transparent clothes emphasise this image of vulnerability and dependency (see opposite).

In the Samburu society, married women (*far right*) do almost all the work. A wife's role is far removed from that of an equal and complementary participant in the society (see page 121).

The same patterns of parental affection and teaching occur world-wide (*below*). Denmark, and Kenya (Samburu).

Cheap air travel has brought Western affluence to the more attractive Third World countries, and certain cities have achieved world-wide status as centres of prostitution. Bangkok, in Thailand, is notorious for the range and number of sexual services it offers. In certain hotels, girls sit behind a glass screen to be chosen by clients.

Although still a relatively rare occurrence, male strippers are a dramatic example of changing attitudes to sexuality in Western society.

confidence is the recent popularity, in Britain and America, of performances in which males strip for an audience of women. That would have been unthinkable a few years ago. The response of the female audience is not at all like that of men at a strip show, however. At a 'hen party', the women are never entirely relaxed about their new-found authority over the male, who is obliged to make a kind of sexual display. The event is more of a group celebration of women's emerging independence and shared confidence. It is punctuated by raucous suggestions, hoots and yells, not at all like the decorous public behaviour still widely expected of women.

The development and acceptance of efficient contraception has had an even more striking and real effect on the life-style of many women, and has clearly revealed how much pregnancy and child-care previously determined the options and attitudes available to women. Many women have found themselves able to discover and reveal a degree of sexual assertiveness of which our grandfathers would have assumed them not to be biologically capable. All these factors have combined to increase the frequency of casual sexual intercourse among adults, though to an extent which is hard to judge.

When researching the television films, we visited Plato's Retreat, probably the best known of the several 'swingers clubs' which can be found on both coasts of the United States. Here, people who prefer casual and completely uninvolved sexual encounters can meet, dance, bathe together, and even copulate, without fear of further commitment. So far this kind of establishment exists on such a tiny scale that it is impossible to say whether it exemplifies a kind of encounter becoming more popular in society at large, or whether, as seems more likely, members' interests are as local and idiosyncratic as those of philatelists or bird watchers. Certainly, there are all kinds of implicit but firmly established ideas about who copulates with who at these clubs, and under what circumstances. Whatever the swingers clubs represent, it is not so much sexual anarchy as simply a new sexual order.

Although these alienated sexual activities do occur, they are only a tiny proportion of all the sexual activity which takes place. The vast majority of sexual behaviour still takes place within stable relationships. The institution of marriage has declined, but it is not surprising if, in the increasingly anonymous urban world, the wedding ritual and the public commitment that go with it are less than obligatory. Unless it is witnessed by a number of relatives and long-term friends, and involves the distribution of significant amounts of property, it is not very significant to the larger society whether a couple are married or not. But this does not mean that we are experiencing, in the Western world, an unprecedented whirl of casual, short-lived promiscuous encounters. Behind all the frantic newspaper headlines, the vast majority of both sexes continue to seek and maintain lasting and emotionally satisfying relationships. When couples separate, it tends to be not so much in order to free themselves for promiscuous and casual satisfaction, as to look for more meaningful bonds and attachments. This essential characteristic of the pair bond, its ability to provide satisfying attachment, has become at last its central function. It has produced a phenomenon sometimes described as serial monogamy; where an individual experiences a number of sexual relationships in a lifetime, but only one at a time. It is entirely possible that our primordial ancestors were not allowed this experience simply because they did not live long enough to be presented with the problem of finding another partner.

In order to have special visiting privileges, including sexual intercourse, inmates of San Quentin prison in California must be legally married. Wedding ceremonies are therefore performed once a month *inside* the prison.

Despite the fact that it may vary, the bond between loving adults can be enormously powerful. This is poignantly demonstrated by a procedure which recently came into effect in San Quentin Prison in California. A new warden decided that inmates could have the right to conjugal visits with female partners, but only if the partner was the legal wife of the inmate. For this, and one or two other minor privileges, many of the sexual partners of the prisoners who had known them in the world outside were prepared to come to the prison to marry them. Even more striking, some of these new wives had known the men previously only through letters and public prison visits. This limited contact had apparently not diminished the capacity of these men to excite affection and desire in the women. One woman, asked why she was prepared to tie herself in this way to a long-term inmate, replied, 'When I'm with him, I feel free.' To her, the reality of his identity as an aggressive criminal was less real than his identity as another human being. This attitude to criminals generally is not common, however. Disorderly, aggressive and criminal behaviour, particularly of young people, is a continuing source of worry to many members of the present-day large urban societies.

Aggression caused by stress
To a biologist, aggressive behaviour is a special form of assertive behaviour. Organisms show assertive behaviour as they try to maintain their identity in the face of stresses from a constantly changing environment. We still do not fully understand what kinds of pressures the large anonymous environment of the super-tribe places on its individual members, but we do know that each one will seek to maintain, and if necessary defend, his sense of his own identity. This identity is initially gained from his parents, the ambassadors from the larger group to the growing child. To an extent, the way they have behaved with him defines to him what being a member of a family group is all about. The parents, in their turn, reflect beliefs and behaviour typical of the larger group. So, just as an animal will assert itself to protect its territory or define its status in a group, a human has the potential to become assertive and even aggressive if he has to in order to defend his personal identity, his family identity, or what he believes to be his larger group identity.

It is this enormous power of a sense of identity to determine human behaviour which the Samburu channel and exploit in their young men. Since, like most traditional societies, the Samburu have a relatively low sense of the importance of personal identity, it is only in situations where there are threats to the Samburu *as a whole* that reactive aggression is aroused. As symbols of their own past vitality and energy, elders regard the morans with respect and affection. In our more complicated societies, young and old often seem to have no common interests.

It is widely thought that many of our young people are only barely socialised, and that a large minority are actively criminal. This belief does not so much reflect reality, as the way in which ordinary social processes of recognition of one generation by another have become distorted by the vast scale of our communities.

Group identity
In recent years, more and more of our young people seem to meet

their profound need for identity and group membership by aligning themselves with sub-groups, often marked by distinctive patterns of dress. Inside these youth cultures, identities are constantly changing, as groups emerge or fade over a few months or even weeks.

Particularly for the young unemployed, who otherwise lack them, membership of a youth group provides strong feelings of personal worth and confidence.

While they exist, however, they offer the joy of status and recognition by one's fellows, and for some even the exciting possibility of arguments and disputes with other rival groups. For a while, the dreadful anonymity of the mass society recedes and that romantic egocentric energy that is so characteristic of many young human adults is given some expression. However, the wider adult society tends not to accept the expression of ebullient small-group identity. In the minds of many of its older and more resigned members, as they read the sensational headlines in the newspapers, youth groups are synonymous with youth gangs. Youthful rhetoric and extra-ordinary clothes become interpreted not so much as assertive, but as aggressive. We are often cut off from the immediate and direct social reality, which reassures the Samburu elders.

Faced with young people who all look like each other but nothing like us, we may take the human mental ability to make powerful generalisations and degrade it into a tendency to manufacture stereo-types, simple labels to characterise and cope with the strange and uncertain.

Football fans
In these circumstances, every football fan can be seen as a football hooligan. When we analyse the behaviour of real football fans, however, it becomes clear that, though there is often a great deal

of threatening behaviour between rival fans, there is usually very little real violence.

A crowd of football fans actually consists of a collection of smaller groups of friends, many with a recognised leader. His status tends to have been derived not so much from his actual violent activity, but more from his bravery and willingness, for example, to be hauled up on his friends' backs to make slow and careful obscene gestures to the opposition. He may also be an expert in all the many songs and chants in which a loyal fan is required to take part.

Within this vast group of fans, however, there is often a tiny minority of individuals with various degrees of emotional disturbance. They are often older than the other fans. They represent the emotional casualties of our impersonal society. They go to a match not so much to watch the football, or even to earn the respect and affection of their friends, but to look for opportunities to be aggressive and even violent. They are designated by other fans 'headbangers'. To many adult observers, unfortunately, they characterise the whole group in which they hide.

Of course, mass conflicts do, on occasion, take place between groups of supporters, but even when these encounters do take place (as they have been doing in urban communities since the supporters of the charioteers in Byzantine Rome, known as 'pinks' and 'greens', clashed after races), there is still much more display, threat and gesture than there is actual physical contact.

Delinquency
Even so, the sight of large groups of young people in some disorder is deeply disturbing to older people, perhaps because it reminds

them that the smooth flow of the large urban society depends very much on the free complicity of all its members. The light hold which our apparently omnipotent society actually has on our basic social drives is revealed. Among many adults, there is a deep need to try to retrieve the social order, which they fear they may lose, by demands for punishment. They assume that young people are individually vigorous and unstable, not as a necessary part of growing up but simply because their new strength is not sufficiently tempered by upbringing. They believe that punishment will re-establish a proper deference to the social order. This belief is particularly clear when we look at our attitude to the prevention of juvenile crime.

In the vast, artificial and technologically sophisticated world of the city, juveniles may be cut off from a free access to natural resources and to a recognisable community with which to identify. It may well be that weight of the larger society, bearing on the sense of identity in young and under-privileged humans, makes them want to be totally involved in a small, local, male group, and consequently in extravagant expressions of its members' purposes, and in bravery against an uncaring world. In these circumstances petty crime, particularly theft, may not only be profitable, but a gesture of personal autonomy. J. B. Mays, who first studied working-class boys in a central part of Liverpool as early as 1954, showed that crimes were not committed by the deviant or disturbed, but by everyone as part of the process of becoming a young man. Arrest, and even prison sentences, were not deterents, but *challenges*. The more severe the punishment, the more the respect earned when the miscreant eventually returned to the streets. The 'short sharp shock', so beloved of those who regard all delinquency as overgrown naughtiness, provides a splendid initiation rite to the maturing criminal.

These phenomena are all well known and well recorded. But such information does not seem to alter the common mis-recognition of what is often a *proper* human attempt at growth, taking place in distorted circumstances, being seen as a distorted response to normal circumstances.

The demands for longer prison sentences continue, although longer and more brutal sentences simply provide better circumstances in which to destroy any emerging social responsibility and confidence and to replace them with alienation and depression. Whatever the immediate effect on the individual, however, the chances of a return to detention are high, and, if the process of successive detentions is left to run its normal course, it will eventually produce an individual fully adapted to, and in fact only comfortable in, the sub-human status of prison life.

Types of crime
The astonishing and horrific extent to which our modern urban society is haunted by the conception of human beings as naturally selfish, aggressive and destructive is made dramatically clear by our

prison system. The fact that humans survive prison life simply reflects the enormous human capacity to adapt to extraordinary circumstances. This capacity is exploited in the service of the human tendency to create myths, in this case myths about the violent nature of crime and criminals, and the effects of punishment. The facts are that the vast majority of indictable offences in Great Britain, for example, are offences against property – mainly theft. The value of items involved is rarely more than a few pounds. They are almost all carried out by people under 21; many are under 16. In terms of the total misery they cause, the penal institutions we have created produce far more human pain than the individuals they were designed to cope with.

Violence and the media

There are many things we do *not* know about our aggressive and violent responses. We all worry about what effect violence depicted on television might have on our lives and behaviour.

Literally millions of pounds have been spent on surveys and questionnaires designed to reveal what, if any, connection there might be between the two. Unfortunately, television viewing is now so much part of all our lives that the conventional method of research – comparing people who watch television with those who do not – is not available. Any results that have emerged have been hedged about with doubts and qualifications.

One intriguing hypothesis is that when young people watch dramas on television or in the cinema, they place themselves in fantasy in a key role in the film. For them to do this, the structure of the film must resemble the kinds of problems and interests they have, so different ages will prefer different kinds of material. Thus young children, faced with the problems of achieving independence and learning how to make moral choices, prefer to watch traditional westerns. In westerns there are no complicated social issues, but a single individual has to be brave, to defend the weak and to punish the guilty. The guilty are usually conspicuously so, and their punishment is generally to fall down dead quietly and without much obvious pain and damage. These same children, however, will find an espionage drama boring or even worrying because it is aimed at more adult problems. In spy dramas, typically, it is hard to decide who *are* the good or bad guys; difficult choices have to be made, nothing is certain; violent scenes may be explicit and extended. The older child or adolescent will welcome this form of fantasy, because it enables him to test himself out, in imagination, in various difficult situations.

So the fact that some adolescents are preoccupied with violent media material may reflect the fact that they are not yet fully confident of their capacity to deal with the real world, rather than that they are directly learning patterns of behaviour from the screen.

Many of the young people who are convicted of crimes involving violent behaviour do seem to watch more television, and more *violent* television, than the rest of us. But they do not watch more violent television than children of comparable class, background and emotional adjustment who do *not* go on to commit crimes.

A more significant worry is that the constant exposure to simulated violent acts may be dulling the emotional responses of all of us to real violence, or accustoming us to the idea that violence is much more prevalent and normal in human affairs than it really is. A surprisingly large proportion of the population seem to believe that crimes of violence are the most common kind of crimes when actually they represent only about 20 per cent of all serious crime (1980 UK figures; about 13,500 convictions for violent crime).

In our artificially large communities, where most of the people we meet in the street are strangers, the contribution of media to our perception of others is vital. The members of small rural communities are confident in the dense network of face-to-face relationships within which they feel safe and secure. If this confidence breaks down, as it seems to have in public places in some American cities, for example, then we may begin to regard each other with suspicion and to be frankly fearful of those people whom we associate with crime and violence.

A climate can be created in which people think that the vast majority of violent offences involve strangers. Even so, even in the United States, in about half of all cases of serious crimes against the person, the victim and offender are already known to each other.

The vast difference between homicide figures in the United States and Great Britain (in 1979 there were 21,500 homicides in the United States and 796 in Great Britain) does not so much reflect a collapse of public order in the United States, as the common availability of hand guns. Guns are the most commonly used weapons in violent crime in America, and the appalling killing figures dramatically reflect the way in which a gun directly converts aggressive gestures into destructive action, completely by-passing the inherent restraints on effective violence built into humans.

In Britain, by contrast, guns are severely limited, and traditional community restraints and values still have considerable influence.

We do not deny the reality of crime, but violent, serious crime, of the kind that frightens people and of the kind that demands detention, is far less common than most people imagine. Most of the violent offences which are recorded in Britain consist of disputes between relatives, or people who know each other well. They occur in predictable locations, like private homes, pubs and dance halls. They rarely involve dangerous weapons.

The widespread fear of personal injury or robbery, as it may happen in the city, reflects mainly the fact that the urban dweller lives in a situation where the people he knows and trusts are a tiny minority, and so all the many people he does *not* know may be reduced in his mind to simplified categories. Despite his fears, the reality is that, despite their enormous concentrations, the vast majority of the several million members of any large city will spend their entire lives without ever directly encountering any situation in which substantial injury is delivered by one human being to another. Our enormous emotional stability and intelligence ensure that the collapse of negotiation which leads to physical disputes is a very rare human occurrence. Those humans who try to profit by violence are a tiny minority. We may depend on it that most of us will die in our beds.

The major exception to this dependable human restraint comes in times of war, when human beings are uniquely able to destroy and hurt one another on a vast scale.

War
War is such a widespread and enduring human phenomenon that it is often offered as evidence either of a continuing human moral failure, or the triumphant emergence of the killer ape in us all. Our uniquely human capacity to respond sympathetically to pain and fear in others and to anticipate our own distress and eventual death makes the vast majority of humans reject and protest against war, often with passionate idealism. Yet wars go on happening, and the super-powers of the world are presently committed to a policy of maintaining the equivalent of about five tons of TNT for every man, woman and child on earth, as the only apparent deterrent to world-wide chaos. To try to understand what dreadful compulsion could drive us to such a manifestly ludicrous state of affairs, it is. important first of all to discard the idea that wars are waged by the wicked in pursuance of an urge to destroy their hated enemies. War draws for its energy and purpose upon every human characteristic which we admire, and a few that we scarcely notice but which are nonetheless crucial.

It is extremely likely that encounters did take place between groups of our earliest ancestors, but, to judge from the behaviour of peoples like the modern !Kung, when our ancestors still subsisted as hunter–gatherers, the range and nature of the resources available meant that there was usually little basis for dispute. If a dispute did occur between groups, as part, perhaps, of a zealous display of group identity by young males, it is likely that it would look rather like the disorganised buffetings between the few individuals at the front of two disputing football fan groups. Closely observed, these reveal a great many weak overarm swings but little real damage. It is very likely that human beings became a real source of annoyance to one another only as techniques of survival changed, and the numbers of humans increased, requiring groups to defend the boundaries of their territories.

Until recently, the hill gardeners of the New Guinea Highlands lived in this way. Rival villages were often seen to wage battles involving much gesturing and spear-throwing, and even the very occasional death. But the main function for New Guinea culture of these ritual occasions was to maintain the boundaries between the territories of different villages, and thus protect the resources they could depend on. For each village the presence of enemy villages and the threat they- represented acted to remind everyone of their common loyalty, and of their common bravery in the face of danger.

Even in large cities, public life is usually so orderly that any disturbance is deeply shocking. This largely ritual display at Basle, during the qualifying game between England and Switzerland in 1981, was described at the time as a 'major riot' and 'a disgrace to football'.

Battle thus acted as a socially cohesive force. The battles also represented an opportunity for warriors to show physical fitness, bravery and flair. It is extremely likely that for a large part of human history, most human confrontations have had an essentially similar character. Although the threat of death would not maintain its force unless there were at least an occasional death or serious injury, the main function of disputes was to demonstrate the bravery of the participants to their fellows, and to *maintain* the boundaries between communities, rather than to *extend* them.

Underlying the whole process, however, was the psychological process by which human beings separate themselves into 'in groups' and 'out groups'. Humans are typically solicitous for, and respectful of, fellow members of their own 'in group', but they do not extend the same sympathy to members of 'out groups'. The natural size of the human 'in group' is probably very small. A group of more than a dozen or so people demonstrates a rapid fall off in the amount of intimate interaction that can go on between all its members. It is unlikely that human beings can naturally identify themselves with a group of more than about two dozen people, unless, as is so elegantly demonstrated by the Samburu, the culture they belong to

Like warriors from many parts of the world, these New Guinea tribesmen paint themselves both to appear ferocious to their enemies, and to demonstrate that they belong to the same group. Much more work has been put into these decorations than into their simple wooden spears.

stresses the common identity of *all* its members through procedures like initiation rituals, common dress, or common traditions. The battles between warrior members of even quite large tribal groups do not usually result in wholesale slaughter since the main aim of the protagonists is to demonstrate their bravery, rather than their effectiveness in killing. The weapons used – spears, knives and axes – will kill only one person at a time, and then with some difficulty. From one culture to another, the extent to which actual violence is considered normal varies, but the function of violence remains essentially similar across a wide range of traditional cultures. It reflects a stable and unchanging balance between groups of human beings, and their environment and resources.

Modern war is quite different. It has evolved from the needs and problems of those centralised city-states which emerged as humans extended their techniques and technologies in the attempt to control their environment. Starting about 6,000 years ago, in four separate sites, Egypt, Mesopotamia, India and China, new farming techniques, particularly of irrigation, began to lead to much greater crop yields. These new techniques required central organisation, and the building and guarding of central stores of crops. The new prosperity they produced meant that members of these new societies were free to begin to develop techniques of manufacture. The first smelting of metals was done in the first cities, producing not only decorations and tools, but much more effective weaponry than that available to the members of smaller, simpler, societies.

As their technological power increased, the city-states were able to extend their territories, usually by conquest of smaller, weaker communities. Indeed they had to, once large-scale agriculture had disturbed the relatively stable balance between humans and their environment, since an expanding population meant a constant pressure on each state to control more and more resources. In its essential elements, this imperative has not changed for modern states.

Inside these new and increasingly complex societies, social order was maintained by organising hierarchies and making laws, but this imposed system is never completely stable. There is always the chance of disputes within such a society, particularly between the minority of rich people and the majority of poor, unless its members are forced, or at least constrained, to obey the rules. To maintain internal order and defend and extend the borders of territory, the city-states developed a new special class of disciplined fighting men – soldiers. Soldiers were to support the power and authority of city-states all over the world for the next 6,000 years. In the city-states, the concept of independent warriors gradually disappeared.

Eventually the warrior qualities of flair and initiative were expected to be shown only by a minority officer class. Soldiers were recruited from the economically dependent majority, and the human potential to learn and accept training enabled the new military authorities to produce a special class in which personal initiative and a sense of responsibility were blunted. Their behaviour was organised into simpler patterns than that of normal human beings. They began almost to resemble machines, as they became the weapons of their commanders, designed to kill. Intensive training not only enabled them to be directed and organised, but was aimed at diminishing the natural human restraint on killing. The ability to kill humans was further facilitated by the development of better weapons, which both reduced the physical action necessary for exerting violent action and allowed the enemy to be killed at greater and greater distances. This has the important implication that it enabled the enemy to appear less and less human. Bows and arrows for example are a poor weapon for a warrior, but, particularly *en masse*, a fine one for groups of trained soldiers. The modern descendant of the bow and arrow, the gun, exploits the human fascination with aiming and striking at a distant, and thus impersonal, object even more effectively.

Although their behaviour is far more destructive than that of most other human beings, the fundamental human motivations of soldiers remain unchanged. They are loyal, in the abstract, to the sources of their identity: to their homeland, its traditions, and the families and friends it supports. In immediate terms, however, they are trained to be loyal to their regiment, their company and finally to their platoon, the basic small group of ten or twelve which, from the time of the Romans at least, has been one way in which military

The Human Race

The origin of guns is obscure. Gunpowder had been used by the Chinese from the ninth century, and was instrumental in the military defeat of the Sung dynasty in 1126 by northern invaders. By about 1275, very primitive guns were in use in India and China. In European history, the first significant use of guns was by the English at the battle of Crecy in 1346. They do not seem to have made any important contribution to the victory, however, and this contemporary woodcut stresses the success of the English long-bows.

Paradoxically, human wars would not be possible without the human capacity for loyalty and affection. This picture was taken during the Vietnam War in 1967.

authorities have exploited the ancient human enthusiasm to protect and defend members of their own small group.

The rewards of loyalty for human beings are so intense that despite the terror and horror of modern war, contemporary ex-soldiers will often recall their wartime experiences as among the best times of their lives, simply because of that sense of supporting and being supported by other caring human beings while executing a vital and necessary task. This same sense of intense common feeling is often achieved by members of the larger society during wars. It is recalled by those Londoners who together suffered the Blitz, for example. For a brief period, all the divisions and uncertainties of the larger society are forgiven and forgotten in a common defensive effort. In war, the inherent alienation and anonymity of mass urban life recedes for a while, as members of the society achieve some echo of the common purpose and shared objectives which typified the lives of our primeval ancestors.

'In war, for a brief period, all the divisions and uncertainties of the large society are forgotten in a common defensive effort.' Sir Winston Churchill and General Montgomery meet the troops at Caen in 1944.

When, however, as in civil war, rebellion or revolution, a large society fragments into violent dispute, the behaviour of its participants is often even more ferocious than that of soldiers in an intergroup war. This is perhaps because the participants so often have a passionate loyalty to abstract values and ideals which they believe to be so vital to the future happiness and prosperity of the society, that they license almost any action. The opposition must have some deliberately wicked or perverse reason for fighting. The enemy can even become, in the minds of the enthused, sub-human or even demonic and as such they can be violently attacked in defence of these greater human values. Thus terrorists can calmly bomb their opponents or those who by inaction support their opponents, especially since the act of triggering a bomb is so far removed from the destruction it produces. Similarly, the agents of authority can torture, imprison, or execute, because they too defend abstract values of freedom, justice and tradition, as well as the values of property, from an enemy who has already breached the defences, and who often cannot be recognised by clothing or language but only by the loyalties which must be revealed within him. This viciousness particularly characterises sectarian wars.

The men being killed here are 'enemies of the revolution' in Teheran. The cruel mass killings are sadly typical of societies which collapse into civil war.

The ancient weakness by which human beings lose empathy with out-group members means that, to us, the pain we inflict on our enemies is no more than they deserve in payment for the atrocities they visit on us.

The power that symbolic language has in directing human behaviour is discussed elsewhere in this book, but the power that 'stereotypes', the simplified prejudiced labels that we apply to those who worry or threaten us, have in facilitating aggressive or violent behaviour cannot be underestimated. Stereotypes can make it easier to reduce other humans to sub-human or even non-human status. Combined with military training and indoctrination, this has produced the dreadful tortures, deportations, and mass murders which haunt the twentieth century as they have haunted so many others.

The memory of those Nazis who assisted in running murder camps and then returned to their homes to bestow benign parental affection on their children sends a chill through all of us. Yet it is only a grotesque extension of a personality split which is potentially available to all human beings.

In day-to-day terms, the loyalty of the members of a large modern urban society is directed not so much to the greater society, as

Despite the nuclear stand-off of the major powers, disputes still continue. Rivalries in the Middle East seem the most likely catalyst for open international war. This area is crucial because of the modern world's dependence on oil resources (see page 229), the continuing antagonism between the Arab nations and Israel over Palestine, and because of the region's territorial proximity to Russia. El Fatah guerrillas (*above*) practice hand-to-hand combat not only to enhance fighting skills, but also to encourage group loyalty (see pages 141–4).

The crew of a tank (*left*) – here in Cambodia – have a group loyalty of this kind, combined with a strong ideology (see pages 204–5).

Since 1960, when development began, British Aerospace have spent billions on the Harrier 'jump jet' (see page 229). Once again, loyalty to a small team licenses the use of such destructive technology (see pages 143–4).

In Britain, active support of a football team supplies for many people those satisfactions of group membership and common purpose which can be lacking in modern life (see page 133).

Adolf Eichmann at Prague with his son Horst, to whom he is known to have been a loving father. At the time that this picture was taken Eichmann was consigning thousands of people to concentration camps every day.

towards the small groups of which they are members: relatives, friends and work mates. These groups often also define the sphere of influence of their members. Only a tiny minority of very powerful people have any real direct influence on the activities of society as a whole and even they ultimately organise their power along the lines of loyalty to small groups of a dozen or so; the Board, the Cabinet, the General Staff. This fragmentation of effort and influence facilitates the process by which members of large warring societies can engage in mass wars of inhuman ferocity. The small team that design a bomb, the factory that make it, the staff who direct it, the bomber crew that drops it – all feel human loyalty and affection within their small group. All apply their ingenuity, hopes and ambitions to the task with which they are presented. Each separate group is freed from final total responsibility for the death and destruction the bomb finally produces. Even the bomber crew sees only a far-away pattern of explosions. Even so, the technology which so easily separates us from our ability to break and burn other living, breathing, human beings can also be used to bring our actions home to us in the form of films and television programmes. The contribution of the extensive television coverage provided by the new 'warrior' teams of war reporters and cameramen, towards ending the Vietnam war, for example, was enormous.

Mass war concentrates our technologically ingenious minds wonderfully. Ever since wars started to be waged to maintain and extend the power of centralised states, instead of to demonstrate the loyalty

The large-scale ferocity of
modern man depends
ultimately on the skill and
enthusiasm of small teams
of dedicated human beings.
When this photograph
appeared in 1941, it was
captioned 'Making a
beautiful bomb'.

and bravery of gesturing warriors, the technology of weaponry and
strategies for using them has been rapidly evolving. This technological evolution has proceeded at an accelerating rate during the
last hundred years or so. This is the result of several factors. Modern
economies have become organised into larger and larger groups, and
thus have a greater ability to provide the capital base and manpower
necessary to develop and manufacture more and more expensive and
effective weapons of war. Consequently, the production of weapons
has become an increasingly large component of the economic activity
of the larger countries. The evolution of weapon technology is also
accelerated by the need for the war technology of one nation to
evolve constantly to match the counter-measures of another. This
applies even when an actual war is not being fought, since, just as
the gestures and shouts of our primeval ancestors were important
because they *threatened* the possibility of conflict, modern weapons
are developed as much for their power to threaten attack, as to
actually carry it out. Finally, it is indisputable that the maintenance
of war-like preparations, and the development of increasingly
sophisticated weapon technology, helps to maintain the authority
of those who direct the major nations of the world today.

In recent history, the First World War can be regarded as the
war in which it was finally demonstrated that victory could not be
achieved solely by destroying enemy soldiers, though several million
men had to be killed in order to make this clear. Their deaths also
made clear how vulnerable the inherited human drive to loyalty
makes us to our new destructive ability.

No matter how reluctant each one of those millions was, he was
able to be placed in the trenches through a combination of loyalty to
his country, the fear of the contempt of his fellows, and his willing-

ness to obey orders. Taken together, these factors made it extremely difficult for each individual human being to refuse. The new machine guns and explosive shells converted these individual vulnerabilities into an unprecedented carnage. By the end of the First World War, it was clear that the primary objectives of modern war must be to destroy the enemy's *weapons* and the resources that produced them. The traditional distinction, between home and the boundaries of territory that were being defended, also began to weaken, as, in the years that led up to the Second World War, it was realised that aeroplanes made it possible to attack even the factories that made the weapons.

The end of the Second World War saw the introduction of the flying bombs that took only minutes to reach their target, and also the emergence of the first small atom bombs. The moral validity of the decision to use those bombs in Japan is still a matter of debate, but the results of their action, in which so many people were killed in Hiroshima and Nagasaki, were unarguably horrifying, and so spectacular that they closed, to a great extent, the psychological barriers of distance which facilitate our killing of others in a war.

The First World War was responsible for the deaths of between 10 and 13 million soldiers, and 20 million wounded. These men were part of the force which gained the Allies a mere seven miles of ground in the five-month Battle of the Somme in 1916. About one million men were killed on the Allied side in this action alone.

The use of aircraft to convey bombs into the heartland of the enemy irreversibly altered the nature of modern war.

Atom bombs, and the hydrogen bombs which evolved from them in 1952, also finally ended the obsolete mental distinction between 'home' and 'the front', and considerably weakened that natural optimism of human beings which allows them to believe that somehow, even in war, they personally will not be killed. With the development of powerful rockets with nuclear warheads, weapons could proceed immediately to the home base that troops and aeroplanes were no longer able to defend.

When the major powers first achieved a common nuclear status, in 1949, it seemed that stalemate had inevitably been reached, and

that a profitable war could not be devised. Wars continue to be waged, however, by the major power blocs – often symbolically by the exchange of propaganda or by the covert encouragement and development of sources of tension and dispute in the enemy's society. Alternatively, those nations not firmly aligned with the major blocs can provide a theatre within which more orthodox, 'traditional', slightly less devastating weapons can be tested.

The technological escalation of weapon-making persists. The two major power blocs now negotiate around the extent to which they have the metaphysical ability to completely destroy themselves several times over. The generals, acting on the habits of a lifetime, insist on regarding the nuclear bomb as a weapon, instead of recognising that its total power of destruction negates its effective use, and thus its use as a threat to the enemy. It is simply a threat of annihilation to us *all*, and therefore of no real value in military action or in preparation for war. For example, it has been calculated that just five large Russian missiles could launch 800 forty-kiloton warheads to kill about 40 million people in the United States. Faced

The first atom bomb to kill human beings was dropped on Hiroshima on 6 August 1945. Its destructive power was 20 kilotons (equivalent to 20,000 tons of TNT). This is tiny compared with modern nuclear weapons, which can reach 10 megatons (equivalent to 10 million tons of TNT). The Hiroshima bomb killed at least 75,000 people immediately, but the eventual death-toll was probably 200,000 people, subsequent deaths coming from radiation sickness, cancer, and so on.

The Human Race

With the exception of the Biological Weapons Convention of 1972, the record of attempts at arms control since 1945 has been lamentable by any standards. Agreements have been negotiated, by all parties, as 'deals' rather than serious attempts to limit the development of weapons. The two SALTs (Strategic Arms Limitations Treaties) have both set limits on weapons far beyond the major powers' conceivable needs. For example, SALT 2 (1979) allows each of the super-powers to add 4,000 nuclear warheads to their armouries by 1985. There is no record in human history of an arms race which has not ended in war.

with these realities, and a relative weakness in orthodox military strength compared to Russia, America appears to be presently trying to give the nuclear bomb some credibility as a threatening weapon by implying that she can conceive of limited and thus 'practical' nuclear war. She has also released the information that she will have completed, by 1983, the 'launch-on warning' system, organised through a computer which will be capable of reacting automatically to signals from reconnaisance satellites, so as to alert all US bases to a co-ordinated nuclear missile barrage. Coupled with the USSR's commitment to retaliate, this means that humans have so finally detached themselves, by their technological ingenuity, from the act of killing, that, by pressing *one* button, a system could be set off which would destroy most of the world's population within a period of about thirty minutes. It is stressed by the US Information Centre that this system has considerable fail-safes, including a manual over-ride available to the President; readers may not find this totally reassuring.

As more and more countries get possession of nuclear weapons, it is quite clear that the chances of world-wide nuclear annihilation will increase unless the full implication of the fact that nuclear bombs *cannot* be considered as effective weapons is grasped by a new generation of military strategists.

Ever since we abandoned the situation in which technologically simple tribesmen maintained orderly boundaries by largely ritual displays, we have been following a continuous (and almost inevitable) process by which weapons were developed in ferocity by expanding states as a means of threat during peacetime and then as a means of destruction in war. As the range of these weapons has increased,

In the early 1980s, plans
by military strategists to
deploy a new generation of
nuclear weapons in Europe
evoked fresh anxieties
among civilians. One
response was a series of
enormous rallies to demonstrate opposition to nuclear
armaments. The evocative
power of Munch's 'The
Scream' is here used as a
banner to communicate the
anxiety of the protestors.

our willingness to use them has increased, as the targets diminish
in perceived humanity. With the nuclear bomb, the evolution of
weaponry has ended, and with it the value of threatening displays.

We have to realise, collectively, that if *Homo sapiens* is not to
become distinguished as one of the shortest-lived species ever

to appear on earth, we must somehow redefine the ways in which we maintain human social stability within and between societies. A vital first step is to abandon those limited and naïve conceptions of human nature, which stress the possibility of reaching some semi-divine state, which we humans never quite achieve for lack of willpower and moral discipline.

We must use our enormous analytical abilities to take a cool look at ourselves, as a *unique* animal, but an animal for all that. We need to see how we can control it. The animal has an enormous memory, but a limited imagination. It finds it difficult to believe that black children starving far away are as real as the children asking for ice cream in its own sitting room. It is relieved to come back to a familiar home after a two-week holiday in a comfortable hotel, but recommends years of close and austere confinement to improve the attitudes and behaviour of its rebellious young. It can make jokes about the Spanish Inquisition or the Nazi gas chambers, where millions of people died in unbelievably cruel circumstances, simply because they happened somewhere else to someone else, and at another time. It rushes to help a child with a bruised finger, but the same day endorses a government committed to apocalyptic nuclear war.

We must not condemn this short-sightedness, but recognise and respect its force in national human affairs. If we lack the capacity to *feel* that we are all members of the human family, we must devise schemes by which our actual mutual interdependence is given a legal and economic binding force. The history of the evolution of the parliamentary system shows that human beings can happily embrace and respect complex systems of rules and procedure to arbitrate in their affairs. Our leaders, who presently waste their energy and the earth's resources in grotesque strategies for appropriate balances of terror, can, and must, devise systems of international arbitration which can harness the human race's enormous symbolic and rule-making ability, before we inevitably descend into world-wide nuclear war. They will have little chance to do so afterwards.

'Family Group' by Pablo Picasso, painted during his 'blue period' (see page 187).

Defiant Optimists

Although the evolution of human beings probably spans more than five million years, we have very little record of substantial human artistic or religious activity until comparatively recently – not more than 40,000 years or so ago. *Australopithecus*, our ancestor of about two million years ago, leaves us some pebbles and simple tools which are marked with red ochre. Neanderthals, the humans with bigger brains than us but probably less language ability, flourished during the period between 35,000 and 70,000 years ago. They left us a few simple pendants of teeth and bone, bearing scratches and also daubed with red ochre. There is also evidence from Iraq that Neanderthals buried their dead, and with them tools and bones, red ochre powder, and even flowers, which suggests that they performed funeral rituals.

The mystery of the caves
The first clear evidence of extensive artistic and religious activity among early humans is found in caves in Europe and Australia: paintings and objects which were made at least 35,000 years ago, around the beginning of the last great Ice Age. They coincide with the appearance of modern man (*Homo sapiens sapiens*), with a complex tool-kit and well-developed hunting culture, who, in Europe, hunted reindeer, mammoth, bison and boar. As well as paintings, these people left us well-made bracelets, necklaces, headbands, rings and buttons. They decorated the tools they used, and they made animal statuettes and human figures.

What is most striking about human cave art is its sudden widespread emergence, and the fact that its appearance is not at all primitive. The sophistication, fluency and vividness of the images suggest that human artistic ability is far older than its appearance as cave art, but that either the materials used have all rotted away, or else that earlier artistic expression was confined to the manufacture of symmetrical and well-made tools, and to creating poems, songs, dances and rituals during the preceding several thousand years. Another remote possibility is that artistic activity began somewhere else, and that we have not yet found the remains.

The images we find in more than a hundred caves in France, Spain and Italy cover that Ice-Age period of over twenty thousand years, usually called the Late Paleolithic (Late Old Stone Age). They reflect the coherent and continuous hunting culture which thrived in that period.

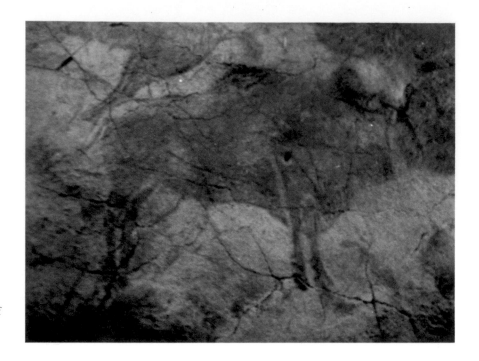

A bison (*right*) on the wall of a Spanish cave (see opposite).

The wall painting (*below*) is from the tomb of the Eighteenth-Dynasty Egyptian King Horemheb. As the first Egyptian kingdom was formed, the various animal spirits worshipped by the tribes within it came together in a pantheon of gods. Sometimes, several spirits were combined into one god. In many cases, reflecting their new status, they were given human bodies. Egyptian religious art was densely symbolic. In this painting, Osiris, God of the Dead, is seated on a throne interwoven with lily and papyrus. This symbolises the successful union of the older kingdoms of Upper and Lower Egypt. Behind him stand the jackal-headed Anubis, and falcon-headed Horus. Every item in the painting had a profound religious meaning to the Egyptians.

The modern Aboriginal bark painting (*below right*) is executed in a traditional style which is probably 15,000 years old.

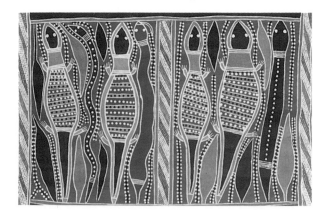

'Venuses', small figurines of limestone, ivory or baked clay, have been found at sites varying from France eastwards to Siberia. This is one of the most beautiful examples; the 'Venus of Willendorf', a limestone statuette from a site in Austria, probably made about 30,000 years ago. The majority of figurines found, however, have no discernible sex.

Nowadays we are impressed how old our cathedrals or the ancient pyramids are. The awe we feel when observing these creations of men past is dwarfed when we look at an image of a leaping bison, still brightly coloured, which is 35,000 years old. No doubt later members of that same Paleolithic people, towards the end of the Ice Age, 12,000 years ago, were equally impressed by the antiquity of the images to which they added.

In several of the caves, the images are in a rich jumble, different from one another in size and the angle at which they are drawn. They show differing styles of drawing and predominant colour, and come from various periods. The images left represent the continuous work of many people over hundreds of generations.

Although only a few of the abundant species of the last Ice Age were killed and eaten, we still find pictures of virtually all of them in the depictions of the Ice-Age artists. At least thirty-five species of animals and plants are all carefully described. They include woolly rhinoceros and musk ox, wild goat and chamois, lion, leopard, seal, bears, snakes, birds, frogs, salamanders, woodchucks, fish and insects. If nothing else, this reveals to us the intense interest of these people in all the life around them, and their detailed knowledge of its behaviour and breeding patterns. By comparison, the human beings painted are usually small and smudgy, virtually stick people.

There is, however, an exception to this. Paintings were recently discovered, at La Marche in France, where the pictures of humans are much more detailed. We can recognise people of different ages, men in long gowns, and women with elaborate hair styles. We can see what looks like praying and dancing.

The beginnings of culture
The perennial question for modern observers of these and all the other magnificent images is: Why were they painted? There is

evidence that many of the cave paintings were visited only seasonally, or even more rarely. For example, the famous clay bisons which are sculpted on the floor of the last chamber at Le Tuc d'Audoubert, in central southern France, seemed to have been made and then never, ever re-visited. Many paintings can be seen only by standing or lying in a particular position in the cave, or as they appear suddenly around a corner. Many of them lie deep in the recesses of a series of caves, and can only be reached with some difficulty. Often, in the last of several chambers, there are sets of completely abstract-looking patterns (some of which have been interpreted as records of seasons or lunar movements), and there are often the hand prints, footprints and finger-marks of both children and adolescents as well as adults. All this suggests that the cave paintings must have played a part in ceremonies or rituals.

The first emergence of sophisticated human cultures, with regularly produced artifacts, and continuity, from one generation to another, of beliefs and customs, is accompanied by the appearance of larger groups of humans than the two dozen or so of the earliest simple hunting groups. The social activities which only human beings practise, like dancing, singing and telling stories, were one means by which the earliest large groups of people maintained social unity, and they undoubtedly reflected the world picture of the people who performed them. They are all lost to us now. The objects they made, however, and their cave paintings, were a lasting reflection of the skills and experience of the cultures which produced them. Cave art might have been made to provide a magical store in the caves, of the power and wisdom of the adult group. Young people could be taken to the caves for initiation rites to be impressed by the power of their elders. In this way, cave art could have been part of the process by which young people were bound to the main group and restricted from setting off to form smaller, potentially rival, groups. At the same time, rather like the initiation rituals of present-day Aborigines in Australia, the rites might provide, with the help of marks and symbols, a kind of cram course in tribal law, long before the existence of orthodox written records.

It is only recently that anthropologists have realised that the apparently abstract line patterns which the Aborigines make and preserve can convey far more information, to them, than apparently more comprehensible animal images. Mastering the information in some of these lines and patterns was such a vital component of male identity for Aborigines that a woman could never be allowed to see them. It is also probable that the Ice-Age images could have been made as part of specific rituals related to seasonal changes and the cyclic renewal of the sources of life. The appearance of animal images together with patterns of hand prints, finger-marks, dots, circles and grids, reinforces this view. Sometimes, an image has been over-painted and overlaid by symbols over many generations.

Apart from the animal
representations, there are
sets of completely abstract-
looking patterns, some of
which have been interpreted
as records of the seasons
or lunar movements.

The function of cave art

The archeologist Alexander Marshack has argued convincingly that,
taken together, all these facts indicate that the early idea, that cave
paintings were simply images of potential meals and that the arrows
drawn near them expressed the hope that hunters would successfully
kill them or that their numbers would increase, is far too simple
and was based on inadequate observation. Lions and bears, for
example, not the object of the hunt and not a species that Ice-Age
man could conceivably want to see increased, are often shown.
Instead, it is most likely that these, and all the other animals we see
painted in the caves, symbolised for the Ice-Age people the way
that their society coped with all the momentous events of life –
birth, adolescence, and marriage – and the seasonal problems of
survival presented by the bitter winter and the chance of death.
Thus the real and symbolic worlds were intertwined, as they still
are in many primitive communities.

When the last great Ice Age ended in Europe about 12,000 years
ago, this way of life disappeared, but the art had already begun to
spread. Dating from about 15,000 years ago to the present, we find

painted and engraved images on rock faces all over the world, a tradition which only began to end as permanent temples appeared. Clearly, the mysterious legacy of rock-art was left to us by minds capable, like our own, of abstraction and metaphor; unlike us they did not distinguish between art, religion and life. To them, all activities had not only purely functional aspects, but also aesthetic, and what we would call religious, aspects.

Hunter–gatherer societies

This attitude to life is often described by anthropologists who have studied the beliefs and practices of the last few remnants of the hunger–gatherer societies which still exist on earth, like the Mbuti Pygmies of the Congo forests, or the Bushmen of the Kalahari.

Hunter–gatherers seem to make very little distinction between themselves and the natural world around them. In their life-style, they do not so much try to *control* the natural world by their actions, as to *reflect* its mysterious ebb and flow. Like all other human beings, they have a considerable sense that there is more to the world than meets the eye, and that there is some supernatural sense in which all the events and objects in the world have a proper balanced order, as do the affairs of human beings. This order extends into the *past* as a set of stories or myths, which often provide a metaphorical model of how the world began.

In the *present*, simple rituals celebrate the order in the world. Colin Turnbull describes how, for example, the Ituri forest Pygmies would place a basket of food by a central fire every evening to invoke the presence of the God of the Forest to join invisibly in their songs and stories. Then there are specific rituals to celebrate humans' movement from one status to another, to mark birth, adolescence, marriage or even death. These are rarely very complicated and often practised in an easy-going, everyday fashion. The rituals and beliefs of these small groups reflect the coherent way they have come to understand the relation between themselves and their environment. Often it is believed that, just as a human being plainly consists of a body which is animated by a spirit, the rest of the world, its woods and rivers and trees, is similarly animated by spirit forces or by one overall spirit force. These entities are always mysterious and powerful but, like the environment which supports an essentially simple and stable life-style, they are basically benign and approachable.

Hunter–gatherers do not require masses of property – indeed it would only slow them down. What little they have, however, is carefully made, of pleasing shape and often decorated. If they have wealth in any sense, it is in their confidence, loyalty to each other, and in the stories and songs which take up a large part of their lives.

These people usually feel confident and secure in the environment which supports them. Life is constantly interesting and purposeful.

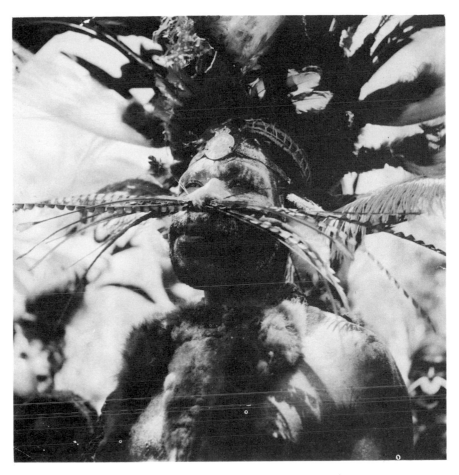

'Primitive humans think of themselves as vital characters in an interesting and important story.'

Their beliefs are not a rationalisation of their inadequacy, or an attempt to cope with the fears and anxieties of life, so much as a vivid and satisfying set of metaphors, reflecting their sense of themselves as vital characters in an interesting and important story.

The move away from nature

Most human beings, including the Ice-Age cave people, probably lived in a similar way, and had a similar approach to life, until about 10,000 years ago. Then, after a transitional period of about 3,000 years, during which gardening was practised alongside hunting, we begin to find increasing evidence of a major change of lifestyle. Agriculture spread from the Middle East, bringing active tilling of the soil, domestication of animals and their gathering into flocks and herds, advances in pottery, sewing and weaving, and the building of permanent housing.

Human beings began to lose their easy confidence in a beneficent, if mysterious, Nature, although this must have been a gradual process. Many of the Indian tribes of North America, for example, were able both to cultivate and to maintain a sense of real affinity for the wild, in which they continued to hunt and gather. This feeling is reflected in their pantheistic view of the wild, in which the wisdom of one god is revealed in all the diversity of bounteous nature, and it is reflected in their thanksgiving ceremonies.

We asked a traditional religious chief of the Iroquois, Mohawk Chief Tom Porter, how some of them still attempted to practise the old religion, and what it meant to them. His verbatim reply gives us a real sense of the elegance and balance of the world which these people perceived.

The religious life of the various Iroquois peoples of the American Eastern Seaboard was distinguished by a concern with giving thanks for the natural processes which sustained them. A number of festivals celebrated various key events in the cycle of the seasons, such as the Maple Sap Festival, the Green Corn Festival and the Harvest Festival. The Mohawks celebrated the dawn of every new day with a simple ceremony in which they burnt tobacco leaves so that their smoke would rise to greet the Great Spirit. (From a painting by Ernest Smith, Rochester Museum and Service Centre, New York State.)

'Every morning, here in this camp, our people get up just before the sunrise, and we offer sacred tobacco. It was given to us Mohawk people from the beginning of time, from the beginning of the world. This tobacco is offered in a sacred fire. As the smoke rises into the sky, it meets all the powers that God, the creator, has made. This smoke will carry our word to the ears of all the living things of the world as it goes to the sky. And every morning that's what we do. We offer this tobacco and this prayer of thanksgiving and gratitude to Mother Earth, to the trees, to all the berries, to all the medicines that grow, to all the animals big and small, to the animals that live next to our houses and help us out, to all the fish, to all the bugs, and to all the snakes, and to everything in the world. And then we go higher, to the trees that give us maple sugar to sweeten our food, and to give us the firewood for the cold winters so our children won't freeze. We give thanks to all the trees, because trees are living, you see. Living. They're not idols. It's nothing like that. Many missionaries thought we were worshipping idols, but the trees are living. They make oxygen, scientists say, make life. We've known that for many thousand years, and so we acknowledge those contributions.

'Then we go to the wind which you are feeling right now, to grandfather-thunder, grandmother-moon, to all the stars in the universe. We acknowledge them all. The unseen forces that we don't know about, we also acknowledge.

'Every sunrise we do that, till we get to the top, to the head of all creation, our creator. Each of those different elements that I have mentioned, the grass, the trees, the people and animals and birds – altogether if you add them up you come to the total. That's the creator. The life is the creator and the creator is that life.'

The religious beliefs described by chief Tom Porter sound perhaps as if they have been influenced by Christian beliefs in one God, but in fact the first white people to encounter the North American Indians discovered that many of them already had a firm belief in one ultimate God. There is no reason to believe that they had not been doing so for at least 10,000 years, and the belief that there is some fundamental unifying force in the Universe – reflected in Nature – may go back to long before the Agricultural Revolution, perhaps even to the beginnings of human consciousness itself.

The influence of tradition
A belief in one ultimate god or spirit is also implicit in the beliefs of many other primitive agricultural societies, particularly in Africa. This was often not recognised by early anthropologists, who were more impressed by the widespread existence of ancestor worship, a common phenomenon in traditional societies. It is common because primitive agricultural societies are strongly directed by tradition. Unlike hunter–gatherers or small gardening communities, their survival depends on the regular and reliable use of fairly artificial techniques of crop or animal husbandry, and on the organisation of large groups into stable families, clans and villages. If all this is to work, all the members of the society must give a regular and reliable obedience to the customs of that society. Members may not be quite sure exactly what it is about their way of life that ensures its success, but they know it is a success, and they know the best way to keep it so is to do everything the ancestors said should be done, in the way they said it should be done.

Traditional art and religion
Both the art and the religious beliefs and practises of these societies reflect this. The materials and designs used for clothes, houses, tools and weapons, and their shapes and colours, are all heavily influenced by tradition. This may produce elaborate and striking artwork, but it is always dominated by traditional themes and symbols. Music, poetry and dance will also reflect these. As in the very simplest communities, members of the agricultural societies expect that all of them will take some part in every form of artistic activity. They use the prosperity and leisure that their way of life brings, to allow them to express their artistic drive.

Just as their arts reflect the authority of tradition in their lives, the religious activities and beliefs of these people are often dominated by regard for their ancestors. Like the traditions which they have left to their children, the ancestors are never very far away from everyday life. Their personalities are often as real in death as they were in life. These personalities are often wilful and arbitrary, as they were in life, but they are always deeply respected. The ancestors may live in a spirit world, which is a supernatural reflection of this one, but they sometimes leave it to speak in visions or dreams to mortals who isolate or starve themselves. The mortals may change their consciousness with chanting and rhythmic dancing or natural drugs, and ancestors may then enter the body of the ecstatic worshipper and speak through his mouth. But they will always recommend a conservative and traditional solution to everyday problems.

Ceremonies
Once a society adopts intensive agriculture, it can no longer depend on the easy support of nature. It may retain some beliefs about forces in the wild, but those forces are no longer the focus of the society's concern. The spirits of the wild may be seen as mischievous or even malevolent, but they are not really important. The prosperity of the small primitive agricultural community depends ultimately on the unchanging cycle of the seasons, the warmth of the sun, the fertility of the earth and the domestic animals.

These abstract forces are often described as personal entities or deities. The continuing human sense that there is some kind of orderly connection between human social activities and the physical environment, both that which can be directly understood, and that which is essentially mysterious, is often expressed in rituals and ceremonies. They reflect the agricultural community's respect for these powerful forces.

Sometimes, ceremonies are carried out which help people to connect with spirit forces within themselves. We preserve this notion when we speak of 'grace', or 'virtue', or of someone being made of 'the right stuff'. Accumulating this spiritual force or fluid is often achieved by isolation or fasting, and possessing it not only gives the individual a sense of power and security, but a sense of rightness between himself, his culture, and the environment in which it exists. Examples of belief in this substance are widespread, and they include the *manitou* of North American Indians and the *sucti* of the Balinese.

As members of a traditional society publicly accept the religious beliefs and rituals which it has developed, they also demonstrate that they accept and respect their society's definition of appropriate behaviour.

In this way, religious beliefs maintain order. The same balance and propriety present in the supernatural also shape the natural world. Traditional customs and religious beliefs influence every aspect of everyday life whether in work or artistic expression. On

The modern performance of the York Mystery Cycle (*above*) gives us some idea of its spectacular impact. In medieval times, it was presented on movable stages, and was a pageant.

'The Adoration of the Magi' by Gentile da Fabriano (1370–1427) (*left*). Like that of other traditional societies, the art of medieval Europe was constrained by traditional themes, symbols and techniques, no matter how brilliant the individual artist. This kind of art helped describe the Biblical stories to those who could not read, and thus shared a function with the Mystery plays.

A typical offering of fruit,
pastries and flowers (*above*)
for a Balinese ceremony (see
also page 18). The elaborate
shadow puppets, the
Wayang Kulit, are an essential part of every Balinese
festival. They are decorated
with a degree of detail that
cannot be observed through
the screen. *Above right*, the
craftsman follows a pattern
in punching the design.
Right, the shadow play is
performed. The decoration
can be seen on the back of
the puppet. The shadow
screen is on the left.

the other hand the rhythms of everyday life, and the special vitality
which art brings to experience, come together in religious rituals.

A traditional society – beautiful Bali

In many modern yet traditional agricultural societies, this integration
of art, religion and everyday life is still maintained. The modern
Balinese offer a particularly striking example of this integration,
although their religion contains some elements typical of a more
complex urban society. For a variety of reasons, Bali, one of the
several thousand islands of the Indonesian archipelago, was not very
easy for Westerners to get into until the late 1960s, and even now,
tourism is mostly confined to a relatively small part of the island. Bali
demonstrates the way a stable agricultural community will integrate
its religious, artistic and practical activity, so that each will support
the other, and also provide a framework of morals, meanings and
purposes for each individual.

The Balinese are greatly dependent on their rice crops to maintain
their large population. This is reflected in a cult which pervades
every aspect of Balinese life. In Balinese mythology, rice was a gift
to man from the Gods. It resulted originally from the cosmic union
of the fundamental male and female forces of earth and water. This
divine origin is reflected in the elaborate rituals which accompany
its daily preparation, and the daily offerings which are made of it.
The Balinese worship their ancestors, and also the pantheon of
Hindu gods, like Shiva, God of Destruction, and Vishnu, God of
Sacrifice.

Each village has at least four temples, and in ten thousand temples
across the island, there are frequent festivals and ceremonies to
propitiate the gods, often involving the sacrifice of domestic animals.
There are festivals to celebrate the rhythmic cyclic renewal of the
sources of life and prosperity, both within the year, and from one
special year to another. There is even a special festival to celebrate
a hundred year cycle, which is conducted at the 'mother temple' at
Besakih on the slopes of the volcano Gunung Agung.

These festivals and ceremonies, in both their preparation and
execution, take up a large part of Balinese everyday life. A festival
will often take all day, and go on into the hours of darkness. The
preparations will usually take even longer and involve a great deal
of artistic activity. This preoccupation with artistic excellence in
the service of religion goes far beyond anything we are familiar
with in the West. For example, both the food offerings balanced on
the heads of the women who bring them to the festivals, and those
prepared within the temple itself, involve exquisite and complex
arrangements of flowers, fruit and specially coloured rice-flour
pastry. The elaborate shadow puppets, the Wayang Kulit, are an
essential part of every religious festival, passing on myths and
legends. They are constructed and painted in a detail which cannot
possibly be seen through the shadow screen through which the
audience watch.

Everywhere in Bali, there are colourful and beautiful pictures, sculptures, towers, altars and offerings. The Balinese do not expect these to last. The humidity of the region hastens the decay of many materials, and in any case, many artifacts are destroyed as part of the religious ritual for which they are produced. There are exceptions of course. Masks are used by the men and women who take part in those dances and dramas which act out the various Balinese myths and legends; they are preserved for many years. These masks allow people to assume the personalities of the spirits they represent, and they are supposed to accumulate power as they are used more and more often. They often accumulate such power that their wearers must possess considerable *sucti* (spiritual grace), or else they may be overwhelmed by the power of the mask. The most powerful mask, the Rangda, is reputed to be able to send those with insufficient *sucti* insane.

The Balinese attitude to the power of the masks reflects their attitude to the disruptive power of what they see as the lower, more animal, parts of human nature, which must be firmly repressed. Life, both here on Earth and in the supernatural world which parallels it, demands a constant conflict between order and chaos, the clean and the unclean, and good and evil. These themes constantly reappear in their myths and plays.

Stability in Balinese society

Balinese life is lived in small densely populated villages, in which there is always the possibility of disagreement. The highly efficient rice cultivation, essential to Balinese life, depends on continuing co-operation. Very little conflict occurs, in fact, and the Balinese generally show very little public emotion of any kind. There is a great concern for propriety and correctness, and, to foreign observers, daily interactions are so ritualistic that it is often difficult to distinguish between religious and everyday procedures. Spontaneous, possibly disruptive, action by individual Balinese is firmly constrained by their religious beliefs and rituals. Instead, individualism is harnessed to the sophisticated and all-encompassing artistic activity which makes Bali such a vivid experience to the visitor.

Religious and artistic activity is in no sense casual to the Balinese. Unlike all their neighbours, they resisted the tide of Islam which swept Indonesia a few hundred years ago. Now they have to maintain that separate identity. Without their own religious and artistic preoccupations, they would not be able to contain the forces which threaten, both from within and without, their existence as a stable and separate community.

The first city-states

Balinese society fascinates Westerners because it is so different from our own; we live in a society in which art and religion inhabit quite separate areas in everyday life. The fundamental separation, in 'developed' societies, between art and religion, and between both of these and everyday life, stems from a change in the relation of human beings to their environment, which began about 6,000 years ago.

The development of irrigation and more effective agriculture laid the foundation for the joining together, usually by conquest, of numbers of tribes. They became confederacies, each with the resources to build large cities and maintain large armies. The cultures based in cities began to organise themselves in an entirely new way.

In sites in Mesopotamia (3,500 BC), Egypt (3,200 BC), India (2,500 BC), and China (1,500 BC), city societies began to organise themselves into hierarchies of status and power, and to allocate particular functions and duties to their members. Members of these city societies had moved far away from the natural forces on which their prosperity ultimately depended, and as they lost contact, they seemed also to lose all confidence in the support of those forces. Urban humans began to distinguish between themselves and Nature.

One sign of this split was the increasing preoccupation with funeral rites. Humans who lived in a society which had lost the easy dependence of the hunter–gatherer on Nature could not expect to return to it when they died. Instead, with a kind of defiant optimism, they looked forward to moving on to yet another society. Just as they had needed equipment in this world, the newly dead were often provided with food, utensils and weapons for the journey to the next. We find evidence of this practice from the earliest agricultural sites, but in the new cities for the rich, these preoccupations could reach new heights, with increasingly complex prayers and ceremonies performed by a new specialised class – the priests.

The new urban dwellers began to stress the distinction between work, art and religious observance. Religious behaviour became increasingly confined to restricted times and buildings; where once the sacred areas had represented merely a concentration of a constant religious feeling pervading everyday life, they now represented its only location.

Artistic activity split in several directions; on the one hand it went to serve the emerging priesthood, providing decoration and architecture for substantial temples and for all the trappings of religious ceremony. On the other, it served the emerging power elite to reflect their increasing wealth and sophistication. Armies of craftsmen and artists could now be employed full-time, to create fine weavings, leather work, metal work in gold and silver, carvings and cut precious stones, portraits, inlaid mosaics, and a vast variety of pectorals, necklaces, ear-plugs, lip-plugs, diadems, head gear, and all the symbolic regalia by which the nobility demonstrated its status.

But the development of the arts as trappings of power did not prevent artistic activity being done by the ordinary labourers; they still had their songs, dances and what we now call the folk arts – the part-time artistic activities of the most lowly workers or slaves.

The angry gods

The new city-states tended to absorb the local beliefs of the various smaller tribes which they conquered into their own religious beliefs, but they arranged these local spirits into 'pantheons' or 'collections of gods'. In Mesopotamia, just as those on Earth struggled for power in the hierarchies which ruled the cities, the local spirits of fields and streams apparently organised themselves into a superstate, with a governing council, which endlessly watched over the squabbles and love-affairs of some two thousand deities. Similar, if less elaborate, pantheons are found among the early Egyptians, Romans, and Greeks.

It is easy for us to feel a smug amusement that people could apparently believe in such a ludicrous multitude of deities, but it is important to remember that, as much as anything else, the creation of these pantheons was a political move, by which several groups of people could be consolidated into one nation. Central government could also be consolidated by assigning divinity to the king. From the foundation of the kingdom of Egypt in about 3,200 BC until about 2,600 BC, the pharoah was regarded as an incarnation of Horus, the sun god. He was not to fully relinquish this status for several thousand years. As the various gods had the power to influence the natural processes on which city life ultimately depended, the new religions offered explanations for the various problems which beset the rulers of a culture which was increasingly exploiting its environment to its limits, and was thus particularly vulnerable to floods or crop failure. They also offered means by which these might be obviated, such as sacrifice or prayer.

The new priesthoods had the power and affluence to develop elaborate and complicated ceremonies, and even secondary ceremonies of purification which ensured that the primary ones maintained their efficacy.

In so far as these new religions claimed to help their believers control the world, they were, in one sense, pseudo-science. If ceremonies and sacrifices were carried out and the desired result was not achieved, then there were endless explanations for this; the ceremony had not been carried out properly, the supplicant was not pure in heart, or the gods, in their wisdom, had simply decided to withhold approval.

The hunter–gatherers and members of the simple agricultural societies had believed themselves to be in balance with the supernatural, having special and privileged relations with certain natural spirits and the ever-present ancestors. The religious beliefs of these newly alienated human cultures, however, are characterised by feelings of powerlessness and fear.

The new religions often demanded a supplicatory approach to irascible and powerful gods. These demands could reach appalling proportions, as in the dreadful sacrifices by the Aztecs of Mexico, in which hearts were taken from live humans as part of ceremonies involving the deaths of thousands of victims. These practices continued until the liquidation of the Aztec empire by the Spanish in the early sixteenth century.

New attitudes to death

The new state religions prescribed proper public behaviour: who might marry who, what the duties of a servant were to his master, what the punishments for failure to comply should be. They were not particularly concerned, however, with the individual moral choices which ordinary individuals had to make, nor with offering them a meaningful system by which they could understand the purpose of the frustrations and problems of their own everyday lives or of their mortality. The urban religions were mainly concerned with maintaining a proper relationship between the state and its rulers, and the often cruel and powerful gods they sought to propitiate.

The controllers of these centralised hierarchic societies accumulated wealth, both because it represented power and authority, and perhaps the possession of many and beautiful objects acted as some reassurance to them. They had lost contact with the comfortable and meaningful simplicity of primitive life.

Whereas to the primitive humans death was not a great problem, but only a means by which the personality went off to join the ancestors, to the rich and powerful it was an enormous problem because it meant leaving all their wealth behind. In many cases they decided to try not to. A great part of the activity of these rulers' subjects was devoted to making sure that they took the many possessions and servants they had required in this life with them into the next. The rich, however, did not return to the ancestors of the tribe, they went on in death to join the powerful gods they had attempted to appease in life.

The great world religions

By the time the Spanish wiped out the Aztec culture, the fierce ancient religions which it represented had all but disappeared in the rest of the world, to be replaced by the great monotheistic world religions which had first originated in Asia about two thousand years before. The ancient religions of the first city-states had not offered much satisfaction to the increasingly large numbers of ordinary people who had to endure the poverty and difficulties which the new centralised economies produced, and whose problems were made even worse by frequent wars and conquests. Some 2,500 years ago, however, a new kind of religious belief began to emerge, one which stressed the *personal* relation between the individual and one universal force or god, whose power transcended the immediate and local interests of the gods of the state, and gave some sense to the inherent suffering of life.

In the East, Gautama founded Buddhism as an offshoot of the

Well-established religions are able to make elaborate demands on the human predilection for ritual behaviour. Here a group of Muslims, followers of Islam, gather at the site of the mosque subsequently built in Regent's Park, London. They pray towards Mecca.

many-godded Hinduism. Buddhism stressed the personal redemptive power of self-denial. This religion spread along trading routes, so that by about AD 500, it had become as important in Japan, for example, as official Shintoism, and had joined Confucianism and Taoism in China.

Christianity

European history was to be dominated by the one God of the Christians. The Jews, more than 3,000 years ago, had already adopted one god with a secret name, which could not be spoken but whose initials approximated to the sound 'ya-weh'. Although this god had guided their escape from slavery under the Egyptians, he was a stern and demanding god of the old tradition, more concerned with maintaining the solidarity and discipline of a nomadic battling people than with their individual problems. He did, however, give them dominion over all other forms of earthly creation, a theme which was to be maintained by the Christian beliefs which were to evolve from Judaism.

Over thousands of years, and in a variety of circumstances, Judaism was revitalised by a succession of prophets. The most dramatic change in the Jews' fortunes came when the area we now call Palestine, in which they lived, became part of the confident and authoritative Roman empire. This aroused enormous conflicts in

Jewish society, as the success of the Romans' pragmatic colonialist policy seemed to make nonsense of the old traditions. Roman authority seemed to defy that of the orthodox religious Jewish hierarchy. Out of this conflict emerged the humane and powerful revelation of the prophet Jesus: the identity of God and love.

Although some of the basic themes of Christianity had been rehearsed in certain early religious cults, for example by the followers of Zarathustra, Jesus's synthesis was entirely new. To Christians, he was more than simply a prophet: he was the Son of God, God made flesh on Earth. His ideas had enormous force and clarity for poor and culturally outraged people all over the Roman empire.

The same efficient communication system which had provided the conditions for the emergence of Christianity ensured that it spread rapidly. After two hundred years of sporadic repression (with which epic Hollywood films have made most of us familiar), Christianity was adopted by the Romans early in the fourth century as the first imperial state religion to be specifically concerned with the needs and hopes of individuals. It also defined for them a personal morality.

The Catholic Church and Nature

When the Roman empire collapsed, the Church remained as a powerful cohesive and political force among independent warring city-states, at the same time disseminating its personal redemptive message through the hierarchical structure and competent professional organisation which it inherited from the empire which had founded it.

The Pope is the most spectacular high priest in the world's religions. The identification of this office with the voice of God is still so complete for Roman Catholics that he can, in certain circumstances, make infallible pronouncements on matters of religious belief and practice.

Christianity continued to spread across the world, being halted in the East only by the power of Islam in the Mogul empire of northern India. Islam, another state religion of personal hope, was founded by Mohammed in about AD 500, as an offshoot of Judaism. It had spread rapidly as the separate Persian empires collapsed.

In Europe, despite various minor heretical rebellions, the Christian Catholic Church spread rapidly, mainly as a result of the missionary fervour of various conquering Christian kings, and the way in which it could easily absorb local beliefs and practices into the Church calendar. In those European countries which had worshipped a fertility goddess for example, Mary, the Mother of Jesus, was now worshipped with similar intensity. Because of its attitude to nature, however, which was that it was there to exploit, Christianity destroyed the balance the old pagan 'primitive' religions had maintained between humans and the environment, and helped to catalyse the increasingly effective exploitation of resources. It also ensured the destruction of the old social order and of the artistic and religious traditions which went with it – the songs and dances and rituals that are completely lost to us now, and remain only as a few isolated stones on lonely moors.

Christianity and the arts

As the Church gained in power and wealth, its officials became major patrons of the arts. To celebrate their power and the power of God, whose earthly representatives they firmly believed themselves to be, they constructed enormous and elaborate cathedrals, filled with beautiful and precious decorations, as well as thousands of simpler churches as beautifully decorated as people could afford.

The human drive to create order and pattern in the supernatural world in the same terms as those of the living world was exemplified by the Catholic Church in a system of belief which was so tightly interlocking that it could account, and vividly, for every event in an individual's life and after-life. Medieval Catholics saw the universe as a complex bureaucratic system of saints and angels who, like the officials and priests they dealt with in this world, had to be approached via the proper bureaucratic channels.

The currency of this spirit world was 'grace', achieved by prayer, denial, suffering and the cash purchase of indulgences as well as by good works and the acceptance of the sacraments. Grace is a kind of spiritual fuel which gives the soul life and energy. Those who accumulated sufficient grace could hope to join the elite of the great and the good in a perpetual paradise, while those who lost it were condemned to make up the eternal balance of good and evil by their eternal suffering. Once again art was put to the service of religion, as this view of the universe was spread among the many who could not read the few official Latin books, by putting pictures and statues in the churches, by the hymns and chants of the Mass, and by the acting out of the major Christian myths.

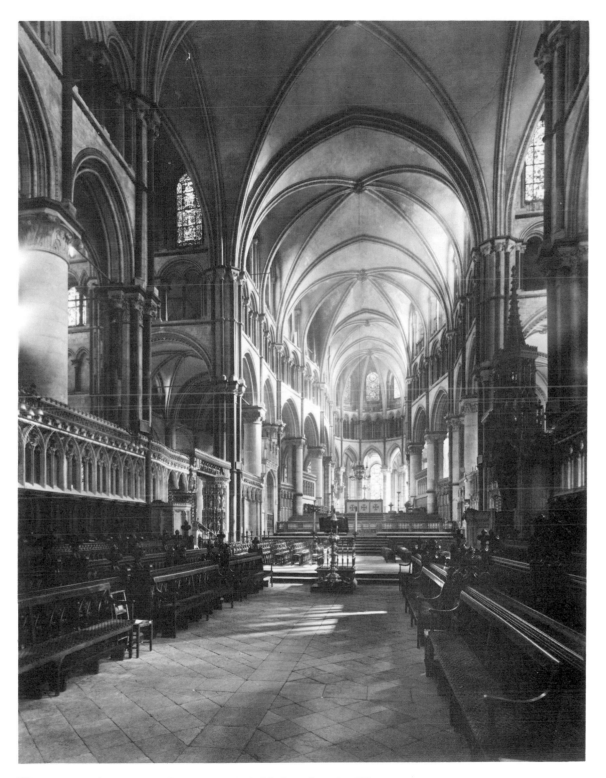

'They constructed enormous and elaborate cathedrals': Canterbury (twelfth century).

Mystery plays

These performances evolved from relatively simple medieval Latin liturgical plays, which we first see in the tenth century, into the Biblical pageants of the fifteenth century. The York Mystery, or Miracle, Cycle is probably the most magnificent example.

The cycle consisted of 48 pageants, which enacted those episodes from the Old and New Testaments which their producers believed best demonstrated the whole Christian scheme of salvation. The pageants were traditionally enacted on Whit Sunday or on Corpus Christi Day (the Thursday eleven days after Whit Sunday). The first recorded performance in York was in 1376, though the cycle may go back even further. The municipal authorities were in general charge of the whole production, but each of the many trade guilds of the town paid for, and produced, each individual pageant. As far as possible, the pageant enacted was the one thought to be most relevant to the guild which produced it; so that, for example, the Water Drawers enacted the pageant 'Noah's Flood' at Chester. Each guild performed its pageant on a waggon which was dragged round as part of the Corpus Christi procession and then stopped at pre-arranged places.

Very little is known about the able people who wrote these pageants, though the fifteenth-century manuscripts still exist and we know the writers brought together religious and secular, Christian and pagan, themes, and put them into verses, which often follow complicated and elegant rules of rhyme and metre.

'Who eats the fruit of
   good and ill
Shall have knowing as
   well as He.'
The York Pageant of the 'Fall of Man' is fifth in the Cycle. The craft responsible for producing it was the Guild of Coopers (makers of casks and buckets).

Although the pageants were essentially religious in nature, they retained humorous and popular themes, which made them fun as well as educational, and they produced a form of drama which we can still enjoy, and which can still move us. The Crucifixion pageant, for example, at York is particularly moving. It is the work of a talented un-named playwright now known only as 'The York Realist'. He was unusual in that he obliged his audience to follow every drawn-out detail of fixing Christ to the cross, including the cruel stretching of his body by cords, so it reached the nail holes, and several awkward attempts to fix the cross upright. By the time it is up, the audience is emotionally exhausted.

The York plays and those like them were a vital feature of medieval life and they were enormously popular. They are an excellent example of the human drive to integrate religious and artistic activity into everyday life. They came to an end in the reign of Elizabeth I, only as a result of Reformist zeal, reinforced by state opposition to 'idolatry and superstition', and they were not to be performed again for over three hundred years. Since 1958, however, they have been performed every four years by local inhabitants at York, giving us some idea of the energy and vitality of those ancient traditions.

Christ is crucified. The Crucifixion is one of the 48 pageants which together constitute the York Mystery Cycle. They still have considerable emotional impact. This comment of one modern audience member is typical: 'The crowd were clamouring, "Crucify him, crucify him," and then I began to realise that it's not Christ we're trying; it's *we* who are on trial!'

The Church and authority

With time, as the Church aged, and as plague and conflict ravaged Europe, Catholicism became, like the older state religions from which it had emerged, increasingly concerned with maintaining the authority and prosperity of the state into which it was now so firmly infiltrated; it did this by attempting to resist change. The Church's concern for maintaining its position was reflected in the philosophical beliefs held in Europe during the long period between the final collapse of the Roman empire in the fifth century, and the period of intense philosophical artistic and scientific activity, beginning in the fifteenth century, which we call the Renaissance, and which coincides with the fall of Constantinople, and the brain drain of its various scholars into European cultural life. During the long periods of the Church's domination, it had been widely believed that all real knowledge had been previously accumulated during an earlier Golden Age (particularly by the Greeks) and that there was little point in arguing with these ancient philosophies. One of these philosophies stressed the enormous difference between the integrity of the spirit, and the mere earthly body with its puny senses and carnal lusts. It was widely believed that the evidence of these earthly senses was inferior to the evidence of spiritual revelation, particularly as this was mediated by Holy Mother Church. Sight was considered a particularly suspect sense, because of the existence of optical illusions; it could thus provide a channel by which the Devil and his followers could deceive the unwary. For example, Plato had said, 'Every soul possesses an organ, the intellect, better worth saving than a thousand eyes, because it is our only means of seeing the truth.' St Augustine said, 'Go not out of doors; return into yourself. In the inner man dwells truth.' It was thus perfectly logical to the Church fathers that even as late as 1633, they should demand of Galileo that he deny the evidence of his telescope and ignore his calculations, as they showed that the ancient model of the solar system, which the Church endorsed, was inadequate and wrong. The Church was concerned not with the propagation of information which was technically correct, but of that which was spiritually proper, and which would maintain the status quo.

The Church had always been helped in that task of maintaining order by the way it accorded the status of true human beings only to those who truly met its demands. Where primitive man saw personalities everywhere in nature, as well as in his own society, the Church recognised as real only the personalities of its faithful adherents. From the time of the Crusades, members of other religions were not regarded as true humans, and could thus be destroyed. Even its own people, if they held the wrong ideas, could be classified as witches, and put to indescribably vicious tortures until they confessed to Satanic possession, when they could be executed.

The impact of printing

Some of the first books printed from moveable type, by Johann Gutenberg and his fellow craftsmen from about 1440 onwards, were more concerned with proper procedures for the inquisition of witches, than with spreading the results of scientific enquiry. But as more and more books were produced, and popular (vernacular) literacy spread, the conditions were created in which the Church's imperial hold over Europe's ideas could collapse dramatically. By the end of the fifteenth century, ten million books had been printed, including several editions of the Bible and various religious polemics. The Greek text of the New Testament, translated by Erasmus of Rotterdam and published in 1516, revealed the shortcomings of basic ecclesiastical writings. Erasmus's *Praise of Folly*, published in 1511, had already satirised the Church, among other institutions, and between 1517 and 1520, Luther alone published 300,000 copies of more than thirty anti-Church books and pamphlets. The new books were very efficient in spreading the new ideas about Christianity that came out of the Reformation of 1517, and hastened the spread of the new versions of Christianity which followed.

Science and technology

The books could also carry the ideas and results of the new breed of scientists. As evidence accumulated, a general concept spread, that the truth about nature could be acquired by experiment and vigorous enquiry. The essentially exploitive approach to nature which the Church had first established, however, had not changed. Francis Bacon (1561–1626) said, 'We shall torture Nature to make her yield up her secrets,' rather as the Inquisitors had tortured people to make them yield up theirs, and as the witch-finders of the new Protestant churches continued to do, well into the seventeenth century. As the 'torture of Nature' revealed her secrets, new technologies were developed to make use of the new knowledge. The primary issues in people's minds became not so much religious as political, concerned with the development of new resources, and the distribution of new affluence.

Despite all the complex and dramatic changes which were to occur in the Western world over the next three hundred years, it is clear that the new strategy for the application of science and technology, which was to transform Western society, continued to reflect the fundamental Christian attitude to nature: it was there to serve Man.

The Industrial Revolution

The revitalised and simplified forms of Christianity which emerged out of the chaos and confusion of urban life in the early nineteenth century also maintained this approach. The main function of these new fundamentalist religions was to provide a background framework for individual moral behaviour, in a complicated and rapidly changing society which was committed to the acquisition of wealth by exploiting new technologies.

In this rapidly changing society, only the individual himself, in a personal and secret relationship with God, could define appropriate moral behaviour, as he interpreted God's fundamental word as revealed in the Bible. The complicated rituals of the Catholic Church were replaced, in the fundamentalist religions, by austere meetings in which believers met to remind one another of their personal commitment to Jesus Christ, and His message of brotherly love. To them, the rituals, decorations and statues of the Catholic Church represented rigidity and inflexibility, putting up a barrier between them and their personal God. This further speeded the separation of art and religion which we now take for granted.

'The Grocer and his Family at Prayer'. Drawn and engraved by J. Franklin (1800–1868), it is a typical scene of formalised religion penetrating every home.

Music, however, with its power to move the individual and enlarge his self-perception, was retained as hymns, accompanied for a while by church orchestras, and then by the celestial notes of highly developed church organs. Later still, with mass production of the harmonium after about 1840, even the smallest church could afford music.

Art in the Industrial Revolution

By the beginning of the nineteenth century, Western society was split into two quite separate groups: the middle and upper classes, and the mass of the working poor. This split was reflected in two virtually separate economic systems, one which traded in pennies, and the other in pounds. Most of the time, the mass of the poor wore the same drab clothes that they laboured in, and their mean dwellings, thrown up as the new workers flooded in from the country, offered few visual stimuli to please aesthetic sensibilities. The overt artistic expression of these people was confined largely to music; to the songs and stories that had been brought from their rural villages, the new songs of the public houses, which many of them attended, and to the performance of villagers' and miners' brass bands. They also poured their creative energy into hobbies, breeding small birds and animals, or gardening.

Fine art

183 Defiant Optimists

None of these activities was regarded as of any artistic significance, however, because, in the period after the Renaissance, the concept of 'fine art' had emerged to dominate most people's thinking about the place of art in Western society. The artists and craftsmen who had laboured for the Princes of the Church had been admired for their work, but were expected to restrict it to meet the traditional demands of their patrons. As the concept of patronage extended outside the Church, it was still confined to certain set themes – particularly classical mythology – but the range of expression which art could take was extended, and could more and more directly reflect the sensitivity and creativity of the artist. Increasingly, the rich and noble vied with one another in acquiring the service of the best artists, whose perceptions, transformed into music, painting and sculpture, would enlarge the patrons' own delicately nurtured sensibilities. In the eighteenth-century courts and salons, the idea was developed that there existed a separate world of refined aesthetic sensibility, to which the great artist could lead the sensitive and noble. This world existed quite apart from the dull and gritty reality of the labourers on which the nobles' wealth depended. There emerged a grand distinction between Life and Art.

The distinction between the artistic professional and his audience was reflected in an enormous new respect for competence and creativity. Ordinary people might dabble in painting and playing music, but *artistic* painting, ballet and music, could be produced only by genius craftsmen who possessed an almost mystical ability to transform the experience of the sensitive observer. Thus Fine Art had qualities which were not present in the mere decoration, dance or song as practised by ordinary people.

Art and organisation

As the number of people rich enough to identify themselves with the aesthetic preoccupations of the nobles increased, there emerged the great expensive classical performing arts. They reflected the affluence and organisational ability of the societies which produced them. Ballet, opera, and orchestral concerts are essentially the production by the few of highly skilled spectacles for the many.

The same spectacular effects were to be achieved by the new architecture, which celebrated the new technological power of Man over Nature. It also reflected the persistent distinction between mere life and Great Art. The new architects constructed factories which looked like the Gothic cathedrals which had once celebrated the power of the Church, and railway stations which resembled the medieval castles of the old barons were built for the new ones.

New materials and new techniques did gradually evoke more innovative design, however. For example, we begin to see the first steel skyscrapers appearing in Chicago by the 1880s. About the same time, the Galérie d'Orléans was built by Fontaine in Paris, and Paxton produced the unprecedented Crystal Palace for the Great Exhibition of 1851 in London.

Not until 1919, however, when the German Walter Gropius founded the Bauhaus school of architecture, dedicated to realising the full potentialities of new materials and methods of production, do we begin to see those blocks and towers now so typical of all developed urban communities. The use of concrete reinforced with metal strip allowed the construction of multiple-dwelling blocks which exactly suited the heroic ideas of a generation of city planners. The distress caused by the environment so created to those who had to live in it, however, underlines the inherent human need for an environment with a human scale, which allows room for 'personal space' and the opportunity to establish individual and distinctive homes.

Art and revolution

The drive to experiment and change was not only apparent in building: it had already pervaded all of Western society, as artists began to extend and develop fine art forms. Beethoven (1770–1827) had shocked his audiences in the early nineteenth century by revealing, in a revolutionary way, the enormous metaphorical power of music to express feelings and relationships which could not be articulated into words. He began a continuous tradition of artistic development in fine orchestral music which is still with us.

In painting, artists like Goya (1746–1828) began to use fine art traditions to demonstrate their revulsion against the more brutal aspects of modern society.

The new and improved techniques of printing and engraving provided a means by which a minority of artists could begin to rebel against the political and social status quo. The work of one person could now reach a vast public. Hogarth, Daumier, Doré, Cruikshank, and the Punch artists, all made explicit criticisms of the contemporary social scene through their art. The new techniques made them widely available to the public.

This new ability of technology, to carry out many of the craft functions previously associated with art, had other dramatic effects. The early images produced by photography, for example, were so like the objects they reproduced that many people thought that they represented an absolute likeness of the objects photographed. Since to many people a good picture was a picture that looked real, it seemed that the need and desire for representational art was virtually finished. Elizabeth Barrat Browning wrote to one Miss Mitford in 1843: 'The fact of the very shadow of the person lying there fixed forever! It is the very sanctification of portraits, I think.' However, many artists, looking at these grimly accurate representations, realised that a painted picture could contain many more elements than a photograph and they began to explore and extend those elements. The Impressionists attempted to 'paint with light',

Joseph Paxton's Crystal Palace (*above and left*) was built in Hyde Park for the Great 1851 Exhibition, and later re-erected on Sydenham Hill.

Hogarth's cartoon 'Canvassing for votes' (1757) criticised the corruption of the eighteenth-century electoral system.

shocking many observers, but they were soon followed by other playful and experimental but often obscure schools, which took representational art merely as a starting point, like the Cubists, the Abstractionists, and the Surrealists. The notion emerged that, through art, an observer could be abruptly directed to understand the world in an unprecedented way. Artists in various media began to talk about the need to shock and alarm their audiences by their choice of subject and the treatment they gave it.

The rationalisation of this activity was that it was the only way to counter the deadening and conservative forces of humdrum and bourgeois urban life. Where primitive art, practised by many, exemplified the values and traditions of the whole society and celebrated the orderly drama of its relationship with the wider universe, fine art became a radical activity, practised by a few in a lonely attempt to revitalise the dull perceptions of the industrial mass society.

'Mandolin', painted in 1910 by Georges Braque (1882–1963). (Tate Gallery, London.)

The artist now saw himself as a lonely force, engaged in a very personal and individual campaign: a revolutionary of the senses. Artists felt free to attempt to investigate all the ways in which aspects of paintings and sculpture could be distorted and extended according to entirely new rules. Some artists became particularly interested in the fact that we do not just *look* at pictures and sculptures but *read* them in terms of symbols; they wanted to investigate the way those symbols affect us.

Art and symbols

The artist Picasso, almost single-handedly, taught the modern Western world how to recognise the beauty of much primitive art,

'Negro Dancer' (1907) by
Pablo Picasso (1881–1973).
Picasso was the first
European artist to use
African symbols as a basis
for his art. Similar forms
and images have so
thoroughly infiltrated
Western consciousness that
it is now hard for us to
believe how revolutionary
it once was for an artist to
take 'savage daubings'
seriously.

as he incorporated the symbolic vocabulary of African and Poly-
nesian artists into his pictures. Primitive art is often highly symbolic.
Relative size may be used to indicate importance; perspective and
anatomical proportions or fidelity of features may be ignored and
distorted. The mechanical regularity of lines, circles or curves is
often ignored. Characters may have to stand or sit in certain fixed
ways, or, as in Egyptian or Balinese pictures, always be seen in a
particular profile. Unless we know a great deal about the traditional
society which produced it, however, the symbolic elements of an
art-form may entirely pass us by, or be mis-recognised. Picasso
helped us to understand that these simple shapes and forms can
have enormous metaphorical power.

Often, young children draw and paint in this metaphorical way.
When painting people, for example, they may, when very young,
draw the most significant part, the face, with no body attached.
Later arms and legs will grow out of the bottom of this face, and
only much later will they draw a recognisable body.

Children often draw what an object is known to be, rather than
how it looks. A table may be drawn flat, with a leg sticking out
sideways at each corner; the sky may be a band of blue across the
top of a page and the earth a band of green at the bottom. We must
not imagine, however, that primitive art is simply child-like or
undeveloped, any more than the simple pictures of Picasso represent
primitive efforts at more complex representation. Primitive art
resembles that of our children only inasmuch as it reflects an artist's
attempts to model the world as it is *significant* to him and his culture,
rather than trying to present the image a camera would produce.

Primitive art has become such an accepted part of Western art styles, that at first glance it is difficult to say where this figure was made. Actually it is from Melanesia.

Modern fine art

The sheer vitality and energy of the work of painters like Picasso speaks for itself. It has helped us to begin to recognise the value of our own and our children's artistic efforts, as we gradually move away from the nineteenth century's inhibiting respect for recognisably professional fine art.

However, within the revolutionary tradition, the Fine Artists continue to present the public with disturbing and unfamiliar representations. They may have gone too far. The idea has grown up that there can be no limits to the form of art or to its subtlety of expression. The Surrealists introduced the idea that 'art' was simply a way of considering experience. For example, a lavatory seat could be an art object if it were hung on a wall in an art gallery. Increasingly, the art public has had to try to appreciate subtle patches of colour, simple pieces of wood and metal, or the arrangement of strings or stones on the floor.

In part, these developments have been due to the artists' rebellion against the paradoxical situation in which they found themselves. Art was now widely recognised as an essential, revolutionary and mind-expanding activity, reacting against the mundane world of cash and profits, yet in an age of mass production, any unique handmade products of individual creativity had a real cash value. If an artist was fashionable, then his pictures could be worth vast amounts of money.

One desperate reaction against this inexorable process, in recent years, has been the development of 'conceptual art' – the arrangement of *events*, which by their very nature cannot be bought and sold. But this is still a minor part of the art world's activities.

To a large extent, the world of orthodox fine art has now retreated to the fashionable art galleries of the world's major cities, and become of direct interest only to a few thousand jet-setting patrons. The ideas and approaches of fine artists do, however, filter their way into our consciousness, as they affect those designers and artists who produce the more popular goods which we all use. For the great mass of people, however, Art has come to be a difficult and sophisticated activity, which only the highly sensitive and trained can appreciate.

The idea of the masterpiece is now fixed firmly in Western consciousness. In a tradition which goes back several hundred years, many art students are still required to make copies of major works as part of their training.

Art as property

The idea of respect for 'artistic genius' is now so firmly fixed in our minds that the remaining work of previous cultures is worth absurd sums of money. The 'Mona Lisa' in the Louvre in Paris, for example, is now so famous and so valuable that it has to be separated from the millions who come to see it by a huge bullet-proof safe with a thick glass front.

Almost all old and original art now has some value. If it occurs in big enough quantities for collections to be made, it can provide, for its enthusiasts, the pleasures usually associated with stamp collecting, combined with those of aesthetic and capital appreciation. Recently, the exquisitely detailed religious pictures known as 'icons', which were produced in large numbers to concentrate the religious devotions of members of Christian sects in Eastern Europe, have achieved this kind of cult status. We recently observed an auction of these curious objects. It was particularly striking that these objects, whose aesthetic component was once entirely subsidiary to a religious function, should now provide not only an aesthetic satisfaction, but a means by which their possessors might resist the ravages of worldly inflation.

Contemporary art

As the nineteenth century merged into the twentieth, the First World War accelerated the development of large-scale production and distribution of goods. In America particularly, more and more goods were specifically made for an increasingly affluent working class. Ordinary people could now buy fashionable, if mass-produced, clothes, cars, and furniture, and be provided with mass-produced entertainment, and even mass-produced art.

In the 1920s, America created the prototype of contemporary world-wide urban society, which now offers us a vast range of specific aesthetic experiences in packaged form: books, records, films and reproductions. A distinction is still drawn between reproductions of fine art and the various artifacts of popular culture, although these too often contain a strong aesthetic element. In the affluent society we live in today, almost *all* the materials that surround us, and the products that we consume, exhibit a professional expertise which includes an aesthetic component. The cars we drive, the cans of food we buy, the television programmes we watch; they have all been processed by professionals with training in design.

In relation to all these objects, the only aesthetic activity available to us is to make a choice, based on our taste, from what is offered to us. We do not make our choice only on aesthetic grounds, however. We select those items which we believe reflect our membership of our preferred sub-section of the larger society, and our special and individual role in that group. Just as for primitive man, the symbolic meaning of items is as important to us as their functional or directly aesthetic qualities. However, the confidence and security in both his culture and the wider environment, which primitive man took for granted, is now lost to us. The confident, secure and happy group to which we all aspire to belong – through our possessions –

In the late 1970s, commercial photographers began to draw increasingly on the special vividness that surrealism gives to objects, so as to reach the consciousness of the consumer. In this typical advertisement, the only objects which could conceivably exist in the real world are the shoes which it is intended to promote.

is represented in advertisements, magazines, popular books and films. Yet it is as mythical as the happy hunting grounds of primitive man's ancestors; it requires its own rituals of consumption. So completely have the popular media taken authority over the beautiful and meaningful, that many people, as they try to describe the transcendental beauty of a scene, will now say, 'It was just like an advertisement on TV.'

Art for *all, or art* by *all?*
This is not to say that many members of modern urban society do not actively use artistic skills, but we still make a sharp distinction between the professional and the amateur, between 'full-time' and 'hobby'. The wealth of popular music now available to us has effectively destroyed our links with the folk songs of our grandfathers, which were passed on from mouth to mouth. Those amateurs who sing together in folk clubs now are as specialised a minority as water-skiers – and probably about as significant to the culture as a whole.

All artistic activity requires some kind of creative tradition in which to operate, and this considerably restricts non-professional artistic activity in our society. But actually using our artistic skills is a vital part of the inherited human drive to establish and maintain identity

Where a tradition of 'amateur' public murals exists, as here in the Spanish–American section of San Francisco (*opposite*), 'graffiti' can become 'art'.

The modern urban dweller is subject to a continuous stream of stimulation, processed by professionals with extensive training in design. Most of it is aimed at motivating us to buy goods. These Piccadilly signs (*opposite, far right*) are typical 'commercial' art.

Another kind of graffiti, that which covers many of New York's subway trains (*opposite, far right*) also reveals a curiously creative way in which modern technology – in this case aerosol spray paint – can be exploited in the service of the ancient human drive to decorate.

'Increasingly, the art public had to try to appreciate subtle patches of colour, simple pieces of wood and metal, or the arrangement of strings on the floor'. New York Museum of Modern Art (*opposite, far right*).

'L'enigme du desir' (1929) by Salvador Dali (b. 1904) (*opposite, bottom*). During the early twentieth century, the idea grew that the artist could direct the spectator to understand the world in an unprecedented way. The artist became a revolutionary of the senses.

and assert personal integrity, as well as being satisfying in its own right. Making art, as opposed to simply consuming it, is a small but definite gesture of personal authority. It constantly resurfaces in urban society, sometimes under the most curious conditions.

Grafitti, the writing and spraying of public walls, can rapidly evolve from a mindless violation of clear space to the complex and even beautiful patterns, which mysteriously appear, for example, on New York subway trains. The mildly deviant fashions of the young people in Britain in the 1950s have now become the extraordinary punk costume or the exotic Romantic look. Even the popular music, which has had such a destructive effect on our folk-music tradition, is constantly regenerated by infusions of new talent, as its simple and over-amplified songs demonstrate the artistic yearnings of young workers in Western society. But until we drop the 'uncrossable' barriers between fine art, popular art, and popular entertainment, many ordinary people will be inhibited from enjoying the best products of their own culture. We must somehow overthrow the rule of the professional, and ensure that every member of the urban society is able freely and joyfully to exercise his own artistic potential.

Religion and the Industrial Revolution

Our modern religious beliefs also reflect the enormous impact of technology on Western civilisation. In the nineteenth century, overt Christian belief performed two main functions: it provided individuals with a personal and secret relationship with their God, and a personal moral system by which to guide their actions in a time of unprecedented change. It also provided them with membership of a group within the larger urban society. This was especially important at a time when many traditional stable communities had largely collapsed. When, as in Northern Ireland, these religious divisions harden into actual lines of division between communities, reflecting a failure of political reconciliation, we are made to realise to what extent religions still have an enormous binding and directing force in human affairs.

By the mid nineteenth century, however, religious belief in developed countries had become increasingly subordinate to economic and political realities, retreating to become a set of respectable sentiments which guided the actions of individuals only if it suited their personal needs and preferences. Wealthy Victorians used the Christian model of the world, with its emphasis on redemption through personal suffering, in an attempt to excuse the suffering which the harsh forces of the Industrial Revolution had caused. Victorian religious literature was dominated by worthy works which exhorted their readers to uncomplaining hard work and personal sacrifice. The Protestant ethic was used to validate the work ethic and to maintain the status quo. The hymn goes, 'The rich man in his castle, the poor man at his gate.' To reflect the Christian emphasis on love,

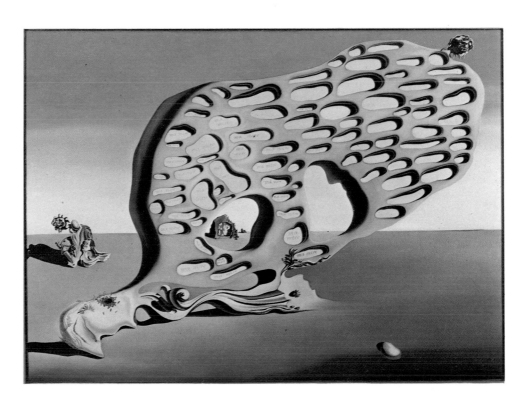

In the eighth century, 338 bishops of the Eastern Church broke away from those of the West to set up the Eastern Orthodox Churches. Although the ostensible reason for their departure was the Western Churches' acceptance of idolatrous images, vast numbers of carefully made sacred pictures, or icons – particularly of a slant-eyed Virgin Mary – were subsequently produced to concentrate the religious devotions of members of the Eastern Orthodox Churches. Rare examples now have enormous value for lay collectors. This example is Russian.

Through his work, an artist can articulate an intuition about how the world is changing long before it reaches public consciousness. This picture by Max Ernst (1891–1976), painted in 1940 and called 'Europe after the Rain', seems almost to anticipate the grim aftereffects of nuclear war.

The idea that all processes ultimately return to their beginnings, often through disintegration, is a recurrent theme in several Eastern religions. It is often expressed in religious imagery by the circle or the wheel. Jung believed that it represented an intuition about an innate human capacity for spiritual regeneration. This Buddhist mandala from Tibet depicts the stages after death and before reincarnation, which all souls must go through, as a series of circles.

however, pious Victorian middle-class women spent a great deal of their time in charitable good works, trying to ameliorate the suffering which was a byproduct of the system which had made them wealthy. Nowadays, it is fashionable to be cynical about their efforts, but the Christian emphasis on the duty that every human being has to others clearly energised the reformers like Howard, Fry and Wilberforce, who fought for the liberal reforms which were eventually to end the worst abuses of human rights.

What did not change, however, was the fundamental approach to the relation between Man and Nature, which the early Christian Church had established and the later ones maintained, and which was so radical a departure from the animistic religions of the earliest communities. Nature was for exploiting, and although humans, out of a decent regard for their own souls, might be reasonably kind to animals, there was no real necessity for them to do so. From a Victorian perspective, the primitive man who apologised to the animal he was about to kill and thanked it for its cooperation was a ludicrous and superstitious savage. When Charles Darwin (1809–92), in his book *On the Origin of Species by Means of Natural Selection* (1859), suggested that both animals and men were all part of one dynamic process of evolution, the outrage that greeted him was not

After returning from a voyage around the world as naturalist on the *Beagle* in 1836, Charles Darwin (1809–82) spent nearly twenty years accumulating evidence towards the theory of evolution advanced in *The Origin of Species by Means of Natural Selection* in 1859. Although the general idea of evolution was not new, his careful and logical presentation of the idea, that modern species had evolved by the mechanism of natural selection, had an enormous impact on the thinking of his time.

only that he was rejecting the myths of Creation and the Garden of Eden, but because he seemed to be saying that men were *only* animals. His idea that the evolutionary process ensured that the most appropriate species, that is to say the most fitting, came to occupy the most appropriate niche in nature, was widely misunderstood as endorsing 'survival of the fittest' – i.e. the victory of the most powerful. Industrial society waged its battle to subjugate nature even more fiercely. To many people, as the belief that the ideas of the past offered any guidance to the actions of the present finally disappeared, the real authority that religion once had was displaced by the authority of the new god: Progress, and his twin lieutenants Science and Technology.

Contemporary religious belief

To the new materialists of the twentieth century, there was no longer any Father in the sky – or anywhere else – to rely on. There was just a set of pretty myths which they taught to their children and expected them to discard as adults. In this spiritual freefall, all they could rely on was their own technological ability to master and control the world. They would no longer attempt to appease the gods; they would would simply ignore them in favour of Progress. This new god has demanded considerable sacrifices; in pursuance of scientific truth, millions of animals have been mutilated and subjected to outrageous treatment; technology has been applied to agriculture and animal husbandry; eco-systems have been destroyed; species have been wiped out; and stable human communities have been destroyed to be replaced by vast anonymous cities of consumers.

Through all this, the fundamental distinction between Man and Nature had still been maintained, and Darwin's message, that we were all part of one system, and its implication that we, as its most powerful members, had the greatest moral responsibility for its maintenance, was not recognised.

In recent years, however, the Pyrrhic quality of our victory over Nature has slowly come home to us, and many inhabitants of our vastly successful technological society are now deeply anxious as they examine the despoilation which their way of life has created all around them and recognise their own spiritual emptiness.

Anxiety and its remedies

The import of Darwin's message, however, has struck home in some curious places. The young psychiatrist Carl Jung (1875–1961), studying the mentally ill, had absorbed from Sigmund Freud (1856–1939) the idea that the forces of recovery often lay within the patient himself. Jung went further, and decided that patients had often become mentally ill because ancient and powerful forces within them were actually trying to correct basically unsound and unhealthy adaptations made to artificial and unhealthy circumstances. Perhaps, when people were anxious and depressed without knowing why, they were right to be anxious and depressed. Jung thought that so-called mental illness was often not so much an illness, as an attempt to grow. To him, there were deeper forces looking after human beings than merely their intellectual abilities. These forces had evolved in human beings over millions of years. He became convinced that they were reflected in both religious and artistic activity. He made a detailed study of the recurrent symbolic themes which appear across a range of primitive cultures, and which he believed reflected these forces.

The idea that there are mystical integrating powers within the human psyche, and that these can be reached and tapped to promote human freedom and mental and physical health, became a key principle in those several schools of psychotherapy which followed Jung, particularly those developed in the United States. Over the years, they have evolved a variety of techniques, which include shouting, deep breathing, massage, body contact, the acting out of drama, and encounter and argument groups. Many of these procedures looked suspiciously like the discredited rituals of traditional and primitive society. All are attempts to help the unconscious personality connect with these inner sources of peace and tranquillity.

Our technological urban society has managed to produce a great many people who feel a considerable lack of tranquillity. There have consequently sprung up, particularly on the affluent West Coast of America, clinics, where various oriental religious traditions like Buddhism, and psychotherapeutic techniques, are brought together in an attempt to help people achieve spiritual growth. An example of this is the Essalen Institute near San Francisco, which has now been running for more than twenty years, and which is distinguished by its eclecticism and lack of dogmatism.

A therapist explained:

'We have experimented with different techniques until we ended up with this combination of controlled breathing, evocative music, and certain body-work techniques. It is done in a way that is a collective experience, in which half of the group is doing the breathing experience with music, and the other half are functioning as "sitters" [helpers]. We have found that the experience can be very meaningful, not only for those who do the breathing, but also for those who are sitting.

'We've started seeing these sequences of "dying" and "being born"; we found out that the techniques provide possibilities for personality transformation which are beyond anything that conventional psychotherapy ever dreamt about.

'To me the spiritual dimension is an intrinsic aspect of existence, and it's also an intrinsic aspect of the human nature, so that every time your self-exploration, your understanding of yourself, goes deep enough, you have to recognise this dimension. In other words, to me, the means to discover spirituality is to go inside, rather than go and listen to somebody who is reading from a book or telling you how.'

The effects can be dramatic:

'At first I got into the breathing, and I didn't feel like anything. I did not feel altered or changed in any way.

'Then something very sudden happened to me – a piece of music started playing. It was the Adagio for Strings by Samuel Barber. What struck me in that experience was a deep and tender sense of sadness. I became very, very sad, and it was amplified so that it became a cosmic experience of the sadness like Wordsworth said: "The still, sad music of humanity". I felt very connected with the whole human experience and the sadness of what it is to be human, and it wasn't a sense of anger or depression, but a very tender sadness, and it was quite beautiful, and as I said quite sudden and quite unexpected.' The therapist concluded:

'I believe that the major reason people come to us is that the present strategies in the world don't seem to be working – and that involves political economic strategies, and it also seems to involve religions. Religions simply don't seem to be meeting the basic needs of human beings. I believe that the more the external world, the external values, are collapsing, the more people are turning inside for the answers. So they're turning to the oriental religions, or to such mystical traditions, where the idea is to discover the divine through self-exploration. It's the beyond *within*.'

The New Fundamentalists
There are other approaches to the problems of urban anxiety. One of these is symbolised by the $14,000,000 Crystal Cathedral at Garden Grove in California. It is presided over by the Dutch Reformed Church Reverend, Robert H. Schuller. His popularity reflects the dramatic return by many Americans to fundamentalist Christian views perhaps more typical of the nineteenth century than the twentieth.

'I believe that the Crystal Cathedral is probably one of the most important things that man has done for God, and I firmly believe that it's scriptural. In the Old Testament, you will recall, God asked the Jews to build a tabernacle, and he said, "Bring your finest linen and your finest tapestry, your finest gold, your finest brass, and build me a temple." I feel like this is what we've done with the Crystal Cathedral; we've brought Him our finest because we love Him that much, and He is a God to be worshipped and a God to be loved.

'People have tried drugs and they've tried total sexual liberation, and they've tried anything that comes to their mind, and they still find an emptiness deep within the soul, and so they're coming back now; "Well, why not try God?"'

The services of the Reverend Schuller, and hundreds of other preachers like him, are broadcast on television all over America. It has been said that what Gutenberg did for the Reformation, Marconi is doing for Revivalism.

The new 'electric church' ministers use all the techniques and styles of the other personalities that people see on television, but the fundamental difference lies in the coherence and sincerity of their one message, which cuts across the alienated trivia of chat shows, crime dramas and comedies: civilisation is on the edge of an abyss; only by a return to tried and trusted values and beliefs can an apocalypse be averted. The Reverend Schuller comments:

'It is very challenging, and the only way we can handle it is to deal with the ultimate basic, deeper issues of life. We can't handle the peripheral issues. We have to get to the deepest issues. We have to deal with faith. We have to deal with hope. We have to deal with love. These are the deepest issues. We have to deal with humanity's need for self-esteem, self-dignity, and this is what we deal with. As long as I stay with these deep central issues, the people that listen to me are all the same.'

The values endorsed by new fundamentalists also include rejection of the women's liberation movement, and repudiation of the legal status of homosexuality and abortion. Increased spending on defence, on the other hand, is enthusiastically endorsed, perhaps because the fundamentalists see a duty to fight for what they believe is the only true and worthy way of life, perhaps because they believe the only way to prevent nuclear war is to match the opposition and maintain the balance of power.

Interpretations of the reason for the 'born again' evangelical movements' popularity vary. It has been suggested that it is a response to the American people's realisation that there are limits to the power and authority that their dedication to progress has previously assured the United States. Internationally, the prospect of nuclear war seems more real and possibly more necessary to many Americans than ever before. The prospect arouses the deepest anxiety. Internally, the zealous application of commercial values to housing, transport and communications has virtually destroyed community feeling in large American cities. Combined with an easy access to guns, this means that many middle-class Americans live in constant fear of their lives, particularly when many believe that deviant minorities have lost all respect for the established order.

The Five Percenters

There are new religious strivings among minorities too. In the black ghettoes of American cities, fundamentalist Christianity has always maintained a powerful hold on the loyalty of disadvantaged people. Through the 1950s, however, it became clear to a new generation of radical blacks that traditional Christian beliefs, with their emphasis on the acceptance of suffering and the common brotherhood of man, worked against the development of a separate and essential black identity.

During the 1960s, the search for that identity found one route of religious expression in the Nation of Islam. The Black Muslims emerged, lead by Elijah Muhammad and popularised by Malcolm X. But in 1964 Clarence 13X Smith was expelled from the movement for posing a threat to its unity, and subsequently devoted himself to saving the 'young black babies'. He declared himself Allah and formed the Five Percent Nation, aimed specifically at poor, young blacks.

The Five Percenters are a relatively tiny movement, but they do exemplify the way religious beliefs can emerge to meet the human need for dignity and purpose, even in the most unlikely settings.

The Five Percenters believe that 85 per cent of the world are cattle, 10 per cent are devils and false prophets sent to mislead the cattle, and the 5 per cent are true and honest teachers who will eventually lead the 85 per cent to freedom. In their teachings, the white man is characterised as the devil who divided the unity of blacks by designating Africa and Asia as separate countries, who brought Africans into slavery, teaching them false religion (Christianity), and who kept them in ignorance not only of scientific knowledge, but also of their own heritage and history. Much of the teaching comes from the Koran, and followers are required to learn by heart a multitude of facts on cosmic and world geography, as well as the history of Islam and rules for correct living.

Although originating in Harlem, the Five Percenters have many groups throughout New York City, as well as up-state New York, Philadelphia, and Pennsylvania. They are particularly numerous in Brooklyn where there were, in 1981, at least twenty groups with a total membership estimated at around 2,000. The vast majority of these are teenagers. Most of the black street gangs, whether with small or large memberships, have almost entirely become Five Percenters. The movement has particular appeal to the young, since it is less stringent in its lifestyle requirements than the Black Muslims. Drinking alcohol, fornication, and drugs are not condoned, but are accepted providing they are not excessive. Some members sell soft drugs as a source of income. Since many of the members were recruited from street gangs and reformatories, they are still involved in small-scale crime. In Brooklyn, for example, arrests of Five Percenters account for approximately 20 per cent of all gang arrests. The majority of these are for robbery, burglary or carrying dangerous weapons.

In spite of these negative aspects of the movement, it has had several positive spin-offs. Members with poor reading and writing skills are coached by older members to learn their religious lessons, which are often quite complex. They are tested on them, and disciplined if their performance is poor. They are very often fluent on the subject of their religion, and will debate its merits. At 'rallies', members are encouraged to stand up and speak – something that many would have shied away from at school. The movement also

unites teenagers who would otherwise have been at war, coming as they do from different 'turfs'. It has also provided a sense of identity and direction that many of the teenagers could not find in school. Though it may seem bizarre to many, the movement demonstrates very clearly the force of the human urge to make order and sense out of life, and to give this order a spiritual dimension.

Religion and the future

There is a rapidly increasing intuition all over the world that the end has come for the approach to nature and its exploitation which was founded in Western society by the Christian Church, extended by the Industrial Revolution in Britain, and is now so dramatically exemplified by the economy of the United States. In a sense, both the new Christian fundamentalism of the wealthy, and cults like the Five Percenters among the poor, are reflections of an attempt to avoid this realisation. This is particularly clearly reflected by the fundamentalists' rejection of Darwin's elegant and rewarding insights into the essential continuity of man and nature. They endorse the Biblical myths of the Creation instead.

It could be argued that the re-vitalisation of both the Muslim and the fundamentalist Christian ethics is essentially no different from similar phenomena which have appeared in other cultures under stress or in those which could not cope with change. The 1890 Ghost Dance of the American Indians, and the Cargo Cults of Melanesia, are examples. These cults all had in common that their members were able to lose touch with reality. The Melanesians, for example, having watched cargo planes land at US bases during the Second World War, came to believe that their rituals and bamboo airports would one day seduce planes from heaven, loaded with the modern goods which they could in no other way obtain. The Ghost Dancers came to believe that their rituals made them impervious to the bullets of the white man who was destroying their way of life.

Such beliefs are clearly ridiculous but they underline the importance of belief in the lives of all human beings. Even in today's largely secular world, many ideologies fulfil the functions of mass religions for their adherents. Marxism, for example, whose founder came from a long line of Rabbis, has its revered father figures, a complete explanation of the history of the world and a complete system of rules for the correct social behaviour of all human beings. Its believers' crusading spirit reflects their intense belief in the superiority of their creed over all others. It seems unlikely, however, that any ideology can resolve the problems that now face the advanced societies unless it can provide a universally respected morality, which determines not only the responsibilities human beings have to one another but also to the environment on which they depend.

The fabric of our Western society is now under enormous strain, and we may expect that if we simply continue to devour the Earth's resources in order to try to buy our way out of our personal and social problems, then our own society will be drawn to increasingly myopic remedies. If we continue the exploitation, we shall have turned away, perhaps disastrously, from any real possibility of regaining the spiritual composure of our ancient ancestors. If we can rediscover a new stable relationship with our resources, we might still re-achieve some measure of that confidence and tranquillity which the earliest humans enjoyed, and which was once the birthright of us all. The first step towards this will be to realise that the insight we now have about our evolution, and the knowledge of human nature which comes from it, does not deny religious belief, but can provide us with a new basis on which to find even more meaningful belief.

An Easter service at the Hollywood Bowl. Symbols have enormous power for human beings. They can compress all the sentiments and belief associated with them into one immensely potent image. The simple cross has an incalculable significance in Christian religious imagery. Such symbolism remains powerful in modern America.

If the power of established religion does fade, however, then in the secular Western world, ancient drives for worship find new expression. Once the power of music to move us was mostly at the disposal of the churches, but now some musicians themselves are the objects of adoration (see opposite). Fans of John Lennon mourn his death in December 1980.

The Crystal Cathedral of the Garden Grove Community Church seats about a third of the church's 10,000 members under its 10,660 panes of glass. Two 90-foot glass walls behind the pulpit open, so that the minister can be seen by drive-in worshippers from their cars. His message can be heard over the car radio.

A key element in the human success story has been our ability to enhance almost every part of our body with technology.

Curious Giants

Compared with many other species, members of the human race are rather puny and vulnerable in their natural, naked, state. And yet, as we have seen, we are the most dominant species on the planet. What is the final secret of our huge impact on the environment? One major factor must be an ability almost unique in the animal kingdom. A tiny handful of other species share it, but compared with *Homo sapiens*, only to a negligible degree. We use tools.

What is human technology?
Such tool use as we see in other species seems to be the result of happy accidents in particular environments. The bird which smashes the shell of its snail victim on a handy rock would not do so if there were not a lot of suitable rocks already around. The chimpanzee poking prey ants out of a hollow log with a long thin stick does not keep a particular special stick permanently to hand. The circumstances in which a chimpanzee uses such a stick are the very circumstances in which there are many such sticks to be found. In other species, therefore, tool use is merely an exploitation of the environment, rather than a dramatic influence on it.

Even the earliest hominid tool use was probably in a different category from this. The simplest fire-hardened sticks and roughly-shaped stone axes were very formidable tools. Combined with our ancestors' increasing intelligence, these implements made our hunting prowess more deadly, and our ability to cut up and use the prey much greater. One species now had a unique advantage over all competing species: 'technology'. Baboons have great cutting teeth as well as speed and strength; chimpanzees, as we have seen, have enough intelligence to use tools opportunistically; *Homo sapiens* inherits a more powerful behaviour pattern: it is a puny but clever creature, that learns how to use sticks and stones to out-perform highly adapted claws and teeth. It therefore has a special place in the history of evolution.

Technology's role in the past and future evolution of the human race is crucial. The mechanisms of evolution are the subject of great controversy amongst those who study them, but the underlying idea, that the continued viability of species depends upon appropriate adaptation, however it comes about, remains the same. To a large extent, form and function are indivisible. Predators like lions, which have to run, chase and kill, are muscular and have built-in weapons. Ungulates, such as cows, move very slowly so as not to detract from

Even the simplest of technologies transforms our relationship to the environment and its resources. This Indian method of irrigation is sophisticated compared to the earliest known techniques, which consisted merely of breaching swollen river banks and guiding water to the fields. The transformation in plants which resulted from even that simple procedure, however, was dramatic. About 7,000 years ago, in the eastern part of the Fertile Crescent, whole new strains of barley occurred with six rows of spikelets instead of the two of wild varieties. The Fertile Crescent is an area the shape of an inverted horseshoe, running from the eastern Mediterranean (modern-day Jordan) to the Persian Gulf, via southern Turkey.

their almost constant digestive processes. For perhaps a million years, and certainly since *H. erectus*, the genus *Homo* has been a dramatic exception to this rule. There have, of course, been significant biological adaptations – bipedalism, the opposing thumb, pair-bonding and above all, brain size and complexity. The adaptations of our anatomy and physiology would have made for a remarkable enough species, but the combination of brain power and tool use – now called technology – has made us unique.

In effect, we have been able to adapt ourselves so successfully, flexibly and *quickly* that we have taken our species' recent development out of a purely evolutionary time-scale. This has given us power as though we had physically evolved to be dominating giants. Every vital part of our anatomy has been technologically enhanced: our arms and hands with weapons; our skins with clothing, armour and shelters; and more recently, our eyes with telescopes and microscopes; our ears with microphones and radio signals. We can be the fastest animals on earth, able to encircle it in a day. We fly highest and quickest in the air; we dive deepest in the oceans; with our technological muscles we can literally move mountains. And, above all, our mighty brains have generated enormous and complex extensions of themselves – from libraries and data banks to computers.

But while technology – in the service of curiosity and inventiveness – has telescoped evolutionary *time*, the evolutionary *process*, of successful innovations surviving, has remained constant. Human technology has not replaced natural selection but it has enabled us to behave almost as though it had. Further, the human capacity for communication means that an invention has only to be made once; others can be informed of it.

Evolution of technology

A distinction must be drawn between *invention* and *innovation*. Invention is having new ideas, and innovation is the process of applying them. Although we are biologically inventive and innately curious, it usually takes some special cultural pressure to make us adopt the new techniques into a practical programme. We feel more comfortable with our old traditional ways. It takes pressure, a crisis of some kind, to make us accept a major invention as a new element in our culture. In evolutionary terms, we can see this in the fact that the earliest stone tools appear to have remained almost unchanged in shape for thousands of years. Later, as the populations and the cultural pressures grew, fairly rapid developments took place, with the technologies of pottery and metals changing in hundreds rather than thousands of years. In the modern era, the speed of technological advance has been breathtaking.

There has always been resistance to change, however. Industrial inventions in the past have been resisted even more fiercely than some factory automation is today. In the early 1730s, John Kay, the inventor of the 'flying shuttle', found it rejected by the weaving industry because it doubled the output of each worker and improved the quality of the cloth. Kay's house was ransacked, and he fled to France, where he seems to have died a pauper. A similar fate befell the house of John Hargreaves, inventor of the Spinning Jenny, patented in the 1770s, which multiplied the productive power of a worker by eight. This resistance to technological progress became very widespread in early nineteenth-century England. It contributed to riots so serious that they led to the formation of a civilian police force on the European model: Robert Peel's famous blue-coated squads of truncheon-wielders first appeared in 1829.

The motive behind machine smashing was fear of unemployment; an understandable anxiety. Perhaps the Luddites do not truly deserve their reputation as mindless destroyers, but were an early example of working people organising themselves to protect their rights. In 1812, Lord Byron defended such resistance to change in his maiden speech in the House of Lords. In specialised modern times, at least, a substantial part of people's identity is preceived and conveyed in terms of their jobs. A bricklayer or a businessman have distinct identities as long as they are in work: unemployed, they lose a crucial element of what distinguishes them.

Even without the fear of unemployment as a barrier to technological advance, there is still resistance. In medieval times, for example, techniques like microscopy were viewed with suspicion. Thinkers saw technological change as a distraction from moral and cultural improvements. Apart from their philosophical reservations, Galileo's detractors were suspicious of the new-fangled telescope,

GRIPEAILO THRASHING MACHINES

Illustrations such as this appeared on broadsheets during the machine-smashing troubles of 1830s Britain. Since the employers had more money, most of the propaganda tended to be biased against the protesting workers.

since the only lenses they knew were spectacles (used to correct *faulty* vision), and the distorting mirrors of fun-fairs. How could they know that what Galileo saw was correct? The equivalent today is the suspicion that some features found in things examined by electron microscopes are artifacts, resulting from the preparation of the specimen, rather than things genuinely there and previously too small to be seen. People have always been suspicious of what they see as 'unnatural'.

Later the arrivals of electricity, wireless, the telephone, photography, television and computers were all, in their turn, greeted with reservations because their potential was incorrectly perceived. The first computer was financially backed by the British Government in 1819. The mathematician Charles Babbage spent thousands of pounds and many years trying to perfect an 'analytical engine'. He was thwarted by lack of precision engineering. It was not until the invention of solid-state electronics, in which numbers are represented electrically, and not mechanically, that his ideas came to fruition. His contemporary biographer noted, 'This extraordinary monument to theoretical genius accordingly remains, and doubtless will forever remain, a theoretical possibility.' A little later, Thomas

Edison himself said, 'They will never try to steal the phonograph. It is not of any commercial value.'

The circumstances must be right for the happy coincidence of invention and the need for innovation. So far, such combinations seem to be best discerned with hindsight. Thinking about technological advance as comparable with biological evolution is essential to the future of our species. In the first place, it can help us to anticipate the dangers of developing and refining the same aspect of technology until we become over-dependent on it. The hairy mammoth and the sabre-toothed tiger were too dependent on their specific body adaptations to cope with a rapidly changing environment; they became extinct. Parallel but unconnected studies in anthropology and botany have independently concluded that extinction is always preceded by over-specialisation. One contemporary aspect of this might be the energy crisis. Too much of our modern industrial way of life depends on dwindling fossil-fuel resources, in the same way that too much of the sabre-toothed tiger's depended on one limited body technology. Secondly, we must be very careful in attempting to make predictions about our future, since an essential aspect of our technological development is the inbuilt likelihood of unpredictable change. Some predictions about the future could be likened, say, to a Stone Age futurologist warning that if every tool and structure were to be made of stone, the world would soon run out of it; or to a London futurologist of a century ago predicting that increasing wealth and population would lead to such a growth in personal transport that the city would be ten feet deep in horse dung within a few years.

Of course, we cannot think of technological development purely in evolutionary terms. There is a crucial difference, in that we *consciously* select what we need to make our life easier, and do not develop a discovery or invention unless we want to. It may be that the happy accident of a discovery is not followed up. It will not be, unless we see potential in it. Furthermore people in different places and at different times may perceive the potential quite differently. Political power is important too; the use to which available technology is put will vary according to where users are in the hierarchy of their culture. But we need to look back to see how some of these differences developed.

Self-sufficient societies

What might our past perhaps have been like? In the tiny paradise islands of the South Pacific a very ancient pattern of life seems, apparently, to continue as though it had never been interrupted. The plentiful fish are still hunted using the simplest technologies – just nets and spears. Unelaborated wooden sticks are sufficient for the minimal domestication of the abundant plant foods. This relative richness and stability points to important aspects of our species' development. Here, technology and intelligence take *Homo sapiens* not into the rat race, but out of the animal race. These appropriately simple levels of technology – just enough to provide plentiful, balanced nourishment and abundant 'leisure' time – are not primitive at all. They are a perfect example of exactly what makes *Homo sapiens* unique. Such people, even today, can be seen as examples of human beings at their most liberated. Freed from the continuous pattern of finding and consuming food, and reproducing – which in different ways is the lot of all other species – they can develop cultures, with legends, traditions, art and religion. Such people typically inherit and continue a complex social organisation and a rich, elaborate language which reflects their society.

Each of the islands of the Pacific Ocean is different from the others because the islands are so dispersed and so small. In a sense, it is only their isolation which has enabled them to survive as they are today. They are anachronistic, but a model, perhaps, of certain early human communities. Observers in recent centuries have felt that the South Pacific islands embody idyllic Garden-of-Eden-like properties. Members of other, more demanding cultures, such as Captain James Cook, Paul Gaugin and Rudyard Kipling, have felt that these islands were a kind of paradise on earth. This eighteenth- and nineteenth-century love affair with 'the noble savage' has been widely criticised. It could certainly be patronising: Darwin himself was guilty of it in certain sections of *The Voyage of the Beagle* (the book in which he described the round-the-world trip which collected the data which led to the theory of evolution described in *Origin of Species*). An example of his condescension is: '. . . man, at least savage man, *with his reasoning powers only partly developed*, is the child of the tropics [our italics].' But the Romantic appreciation that a society without the pressure for innovation is a peaceable and idyllic society, has some truth.

But if it is the case that such a way of life seems like paradise to us today, and if, at least to some extent, we all lived like that at some primeval time – what caused the change?

The Pacific islands give us a clue, because although their people do not live like the majority of primeval hunter–gatherers, they present a less distorted picture than do the remaining contemporary actual hunter–gatherer groups. There are really only two hunter–gatherer groups left: the Kalahari Bushmen in the Botswana desert, and the Pygmies in the rain-forests of Zaire. Both live in harsh environments, so we might think our primeval ancestors lived in such surroundings, locked in a bitter struggle for survival. That would be a mistaken view. Since the Agricultural Revolution, the farming majority of the world's population has taken over the fertile country, leaving the hunters as remnants clinging on in remote regions. Their plight is not a true reflection of what it must have been like in our ancient, affluent, tribal days.

Yap. Far from struggling to survive, small communities with relatively simple technologies have abundant time to develop rich cultural traditions which are passed down through the generations.

Pressure and growth

Thousands of years ago, when only a handful of the Pacific islands were inhabited, there was plenty of room to expand, to accommodate the extra people resulting from human breeding success. We know from the existence of 30,000-year-old *Homo sapiens* fossils in Australia – with no evidence of their antecedents whatsoever – that boat-building technology must have been used as long ago as that. And so, over the years, more and more islands became populated. Human curiosity is a powerful force. We are innately exploratory, and yet to uproot, travel dozens of miles to the nearest island, and, above all, to populate it permanently, indicates a pressure beyond curiosity.

So the islands of the South Pacific also model for us an aspect of what might appear to be one of our species' greatest problems – overpopulation. They show not only how existing technologies can be rapidly adapted to meet the demands of expanding numbers, but also how efficiently we can enlarge the human population to exploit all the available resources. For a long time, non-island-dwelling human societies must have used the same techniques, populating new, unexplored territories when necessary, and expanding into them.

With the advantage that even the simplest technology gave them over all other species, the human race could grow and prosper as long as there were more new territories to colonise. Marginal adaptations of the existing technologies of clothing, control of fire, and the making of tools, made us a globally successful species, succeeding in all but the most hostile climates and environments.

With huge continents to expand in, as opposed to sparse groups of small islands, our control of technology quickly gave us a dramatic evolutionary advantage. Our 'human animal' status, based on simple technology, gave us time to add knowledge to our power. We could begin to solve the problems that only we could create. With the domestication of animals and plants, a population explosion was under way. In 8,000 BC, the estimated human population was 10 million. By AD 1, it had multiplied to 300 million. Once these steps were taken, the previously slow rate of technological innovation was rapidly accelerated with each human 'age' (taking 'age' to mean a period of technological stability), becoming shorter and shorter. Profound alterations in human culture, which once took millennia, soon came about in centuries. Today, they can be measured in less than a lifetime.

Once started, such progress accelerates. Ever more innovative ways of being fed allow ever-increasing populations. Cooking, for example, made previously inedible foods more palatable. It was probably an accidental discovery – perhaps meat once fell into a fire and, surprisingly, it was more, rather than less edible. Cooking soon became a regular part of the human life-style. There is evidence of ancient hearths in the Escale cave near Marseilles, a site close to one million years old, and further evidence is provided by the steady

When the film of H. G. Wells's book *Shape of Things to Come* was made in 1936, it predicted travel to the Moon in 2036. It actually happened in 1969.

decline in the size of human teeth (and consequently, jaws) from the time of *Homo erectus* – the middle of the Pleistocene age about a million years ago. If food is cooked, it is easier to eat; the steady decline in jaw size may reflect this. Interestingly, J. Z. Young suggests that cooking also contributed to man's development by saving time. It pre-digests food. Pre-digestion reduces the time needed to feed and ruminate. Rice, maize, and other such staple crops, now support the majority of the world's population at least well enough to allow them to survive and reproduce. Agricultural technology, from the simple hoes, ploughs and grinding mills and irrigation technologies of the Agricultural Revolution, to the combine harvesters and food factories of the industrial age, has increased immensely the yield per acre. They have matched increased food production to the increased population which they have in themselves made possible.

Many more people means many more brains at work – who (see above) have a greater proportion of their time free. The rate of technological change is inevitably linked to the number of fertile human minds around to promote it. Once writing encapsulated and spread human thinking, another twist was given to the technology/population spiral.

The impact of agriculture

The Agricultural Revolution was the most significant single development of human technologies until weapons of global destruction. What is considered to be the earliest known writing, on Sumerian tablets over 5,000 years old, demonstrates the crucial importance of the technology and creativity which precipitated it. As well as we can decipher it, this combination of symbols, pictograms and heiroglyphics is to do with the trading of food.

One of the earliest specimens of human writing (*c.* 3300–3100 BC), this Sumerian tablet seems to be an agricultural record.

Abstract symbols existed 35,000 years ago in the decorated caves of Europe. We do not yet really understand them, however, and so – although beautiful and fascinating – they fail to qualify to us as writing in a vital sense. The Sumerian tablet is writing, to us, because we can to some extent understand it. It thus fits the fundamental requirement of writing in that it communicates human ideas across space and time. One of the messages that this earliest known example conveys is that, following the advent of the Agricultural Revolution, the human race underwent important changes of organisation.

All primate groups have some kind of social order; many have rigid, formalised hierarchies of authority. There seems to be no doubt that *all* human societies have, in varying degrees, had much the same kind of dependence on organisation and order. Ancient hunter–gatherers presumably lived on environmental 'income', as their counterparts do today. Food was hunted or gathered as needed. They were more concerned with matters of social organisation than with political control of resources. The technologies of the Agricultural Revolution eventually changed this. The surpluses of food and the domestication of animals introduced the idea of property ownership. Increasing social complexity and specialisation inevitably lead to a uniquely human situation in which certain individuals controlled more surpluses or owned more property than others. Where the headman had more status, he now could have more wealth and power. Where dominant males could expect more sexual favours, they could now own more wives. The simple division of labour that had always existed in hunter–gatherer societies, between the hunting

Agra, northern India. Small traders and artisans scrape a living in the city.

males and the gathering females, was re-arranged and extended in many ways.

After several thousand years of agriculture, the first large settlements appeared. In these, it was not necessary for everyone to make their own clothing or pots, and so specialisation and craftsmanship emerged, with techniques handed down from generation to generation.

The old natural order, in which all were equal, gave way to a system of caste and class with rich and poor, lords and peasants, masters and slaves, and there also arose a group of merchant middlemen: the market-place was born. In the noisy bustle of the swelling towns and cities, buying and selling, bartering and exchanging became the new way of life. The self-sufficient tribesmen of yesterday became the mutually dependent citizens of the growing urban world. Losing their independence as hunters and small farmers, the city-dwellers suffered a new kind of vulnerability. They were increasingly at the mercy of the overlords who ruled these expanding communities.

As more people leave the land to come to the city, shanty towns, like this one in Brazil, are a recent additional problem in many already overcrowded cities.

If the pedlars and merchants objected to their conditions, there was little they could do about it. As tribal hunters or subsistence farmers, they would simply have moved on to new territories and started afresh. But for the townsman, such moves were impossible. He was trapped in the city by his own specialisation and the new overlords were able to exploit this to increase their power. Human poverty was born. The affluent days of hunting and gathering were over. The human race was learning a hard lesson: that major technological advances do not benefit all of the people all of the time. Usually they benefit the few at the expense of many. The lucky few take a leap forward down the path towards material comfort, but the many take a step backwards. In place of a healthy, relaxed tribal life, they experience instead an over-crowded, often diseased, stressful, boring life in city slums. Slums, of various kinds, have been with us for thousands of years now, and it is to our shame that there are now slum cities in many parts of the world. For the majority of people living today, the routine of daily life is worse than it was back in our primeval past.

Imbalances

Technology has contributed to human misery as much as to human success. Its failure has not been limited to aggravating the problems of the division of labour. Particularly over the last few hundred years, the scale and nature of the technological growth, particularly in transport and communications, has led us to the point where we have to face the truly global nature of our activities. The twin spectres of over-population and nuclear war, which haunt the modern world, are constant reminders.

Since technology is largely of benefit to the few, at the expense of many, and is now so powerful, we live in a world which is very unbalanced not only in terms of wealth and power distribution, but in terms of population. There is an argument which states that the poverty of much of the Third World is the result of the huge populations of many of its countries. But there is no biological reason why some members of our species should have a greater breeding drive than others. It seems unlikely that the populations of the Indian subcontinent, for example, have evolved with a reproductive drive

Children of a matchmaker near Lucknow, India. In such a labour-intensive activity, the more hands the better. The same is true of the grain harvest. Such requirements for 'free labour' encourage population growth.

three times greater than, say, the Norwegians. In fact, it is likely that large populations are the *result* rather than the *cause* of poverty. In cultures where the majority of the wealth is controlled by a minority of the population, the only hope for most families is to have enough members to generate a reasonable total income. A poor Asian peasant or artisan depends largely on labour for his livelihood. The more working members of the family, the more income. Without welfare benefits and pension schemes, a large number of children is the only insurance against impoverished old age.

The development of Sri Lanka, as contrasted with many other Third World countries, has been widely quoted as an example of what is called the demographic transition. Demographic transition theory, developed in the 1940s, notes that fertility tends to decline in richer nations, and argues that improved economic conditions – and certain related changes in social structure – cause a reduction in population growth. Both India and Sri Lanka (formerly Ceylon) inherited common post-colonial problems – over-development of exportable cash crops, for example – and in 1970 both countries had the same per capita income of about $110. At the same time, however, the deaths per thousand births in India was about 140, compared with 42 in Sri Lanka. Life expectancy in Sri Lanka was 68 years, which approached the average in the developed world (about 71 years), and greatly exceeded the average in India (47) and in the developing world as a whole (51). By 1975, according to UN population studies, the birth rate in Sri Lanka was 27 per thousand population per year (compared with 23 in the developed world) while India remained high at 38.

But this decline in Sri Lanka's birth rate has not resulted from a surge of economic growth. The economy grew only about one per cent per year in the two decades since 1950. What *has* happened is that the resources have been more evenly distributed than in, say, India. Deliberate government policy in Sri Lanka has seen to it that adequate food, health care and education were available to all. There are minimum wage laws and, in particular, welfare schemes to provide security in old age. In 1970, over 83 per cent of the population was literate, compared with 29 per cent in India and 32 per cent in the developing countries. This leads to the conclusion that once a certain modest level of per capita income is achieved, then it is the even *distribution of wealth* which restricts the rate of population growth. In India, top managers typically earn twenty to thirty times as much as their workers. In the West, the ratio is between three to one and six to one.

The difference in the calorific intake of different social groups in India is shown in the graph. Above all, perhaps, Sri Lanka shows that improved medical care, increased life expectancy and reduced infant mortality *reduce* rather than increase population growth.

In many poor countries, a peasant will want to be sure of having children to care for him in his old age. If infant mortality is high,

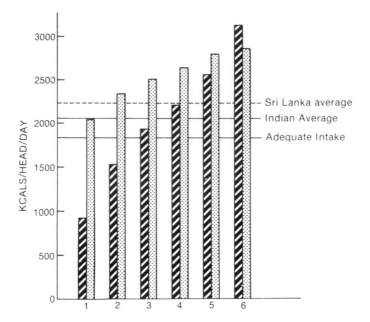

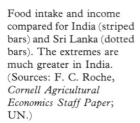

Food intake and income compared for India (striped bars) and Sri Lanka (dotted bars). The extremes are much greater in India. (Sources: F. C. Roche, *Cornell Agricultural Economics Staff Paper*; UN.)

he will have more children than if it were lower, to ensure that at least some will survive. If his particular children survive – against the odds – his family is larger than it would have been. In this way, *high* infant mortality can paradoxically *increase* population.

Distribution

Ownership of resources, and the exertion of power through wealth, are no longer problems simply within cultures. They now operate on an even larger scale; substantial differences now exist between entire nations and continents. Given the evidence to date, it seems that although about a thousand million pounds (UN estimates) is spent annually on attempts to limit population growth in the developing world, it is unlikely to have a substantial effect. Already, we have starvation in one place and mountains of unused food in another. It has been estimated that, in the whole world, there is a 5 per cent overall over-production of food, yet, in parts of Africa, children are kept alive only by charitable handouts, while people in the West spend millions on products to help them lose weight.

According to the yearbooks of the United Nations Food and Agriculture Organisation, enough *grain* alone is produced annually to provide everyone in the world with sufficient protein and more than 3,000 calories per day. This is the calorific intake of the average person in the developed world. It ignores what could be obtained from vegetables, fruits and meat.

In Bangladesh, one of the world's most densely populated countries, enough grain is produced to supply each person with more than 2,600 calories a day. Actual minimum daily requirements for an active person are considered to be about only 2,000 calories. Yet, a recent survey by the University of Dacca showed that over half the population of Bangladesh somehow survive on less than 1,500 calories.

Neither is the problem simply one of population *density*; there is poverty in India with 68 people per square mile (172 per square kilometre), and prosperity in Holland with a density of 128 (326). The problem is *distribution* of resources. There is not much hope of arriving at a balanced world economy while, for example, the United States, with only 6 per cent of the world's population, consumes about 35 per cent of its annual resources.

The United Nations statistical yearbook for 1974, for example, showed that the United States, with a population of just over 200 *million*, consumed 2.18 *billion* (2,180 million) tons of energy, expressed in tons of coal equivalent (2.22 billion metric tonnes). By contrast, the developing world with a population of nearly 2.5 *billion* consumed not even twice as much – a mere 3.5 billion tons (3.6). According to the same source comparative steel consumption is even more disparate. In the developed world as a whole average per capita steel consumption was 1,254 pounds (568 kilograms), while in the Third World it was 46 (21). According to the 1981 report *State of the World Population* from the United Nations Fund for Population Activities, the number of people in the world stood at 4.4 billion, with an annual growth rate of 1.73 per cent, falling. Extrapolating present trends takes world population to just over 6 billion by the end of the century, and to 10.3 billion by 2110, when growth is expected to come to a halt. Between now and then, the estimates show that populations will increase like this:

	Population in millions		Percentage			
	1980	2110	1980		2110	
South Asia	1,400	4,100	31.9		39.7	
East Asia	1,200	1,700	27.4		16.4	
Africa	400	2,100	9.1		20.3	
Latin America	400	1,200	9.1	77.5	11.6	88.0
Europe	450	500	10.3		4.8	
USSR	265	380	6.0		3.7	
North America	248	320	5.7		3.1	
Oceania	23	41	0.5	22.5	0.4	12.0
Total	4,386	10,341	100	100	100	100

In other words, almost 90 per cent of the eventual 10,341 million people will be living in today's developing countries, and the industrialised world's share of total population will decline from today's 24 per cent to approximately 13. According to present gross national product figures, the industrialised nations' share of the world's wealth is now over 80 per cent.

A birth control clinic in Lucknow, India. According to the United Nations, about half of the Third World's women want no more children, but only half of those have access to effective birth control.

The 10.3 billion stabilisation figure is the UN's 'medium variant' projection and depends on population and development policies which will continue to force down the annual growth rate. Different assumptions could see world population go as high as 14.2 billion people or as low as 8 billion. Can the world support two-and-a-half times as many people as it contains today? In 1981, an estimated 450 million people do not have adequate food; 1,200 million do not have adequate water, sanitation or health-care; over 100 million 6- to 11-year-olds have no schools to go to; and perhaps one-third of the world's workforce is either unemployed or earning too little to meet their own and their family's needs. In this context, it will clearly be enormously difficult to cope with a 150 per cent increase in world population in the next 130 years.

Surprisingly, the earth's physical capacity to feed 10.3 billion people is not really in doubt. Some estimates suggest that even four times that number could be fed on *present* land with *present* technology. A recent study by the University of Wageningen in the Netherlands, for example, based on the new FAO/UNESCO soil maps of the world, concludes that the Earth could sustain the production of over 31.5 billion tons (32 tonnes) of grain each year – 25 times as much as at present.

With abundant natural resources (*above*: collecting water melons) and efficient boat-building technology for fishing (*above right, below*), the people of the tiny island of Yap in the South Pacific could be self-sufficient.

Japanese girls mimic Western style as part of their display of appreciation of American rock and roll. This is an example of the cultural homogenisation which rapid communications and telecommunications bring about (see page 227).

Modern Western methods of food production and distribution have considerable advantages. But as long as we depend on costly fossil fuels for energy, the expenditure of ten times as many calories on production as are contained in the final food product is very inefficient. Supermarket in the Home Counties of England; harvest in Colorado, United States.

The root of the hunger problem is distribution. Summing up the recent US National Academy of Scientists World Food and Nutrition Survey, its Chairman, Harrison Brown, said that 'doubling world food production next year, on the present pattern, would not materially change the status of the great majority who are hungry or malnourished today.'

All over the world, people go hungry because they simply do not have the means to grow food or the money to buy it. In many countries where malnutrition is prevalent, up to half of the cultivated acreage is used to grow crops for export to those who can afford them, rather than foodstuffs for those who need them.

Of the poorest and hungriest countries in the world, 36 out of 40 export food to North America. Africa, the hungriest continent, is a net exporter of protein to Europe.

The food problem cannot therefore be considered in terms of too many mouths to feed and too little food being grown. We must also ask whose land is growing what crops, and for whose benefit. If a world of 10.3 billion is indeed to be fed, then we will have to consider most carefully whether basic needs like food can continue to be distributed according to economic demand rather than to human demand.

These besetting problems are not novel or sudden. They have been thought and worried about ever since the English clergyman, Thomas Malthus (1766–1834), published *The Principle of Population* in 1798. But only if we develop respect for the people of the world as a whole and realise that all our futures are interrelated, will appropriate solutions be found.

Technological solutions?
Not surprisingly, technology, so successful for the few, has been applied in attempts to find solutions to world hunger and poverty. Unfortunately a technology developed by the few for the few does not readily translate into a technology which will benefit the many. Huge automated factories are not an answer for cultures where labour is the most plentiful resource and where village life is deeply traditional. The attempted application of agricultural technology – very successful in the West – to the food production problems of the developing world has not met with any real success. Sophisticated super-fertilisers dramatically increase crop yield, but they are inappropriately expensive to produce. In the West, the goal of agricultural efficiency has been to reduce the labour element. So in the United States, for example, each farmer feeds an average of nearly sixty people. A family of subsistence farmers in countries such as Mexico or Peru – all involved in planting and harvesting – will often produce only just enough for themselves.

It might appear that this shows that the Western way is more efficient, but this is a serious misunderstanding. Much more important than the numbers of people involved in food production is the amount of resources consumed by the process. Nearly ten years ago an article in the American journal *Science* contained a revealing analysis.

Whatever our food, whether we eat steak or rice, we can measure its energy content in calories. We all need a basic minimum number of calories each day, as well as certain vitamins and proteins which are essential raw materials. The number of calories available in our food is therefore of fundamental importance. In 1910, according to *Science*, farmers in the United States obtained just over one calorie of food value for each calorie expended in producing it. By 1970 it was taking US farmers ten calories of energy expended to obtain one calorie of food value. The calories used up in human labour are now just a tiny proportion of those used by non-human sources of energy. Subsistence farming is much more efficient than high technology in these terms. Peasant agriculture, using hand tools, animal labour and crop rotation, rather than fertilisation, is the most energy efficient in the world. Food production systems which produce more calories than they cost also include hunting and gathering, all traditional rice production and free-range beef and egg production. Peasant corn production is similarly efficient but, by contrast, to produce a can of corn containing 270 calories in the United States requires the expenditure of 2,790 calories. The average acre of American farmland is cultivated by 15 tons of machinery, and uses 12 gallons of petrol and 203 pounds of fertiliser every year. Add to that the energy consumed by the factories that make the machines and the chemical fertilisers, by the transport systems involved, and by the food processing plants and refineries, and the inefficiency of modern agricultural technology is clear.

It is no wonder, therefore, that trying to solve the problems of the so-called developing world by exporting such inefficient technologies has come to be thought of as an inappropriate strategy.

It will be interesting to see, for example, what happens next in Sri Lanka. The government elected in 1977 decided that the welfare programmes had been too costly and were inhibiting economic development. They have opted instead for foreign aid from the International Monetary Fund and the World Bank, and a free trade zone has been established, allowing foreign investors to export their profits tax-free.

In some parts of Western society the clarion call of the moment is for 'appropriate technology', technology that takes account of the local needs and circumstances. It may well be that, in the long term, when human ingenuity has made energy cheap again with solar or nuclear devices, chemical fertilisers and intensive farming will become the ultimate solution to the problem of how to provide a high quality diet for the whole population of the planet. We have also to be sure that they are not polluting it. In the meantime, however, *appropriate* technology – whether in the form of plant genetics to produce better strains of staple crops, or industrial design

which takes account of existing traditions and labour resources –
seems to be a most promising approach. Oxfam, for example, has
used and given new force to the ancient Chinese proverb: 'Give a
man a fish and you feed him for a day; teach him to fish and you
feed him for life.'

Neo-colonialism
The other advantage of appropriate technology is that it should
obviate the dangers of a kind of neo-colonialism which have beset
many aid programmes in the past. To make developing communities
dependent on developed ones creates imbalances and does nothing
to reduce the overall instability which now threatens us.

Formal colonisation involved not only economic exploitation, but
also the imposition of one cultural system upon another. Whenever
the European colonialists of the nineteenth century spread themselves across the planet, sometimes promising better health and
education, occasionally promoting fairer social conditions, they
always imposed at least some of their cultural values.

Unfortunately even in benign cases those individuals most concerned with this cultural expansion were usually either religious
bigots who believed that their particular faith was superior to
all others, commercially motivated entrepreneurs who exploited
resources, or anthropologically naive politicians with no respect for
human societies other than their own.

Even as this nineteenth-century tide has receded, another wave
of cultural colonisation is sweeping across the world. Modern
technology, particularly in communications, has truly produced what
the Canadian Marshall McLuhan called 'the global village'. Commercial interdependence has accelerated this process into a kind
of self-generating spiral. A telephone instrument is made of raw
materials from four continents and is itself often used to speed up
and intensify the process of obtaining more raw materials for more
products from more places. Trucks, trains, ships and aeroplanes are
in constant motion all over the world, transporting materials,
products and people to such an extent that we are in real danger of
wiping out all local variety, regional identity and special cultural
tradition. To some extent we already live in a world in which all
hotels look alike, all drinks taste alike and all restaurants serve chips.
Not only can it make life difficult for the travel agent, constantly
striving to provide exotic locations for his customers, but this process
of cultural homogenisation can have far more serious consequences.

The tiny Pacific island of Yap is a United States commonwealth.
Its location is considered to be of considerable importance by
American military strategists, and a benign colonisation has taken
place. Since the Yapese are technically almost US citizens, they
qualify for all kinds of Federal aid programmes. On this previously
self-sufficient island, very few people now need to work, and most of
those who do, work for the US government. The population is only

about 6,000, and yet in 1981 fourteen million dollars came to them in aid. Nobody fishes any more and many of the ancient fishing skills are being lost with the arrival of the outboard motor. The surrounding seas abound with fish, yet most of the fish eaten arrives in American transport planes. When a meal is being prepared today, on an island that has never been short of indigenous food products, the can-opener is a dominant feature. Indeed the only real industry to have arisen on the island is the crushing of empty beercans for metal salvage.

In the Yap Co-op the islanders can buy canned and processed American foods.

Although the people of Yap appear to be happy with this state of affairs, since they take no action to change it, it can certainly be regarded as inappropriate. Technological rigidity and conformity are dangerous to any members of a species whose success has been based on ingenuity and enterprise. If the Americans withdrew in a hundred years time, what would become of Yap? Could they possibly revert to self-sufficiency? Would the human ability for rapid adaptation to changed circumstances be sufficient to cope?

If the result of military strategic concerns was just to alter the cultures of tiny islands it would be bad enough, but the greatest shadow over the human race lies, ironically, in the most brilliant and sophisticated of human technologies – the weapons of mass destruction. Buckminster Fuller, who makes his own contribution to this chapter later, has long asserted that if the technological imagination and expertise traditionally applied to the development of *weaponry* were to be applied positively – to what he calls *livingry* – then most of our problems would evaporate. It should be only with astonishment that rational minds can contemplate the fact that perhaps the greatest human efforts in design, engineering, chemicals, nuclear energy, electronics, communications, metallurgy – almost all technologies – are concerned with developing even more efficient ways to destroy even larger numbers of our own species; our leaders appear to have their own logic.

The 'Passionate Survivors' chapter contains a more detailed analysis of the factors involved in this grotesque situation; it is appropriate to point out here that the apparent reason the enormous proportion of national effort and resources allocated to the annihilation industry is tolerated – even in democracies – is because leaders are able to persuade their peoples that their very survival is at stake. Ever since Malthus, there has been an underlying belief that eventually there would be insufficient food to go round and that, by implication, some people would survive and some not. Malthus argued that population grew geometrically (1,2,4,8 ...) while food production could be increased only arithmetically (1,2,3,4 ...). Since Malthus's time, similar arguments have been put forward concerning vital resources other than food: energy sources, raw materials, and so on. But they, like Malthus, reckoned without the advances that modern technology would bring. The world population is now more than four times greater than it was at the time *The Principle of Population* was published and yet, as we have seen, with all our inefficiencies, the world still produces an overall surplus.

When considering whether these arguments are the real justification for weapon-building, we should remember the extent to which much industry now depends on development of new weapons. In other words, there are vested economic interests.

Yet, given the irrational, neo-religious, ideological conflicts of modern times, the potential flashpoints which pose the greatest threats to world peace are still areas where the control or supply of resources is at stake, which has undoubtedly been the genuine cause of many conflicts. Currently, in our state of dependence on fossil fuels, there are several in the Middle East. Previously they have been in parts of the world that could affect the flow of vital but far-flung raw materials.

This relation between politics and economics has a well-established history. As G. M. Trevelyan says in his *English Social History*:

'The Princes and Ministers of the Court of Charles II, as well as their critics in Parliament, were in close personal contact with the City magnates who conducted the great adventures of foreign commerce. The highest persons in the land held shares in the joint-stock companies trading in India, Africa and American waters. James, Duke of York, Lord High Admiral and heir to the throne, was Governor of the Royal Africa company and shareholder in East

Indian stock; he succeeded Prince Rupert as the Governor of the Hudson's Bay company and was in turn succeeded by Marlborough.

'In this way, the magnates who controlled English diplomatic, naval and military policy were in the closest possible touch with mercantile communities and shared its interests and outlook. The wars with Holland in the reign of Charles II and with France in the reigns of William and Anne, were to a large extent mercantile and Colonial wars, on the necessity and profit of which the Court, Parliament and City were agreed.'

Paradoxes

But at the same time as technology facilitates the development of giant instruments of extinction, it also aids the processes of improving the human condition. An obvious example of this paradox is the great advances in medical technology. As the weapons grow more sophisticated so do the techniques to repair shattered bodies. In the same way, other technologies can reverse the process of gobbling up resources and, properly applied, could even increase resources and extend their usefulness, revealing a contradiction to Malthus's pessimism, which would make warring over insufficient resources as obsolete as yesterday's nuclear warhead.

Like a pendulum, the extent to which we benefit from technology has swung back and forth as each new use has generated adverse side-effects. Agricultural technology helped to support larger populations; medical technology in the form of birth control and the reduction of infant mortality then helps to counteract the population explosion. Even newer agricultural technologies are now emerging to help feed those that are still underfed.

Engineering and transport technologies enable large groups to exist in huge impersonal communities, and encourage individuals to travel far from their families; communication technologies such as the telephone enable those same individuals to keep in touch over great distances. The proliferation of media enables cultural identity to be preserved in otherwise anonymous cities, yet simultaneously homogenises cultures.

New technologies constantly come into being to overcome the problems created by other technologies. Whole industries attempt to control industrial pollution, to ensure industrial safety and to alleviate some of the stresses created by the high-speed, high-technology life.

This constant battle with our own technologies, in effect with ourselves, is both fascinating and frightening. Our curiosity, inventiveness, and skill with technology have made us the remarkable, unique species that we are. Sadly, it sometimes seems that we understand the machines we make better than we understand ourselves. In the story of the Human Race so far at least, it appears that we are better at being technologically clever than we are at being socially clever.

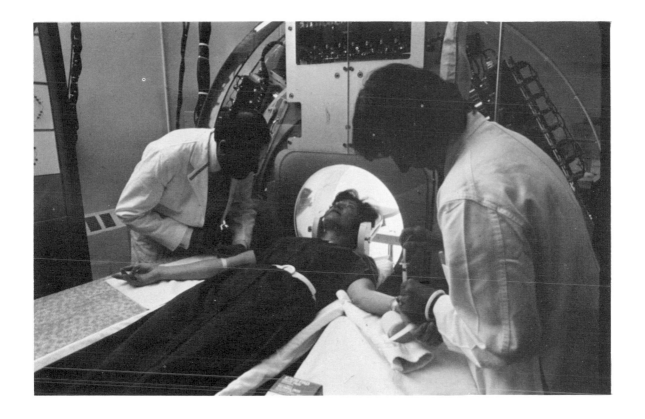

The brain scanner helps to save life.

Elsewhere, even more sophisticated technology is being developed to destroy it.

There can be no doubt that our future is uncertain. We may become the first species on earth consciously to bring about its own extinction, or we could become the super-species that colonises the universe. Trying to anticipate what the human future may be has become a full-time profession known as 'futurology'. Futurology has its institutes, its researchers, its publications and its predictions. It has become an industry.

As Joe Fisher says in his recent book *Predictions*:

'Although the practice of retaining professional predictors wasn't generally adopted until the early sixties, the largest of the futurist concerns, the California-based Rand Corporation, was founded after World War II. Next came the Hudson Institute – the world famous think-tank run by Herman Kahn – that was set up near New York in 1961. Once these installations were operating, professional forums were founded between 1965 and 1970 where futurists could meet and swap ideas. Among the most notable are the International Futuribles Association (Paris 1965), the World Future Society (Washington 1966) and the Club of Rome (1968).'

In Britain there is the highly-regarded Science Policy Research Unit (SPRU) at the University of Sussex. And, as Fisher observes: 'Today, few co-operative enterprises can afford not to employ or contract futurists to sit in the crows-nest and scan the horizons of their endeavours.'

The Human Race has mostly been concerned with what, and where possible why, we are the way we are. There is no doubt, however, that we are a species with a big and spectacular future whatever it may be. Not wanting to make speculations beyond our brief and competence, but wishing to look forward to some extent, we sought the views of three distinguished men who, each in their own way, have an interest in our future.

Sir Bernard Lovell

If one wants to engage in a major piece of scientific research, a major space activity, it is really not a question of whether the nation can afford it: it is a question of a vision, a question of the will of the people.

The most important purpose of space research is to investigate the universe. To help with the study of man's position in the solar system and in the universe. To study the origin of the evolution of the solar system, the evolution and origin of the entire universe.

The position today, alas, is that space has now become dominated not by these visionary scientific activities, but by military purposes, and to a lesser extent, by commercial enterprise. I think it's correct to say that well over 90 per cent of the rockets which have been used to launch the Soviet and American space vehicles have been military rockets, designed for military purposes. The sad feature in the development of space in the quarter of a century since the launch of the Sputnik is the very minor part occupied by the visionary enterprises.

Professor Sir Bernard Lovell retired in 1981 from his post as the Director of the Radio Astronomy Laboratories at Jodrell Bank, near Manchester. After graduating from the University of Bristol, he did distinguished work on cosmic rays and micro-waves, and subsequently built what was the world's largest steerable telescope when it came into operation in 1957. His research included investigation of radio emissions from the galaxy, and the observation of quasars. The author of numerous publications, Sir Bernard has been awarded honorary degrees by several universities in Britain and abroad, and is a member of dozens of national and inter-national scientific associations.

I think the scientific activities in space have enormous potential for human good. The Earth Resources Satellite which had become known as Landsat revealed the possibility of new areas of the Earth which could be cultivated, the possibility of getting the fish out of the sea without upsetting the balance, and of the problem of water supply. So all these problems are soluble. The question is not a scientific one; it is a political one of the distribution of these resources.

During recent years there has been much investigation of alternative energy resources – the waves, wind and particularly the Sun. The Sun, like all the stars, is an almost inexhaustible source of energy. The output of energy from the Sun has been at its present rate for about four thousand million years and, as far as we understand scientifically, it will continue at this rate for another four or five thousand million years. Therefore the energy available from the Sun is effectively inexhaustible, certainly as far as the prospects of the human race are concerned. The problem is how to get it in an available form. One is now getting used to solar collectors for heated swimming pools and so on. There are somewhat more major projects in the desert areas, but this is not a very promising possibility because of the distribution problems of providing power all over the earth. However, as far as space is concerned, the project which is receiving a good deal of attention nowadays is that put forward in America, whereby one builds enormous solar collectors in space, so that there is no problem with obscuration by cloud. You collect the energy in outer space and you beam it to earth with high-powered transmitters. The great advantage with this is that you can put your collecting device – aerial, so to speak – near the centre of the population, and therefore the distribution problems do not arise. Whether or not this will be done, again, depends on political decision and the will of the people. The estimates made for the development of this system of satellites are certainly very big, but in fact the development costs are no greater than those that had to be invested in the extraction of oil from the North Sea.

However, if you are going to provide, by the end of the century, the same amount of energy for 20 billion people as is enjoyed only by a few hundred millions today, then there is a danger, I think, of upsetting the heat balance of the atmosphere: that is the amount of energy being radiated from the Earth compared with the amount of energy being received from the Sun. It's an extremely delicate balance, as one can see when one considers what has happened to the planet Venus, which in many ways is similar to the Earth, but over the last few billion years it has had an evolution which is entirely different and has become extremely hostile. This is undoubtedly due to the fact that it is slightly closer to the Sun, and therefore slightly hotter. Therefore the heat balance is a matter of the greatest importance. This could be a very serious matter, which could lead to the prospect that serious attention might have to be given for the establishment of colonies in space if the human race is going to survive. Now, people always say this is impossible, but if we fly the Atlantic, we are living in a completely artificial environment, and the Soviets have built a city in the Arctic regions, which is a completely artificial environment. So there is no problem in principal about this. Again, it is a question of money.

But the costs involved in this are not completely out of the question if it is an international desire, a world-wide global desire to do these things. If this became a necessity, either because of the increase in the standard of living of the people, upsetting the balance of the Earth, or because of some nuclear disaster, all these things are technically possible. Whether they will be desirable or not is another matter.

I am an optimist because I think a reading of history indicates that we are by no means in a unique state. Throughout recorded history you will find tremendous contrasts between disasters to civilisation and advances which we now recognise to be of the very greatest intellectual importance. The great Persian empire, for example, of 600 to 500 BC is notorious for its greed, corruption and violent expansionism. But while all this was taking place, Pythagoras was living, discovering his famous theorems and propositions and mathematics in the musical scale. Again, in the thirteenth century there was tremendous conflict between science and theological dogma. Since the seventeenth century there has been a tremendous battle between, and largely a separation of, science and religion. It is only recently, I think, that the realisation is growing that neither of these activities has any ultimate validity.

If we want to understand the universe, to understand the relevance of ourselves and the universe, to understand human purpose, then it has to be a synthesis of these two types of knowledge, and this, I feel, is grounds for optimism. That the desire for knowledge will begin to override the kind of news which bewilders us today and fills the newspapers.

Sir Peter Medawar

It is logically impossible and self-contradictory to predict future ideas, and therefore future advances in science. What one has to ask, I think, is what things should we like to see taking place, because modern science and technology are such that everything that is possible in principle can be done, if the intention to do it is sufficiently resolute. Everything therefore starts with a good political decision. And then we do our best to put it into effect. What should we like to see happen in medicine? I have very clear ideas. We must extend to the world as a whole the kind of medical advantages that are enjoyed at present by the countries of

Europe and North America. Infectious disease is pretty well coped with in the Northern Hemisphere. Smallpox is out, so WHO tells us. Polio is on the way out. There are still a number of intractable virus diseases. But in the world as a whole, there are still a number of 'killing' infectious diseases which can and must be brought under control. There is malaria for example: still, I think, the major killing disease in the world. These must be brought under control.

I have not the least doubt that it will be possible to prolong the life of human beings. It can be done already in laboratory animals by comparatively simple means. This causes a good deal of alarm among politicians, because the feeling is that this is in effect exacerbating the population problem, and that we have problems enough already with the proportional ages in the population, without adding to them. This is a very short-sighted view, because all advances in medicine increase the expectation of life. We would not wish to deny medical treatment to the sick or otherwise infirm on the grounds that they are adding to the population problem. The important thing is to ameliorate the life of the aged. Many of the changes that occur in ageing are pathological, and are remediable, and should be remedied.

I think that, as our expectation in life increases, our assumption of youth increases also. The age in which we are meant to be middle-aged or old gets older and older and older. It becomes increasingly important to find means of ameliorating the disadvantages of being old and decrepit. I think this is where the great advances will take place.

As far as the transplant is concerned, the transplant days of lungs will certainly come. Possibly also pancreases, which would be the definitive solution to the problem of some forms of diabetes due to the failure of the production of insulin. But some organs are not physiologically transplantable. Some science writers are conjuring up ideas of transplants of brains. The transplantation of the brain is absolute bunk. It is not a consideration, and need not worry anybody for a moment. Nobody should be caused a moment's unease.

I do not see great advances in genetic engineering for human beings. I think for farm animals there might be important advances. But the benefits and the threats of genetic engineering are both greatly exaggerated in my opinion. We already have a system of genetic engineering applied to farm animals, known as artificial selection. This is by far the most powerful instrument there is for changing the character of animals. It is not applicable to human beings, clearly, unless we lived in a tyranny, in a dynasty of tyrants who ordered human beings to reproduce in ways they fancied to be salutary. You cannot have that with human beings.

Because of the advances in medicine, the control of death and, above all, the conquest of infectious disease, the population problem is now the greatest single menace affecting mankind. A lot of people realise this. A lot of people also do not realise that this state of affairs is not irremediable. The kind of technology and the kind of advances in science that give us this evil can also remove it. It is not wholly a scientific matter, it is a political and educational matter as well. But the population problem is slowly being remedied and I see no reason why it should not be overcome completely, in a matter of decades, not in a matter of centuries.

There are many things going for human beings, biologically speaking. One of them is the youth of our species. If you imagine the evolution of mankind having taken a year, it is only in the past ten or fifteen minutes that we have been able to say, 'We've made it, we aren't going under.' Many species merely disappear from the face of the earth, but ten or fifteen minutes ago in this human day, we could say, 'We're on the map', and the likelihood is that we are going to stay on the map.

I think it is grossly un-biological to suppose that human beings are going to destroy themselves. No instinct, no biological feeling, is more deep-seated than our preference for being alive as opposed to being dead. People with a shallow knowledge of biology talk sometimes about lemmings, because of the widespread illusion that lemmings control their numbers by plunging headlong over a cliff and drowning themselves. This, I believe, is one of the most comical popular fallacies of the day. Human beings are not like that. They will not plunge over any cliff and annihilate themselves.

I think it is essential to keep alive the hope of progress; indeed I will go further and say that to deride the hope of progress is the ultimate fatuity. It is the last word in poverty of spirit and meanness of mind, and, for human beings, self-defeating.

R. Buckminster Fuller

Buckminster Fuller, who coined the famous phrase 'Spaceship Earth', is a much-honoured man, born in 1895, who has spent more than fifty years playing his unique 'World Game'. This massive inventory of the Earth's resources and technologies is intended – as a deliberate opposite to a war game – to provide data enabling us to make the right decisions in order to survive successfully on our spaceship. Fifty years of tireless, painstaking, detailed and radical work cannot be properly expressed here. His fundamental point is that, since technology now enables us to do more and more with less and less materials, we no longer have a resources problem. He points out, for example, that there are enough metals and minerals above the ground to meet all the world's needs if they are recycled fully. Miniaturisation and sophistication can accomplish this. A transatlantic telephone call now uses only 175 pounds (80 kilograms) of copper in a satellite instead of dozens of tons in a cable. Although he refuses to call himself either an optimist or a pessimist, this extract from what he told us is revealing.

Buckminster Fuller. One of his famous geodesic domes is in the background.

I was born more than ignorant. I was born, in 1895, into an incredible amount of mis-information. When I was seven, the Wright brothers flew in an aeroplane. I had been told by grown-ups that it was inherently impossible to fly. I was told that we would never get to the North Pole, that we would never get to the South Pole. When I was fourteen, we got to the North Pole; when I was sixteen we got to the South Pole. When I was twelve a steamship sent an SOS on the radio, it was a wireless – you could not see it – but it was terribly important. Historically, up to this time, Dad and Mom were the authorities to every child. Dad and Mom would tell you what you are going to eat, what the system would let you get away with. Dad covers a little more territory than Mom, because she is carrying the baby and he is the hunter. As well as being the authority in the house and telling you what to do, Dad brings home the news as well. Dad's language is not very inventive, maybe it is even atrocious, but the kids copy it.

Suddenly we have this invisible world of the wireless, the radio is on at home. In 1927, all the Daddies were coming home one afternoon and the kids said, 'Daddy, come listen to the radio. A man is flying the Atlantic.' And Daddy never brought home the news again. This was a very extraordinary change. People would cross the streets and tell each other what the radio man said; and the way the people got their jobs on the radio was by virtue of the size of their vocabulary and their ability in using it. The kids immediately copied the language pattern of the radio. It completely changed language. When I was young, all the people I worked with were beautiful craftsmen and so forth but their vocabulary was about a hundred and fifty words, half of them blasphemous or obscene. Today, all around the world, I find people have beautiful vocabularies.

Television opened up a completely new range of human communication. In the 'sixties, the students who led the dissent at the University of California at Berkeley asked me to come and meet with them. I found that they were mostly born in the year that television came into the American home. And they said to me, 'We love Dad and Mom to pieces, and Dad and Mom love us to pieces, but they don't know what is going on.' They come home from the shoe store and the television makes it perfectly clear that the world is in trouble; the problems are for everybody around the world and not just for the local neighbours anymore. Dad and Mom have little to do with whether we are going to Vietnam or the Moon, or anything else. We have to do our own thinking – the world is in trouble.

Today, each successive child is being born into the presence of an ever larger inventory of viable information. I get letters from ten-year-olds saying that if humanity can do anything it needs to do, why don't we make this world work? And I find that this young world is not mis-informed. It is well informed, reliably informed, and is very liable to take over and make things work.

The discussion of our species' future will continue as long as we continue to have one. Humans alone, as far as we know, can discuss their own future. We should never forget, however, our long past, and the inheritance of that past which defines our present, uniquely human, nature.

In the past, we have all too often been dominated by fixed beliefs, by rigidly held faiths that supposed outside forces operating to control our human destinies. For thousands of years we were subject to the wrath of an angry god, to the dark forces of sinister spirits.

When things went wrong, we were able to blame these outside forces – to pass the buck. It was a comforting naïvety, despite all the terrors and fears it spanned in our earlier, more superstitious days. Now at last we are coming to recognise that most of our problems are self-created, a fall-out from the activity of our intensely curious and inquisitive brain.

We have to face the simple fact that we alone are our own masters, that we alone are in control of our own destiny, that we can have anything we wish, and can take any direction we like. The human race is an exploring race. It is given a fresh impetus every time a child is born, with its new young brain buzzing with the excitement of being alive, in due course to bring fresh and often rebellious ideas to bear on its culture.

In concluding this book, we too tend to be optimistic, not only because of much of the evidence included in this book, but also because we believe that it is inherent in human nature to strive for that which is better. In a crowded world, where not everyone strives for the same objectives, there are evidently built-in dangers. But only the madmen *dream* of disaster, have *fantasies* of destruction. The ultimate human uniqueness lies in the sublime ability to con-

The human thirsts for achievement remain unquenchable despite the most devastating physical disabilities. Only highly sophisticated modern techniques enable Dick Boydell of Milton Keynes, who suffers from cerebral palsy, to realise some of the potential of his high, but previously imprisoned, intelligence. If we use our technological potential in ways which liberate the human spirit and embody our unique compassion for each other, then the future of the Human Race should be even more rewarding.

template abstract ideas, to construct models of our own destiny. As the world grows more crowded, so it enables us to share more with each other. Arts, music, moral systems and strategies for personal happiness often developed in isolation from one another. They are now part of an internationally appreciated human culture. The beauties of oriental art or the opportunities of Eastern meditation, for example, are taking their place in the culture of the West. Books, films, and television programmes now spread human dreams, fears and ideas all over the world. It becomes increasingly difficult to contemplate isolated, selfish futures.

Because we can imagine something better, we can achieve something better.

Illustration Credits

t top   b bottom   r right   l left   m middle

Significant events in the story of the Human Race

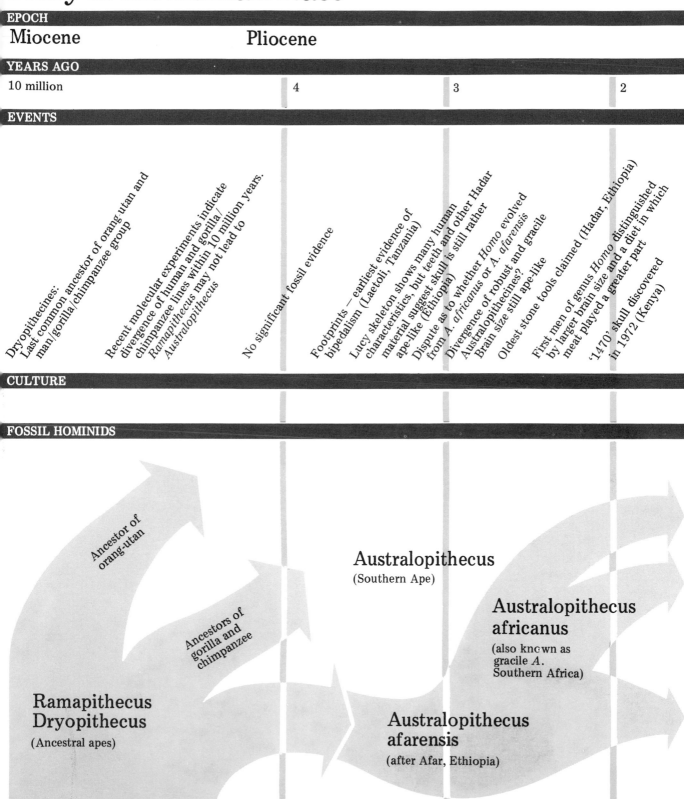

EPOCH			
Miocene	Pliocene		

YEARS AGO			
10 million	4	3	2

EVENTS

Dryopithecines:
Last common ancestor of orang-utan and man/gorilla/chimpanzee group

Recent molecular experiments indicate divergence of human and gorilla/chimpanzee lines within 10 million years. *Ramapithecus* may not lead to *Australopithecus*

No significant fossil evidence

Footprints — earliest evidence of bipedalism (Laetoli, Tanzania)

Lucy skeleton shows many human characteristics, but teeth and other Hadar material suggest skull is still rather ape-like (Ethiopia)

Dispute as to whether *Homo* evolved from *A. africanus* or *A. afarensis*

Divergence of robust and gracile Australopithecines? Brain size still ape-like

Oldest stone tools claimed (Hadar, Ethiopia)

First men of genus *Homo* distinguished by larger brain size and a diet in which meat played a greater part

'1470' skull discovered in 1972 (Kenya)

CULTURE

FOSSIL HOMINIDS

Ancestor of orang-utan

Ancestors of gorilla and chimpanzee

Ramapithecus Dryopithecus
(Ancestral apes)

Australopithecus
(Southern Ape)

Australopithecus africanus
(also known as gracile *A*. Southern Africa)

Australopithecus afarensis
(after Afar, Ethiopia)

EPOCH

Pleistocene

Lower   Middle   Upper

YEARS AGO

| 1.5 | 1 | 500,000 | 200,000 | 100,000 |

EVENTS

Wind-breaks or huts in Olduvai Gorge (Tanzania)

'3733' skull: oldest H. erectus (Kenya)

Human brain nearly modern size

Increasing development of hunting behaviour

Oldest fire claimed: evidence of hearth (Kenya)

H. erectus skulls (Olduvai, Tanzania)

Hand-axe industries in Africa

Typical Java man (H. erectus)

Ice ages become more intense in high latitudes

Heidelberg man: oldest human fossil in Europe

First good evidence of fire in Europe and Asia

Problems in classifying fossils as erectus or sapiens

Hand-axes found in Hoxne (England)

Production of groups of tools in Europe

Oldest hut structures in Europe

Oldest known Briton (Swanscombe)

Uncertain whether Neanderthals evolved into Homo sapiens sapiens or became evolutionary dead end

Rhodesian Man: First evidence of modern brain size

CULTURE

Lower Paleolithic   i.e. lower old Stone Age

FOSSIL HOMINIDS

Australopithecus boisei

(after Charles Boise who funded research)

Australopithecus robustus

(heavier, more robust)

Late *Homo erectus* (Africa)

Homo sapiens

(Thinking Man)

First fossils in Europe

Homo erectus

(Upright Man)

Early *Homo erectus* (East Africa and Java)

Late *Homo erectus* (China)

Late *Homo erectus* (Java)

Homo habilis

(Handy Man)

Recent

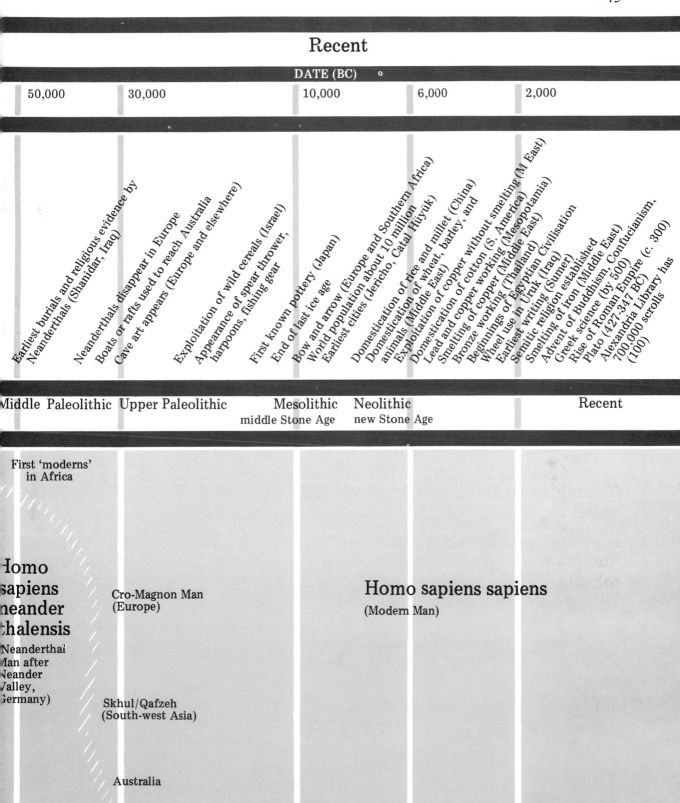

DATE (BC)

50,000	30,000	10,000	6,000	2,000

Earliest burials and religious evidence by Neanderthals (Shanidar, Iraq)

Neanderthals disappear in Europe

Boats or rafts used to reach Australia

Cave art appears (Europe and elsewhere)

Exploitation of wild cereals (Israel)

Appearance of spear thrower, harpoons, fishing gear

First known pottery (Japan)

End of last ice age

Bow and arrow (Europe and Southern Africa)

World population about 10 million

Earliest cities (Jericho, Çatal Hüyük)

Domestication of rice and millet (China)

Domestication of wheat, barley, and animals (Middle East)

Exploitation of copper without smelting (M East)

Domestication of cotton (S. America)

Lead and copper working (Middle East)

Smelting of copper (Thailand)

Bronze working (Mesopotamia)

Beginnings of Egyptian Civilisation

Wheel use in Uruk (Iraq)

Earliest writing (Sumer)

Semitic religion established

Smelting of iron (Middle East)

Advent of Buddhism, Confucianism, Greek science (by 500)

Rise of Roman Empire (c. 300)

Plato (427-347 BC)

Alexandria Library has 700,000 scrolls (100)

Middle Paleolithic	Upper Paleolithic	Mesolithic middle Stone Age	Neolithic new Stone Age	Recent

First 'moderns' in Africa

Homo sapiens neander thalensis

(Neanderthal Man after Neander Valley, Germany)

Cro-Magnon Man (Europe)

Homo sapiens sapiens

(Modern Man)

Skhul/Qafzeh (South-west Asia)

Australia

Thanks to Dr Christopher Stringer of the British Museum (Natural History) for his contributions to this chart

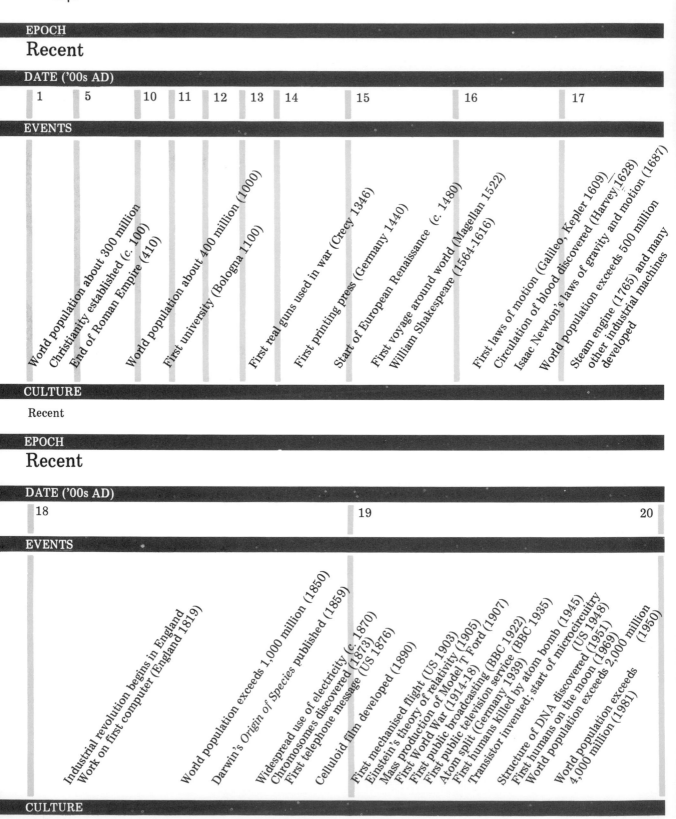

EPOCH

Recent

DATE ('00s AD)

1   5   10   11   12   13   14   15   16   17

EVENTS

World population about 300 million
Christianity established (c. 100)
End of Roman Empire (410)
World population about 400 million (1000)
First university (Bologna 1100)
First real guns used in war (Crecy 1346)
First printing press (Germany 1440)
Start of European Renaissance (c. 1480)
First voyage around world (Magellan 1522)
William Shakespeare (1564-1616)
First laws of motion (Galileo, Kepler 1609)
Circulation of blood discovered (Harvey 1628)
Isaac Newton's laws of gravity and motion (1687)
World population exceeds 500 million
Steam engine (1765) and many other industrial machines developed

CULTURE

Recent

EPOCH

Recent

DATE ('00s AD)

18   19   20

EVENTS

Industrial revolution begins in England
Work on first computer (England 1819)
World population exceeds 1,000 million (1850)
Darwin's *Origin of Species* published (1859)
Widespread use of electricity (c. 1870)
Chromosomes discovered (1873)
First telephone message (US 1876)
Celluloid film developed (1890)
First mechanised flight (US 1903)
Einstein's theory of relativity (1905)
Mass production of Model T Ford (1907)
First World War (1914-18)
First public broadcasting (BBC 1922)
First public television service (BBC 1935)
Atom split (Germany 1939)
First humans killed by atom bomb (1945)
Transistor invented; start of microcircuitry (US 1948)
Structure of DNA discovered (1951)
First humans on the moon (1969)
World population exceeds 2,000 million (1950)
World population exceeds 4,000 million (1981)

CULTURE

Recent

Bibliography and Further Reading

General

CROOK, J. H. *The Evolution of Human Consciousness*. Clarendon Press, Oxford, 1980.

DAWKINS, R. *The Selfish Gene*. Oxford University Press, 1971.

ECCLES, J. *The Human Mystery*. Springer, New York, 1979.

EIBESFELDT, I. E. *Ethology*. Holt, Rinehart and Winston, New York, 1970.

FARB, P. *Humankind*. Jonathan Cape, London, 1978.

GEERTZ, C. *The Interpretation of Cultures*. Basic Books, New York, 1973.

HARRIS, M. *Culture, People, Nature*. Crowell, New York, 1975.

—— *Cows, Pigs, Wars and Witches*. Random House, New York, 1974.

—— *The Riddles of Culture*. Random House, New York, 1974.

JOLLY, A. *The Evolution of Primate Behaviour*. Macmillan, London, 1972.

MORRIS, D. *The Naked Ape*. Jonathan Cape, London, 1967.

—— *Manwatching*. Jonathan Cape, London, 1977.

PFEIFFER, J. *The Emergence of Man*. Harper and Row, New York, 1978.

—— *The Emergence of Society*. McGraw-Hill, New York, 1977.

PILBEAM, D. *The Ascent of Man*. Macmillan, London, 1972.

THOMAS, H. *Unfinished History of the World*. Hamish Hamilton, London, 1980; Pan, 1981.

WILSON, E. O. *On Human Nature*. Harvard University Press, 1978.

Spectacular inhabitants (*clothing, buildings and settlements*)

BUZAN, T. and DIXON, T. *The Evolving Brain*. David and Charles, Newton Abbot, 1977.

DULY, C. *The Houses of Mankind*. Thames and Hudson, London, 1979.

HALL, P. *The World Cities*. Weidenfeld and Nicolson, London, 1977.

HAMBLIN, D. J. *The First Cities*. Time-Life, Amsterdam, 1979.

KUEN, G. *Views of Los Angeles*. Portiga Publishing, Los Angeles, 1978.

LAVER, J. *A Concise History of Costume*. Thames and Hudson, London, 1969.

LYNCH, K. *The Image of the City*. MIT Press, Cambridge, Mass., 1979.

MORRIS, D. *The Human Zoo*. Jonathan Cape, London, 1969.

NANCE, J. *The Gentle Tasaday*. Harcourt Brace Jovanovich, New York, 1977.

RUDOFSKY, B. *The Unfashionable Human Body*. Doubleday, New York, 1974.

WOODBRIDGE, S. (ed.) *Bay Area Houses*. Oxford University Press, New York, 1976.

Masked hunters (*sport and work*)

ARGYLE, M. *Social Psychology of Work*. Penguin Books, London, 1974.

ATTEO, D. *Blood and Guts: Violence in Sports*. Paddington Press, London, 1979.

BENEDICT, R. *The Chrysanthemum and the Sword*. Routledge and Kegan Paul, London, 1967.

COLE, R. E. *Japanese Blue Collar: The Changing Tradition*. University of California Press, 1973.

COON, C. S. *The Hunting Peoples*. Jonathan Cape, London, 1972.

DOUGLAS, M. and ISHERWOOD, B. *World of Goods*. Allen Lane, London, 1979.

DOWNES, D. M., DAVIES, B. P., DAVIES, M. E. and STONE, P. *Gambling, Work & Leisure*. Routledge and Kegan Paul, London, 1976.

FOX, A. *Sociology of Work and Industry*. Cassell Collier Macmillan, London, 1971.

FOX, R. and TIGER, L. *Imperial Animal*. Secker and Warburg, London, 1972.

FREEMAN, C. *The Economics of Industrial Innovation*. Nichols, New York, 1974.

HAYES, J. and NUTMAN, P. *Understanding the Unemployed*. Tavistock Publications, London, 1981.

HELVOORT, E. V. *The Japanese Working Man*. Norbury Publications, 1979.

JENKINS, C. and SHERMAN, B. *The Collapse of Work*. Eyre Methuen, London, 1979.

JOLLY, A., SYLVA, K. and BRUNER, J. S. (eds.) *Play*. Penguin Books, London, 1978.

LOY, B. *Sport and Social Order*. Addison-Wesley, New York, 1975.

NAKANE, C. *The Japanese Society*. Weidenfeld and Nicolson, London, 1970.

UDY, S. H. Jnr *Organisation of Work*. Hraf Press, New Haven, 1959.

VOGEL, E. F. *Japan as Number 1*. Harvard University Press, 1979.

WALLMAN, S. (ed.) *Social Anthropology of Work*. Academic Press, London, 1979.

WEBER, M. *The Protestant Ethic and the Spirit of Capitalism*. George Allen and Unwin, London, 1977.

WEIR, M. *Job Satisfaction*. Fontana, London, 1976.

Golden tongues (language and humour)

AITCHISON, J. *The Articulate Mammal*. McGraw-Hill, New York, 1978.

ARGYLE, M. and TROWER, P. *Person to Person*. Harper and Row, New York, 1979.

BATES, E. *et al. The Emergence of Symbols*. Academic Press, New York, 1979.

BLOCH, M. *Political Language and Oratory in Traditional Society*. Academic Press, London, 1975.

CHOMSKY, N. *Language and Responsibility*. Harvester Press, Hassocks, Sussex, 1979.

COWARD, R. and ELLIS, J. *Language and Materialism*. Routledge and Kegan Paul, London, 1977.

DEICH, R. F. and HODGES, P. M. *Language Without Speech*. Souvenir Press, London, 1977.

DESMOND, A. *The Ape's Reflexion*. Blond and Briggs, London, 1979.

DE VILLERS, P. A. *Early Language*. Fontana/Open Books, London, 1979.

DILLARD, J. L. *Black English*. Vintage Books (Random House), New York, 1972.

DOUGLAS, M. *Implicit Meanings*. Routledge and Kegan Paul, London, 1975.

EKMAN, P. *The Face of Man.* Garland STPM Press, New York.

FARB, P. *Word Play.* Jonathan Cape, London, 1976; Coronet, London, 1977.

FRIEDRICH, H. (ed.) *Man and Animal.* Granada, London, 1972.

FROMKIN, V. and ROODMAN, R. *An Introduction to Language.* Holt, Rinehart and Winston, New York, 1978.

GOODY, J. *The Domestication of the Savage Mind.* Cambridge University Press, 1977.

GUMPERZ, J. J. *Anthropology 4, Vols. 1, 2.* ASUC Copy Centre.

HALL, E. T. *The Silent Language.* Anchor Books, 1973.

HARNAD, S. R. (ed.) 'Origins and Evolution of Language and Speech'. *Annals of the New York Academy of Sciences,* Vol. 280, 1976.

HENLEY, N. M. *Body Politics.* Prentice Hall, Englewood Cliffs, 1977.

HINDE, R. A. (ed.) *Non-verbal Communication.* Cambridge University Press, 1972.

KLIMA, E. and BELLUGI, U. *The Signs of Language.* Harvard University Press, 1979.

LABOR, W. *Language in the Inner City: Studies in the Black English Vernacular.* University of Pennsylvania Press, 1928.

LEWIS, D. *The Secret Language of your Child.* Souvenir Press, London, 1978.

LOCK, A. (ed.) *Action, Gesture and Symbol: the Emergence of Language.* Academic Press, London, 1978.

MCGHEE, P. E. *Humour: Its Origin and Development.* W. H. Freeman, San Francisco, 1979.

MCINTYRE, J. (ed.) *Mind in the Waters.* Charles Scribner's Sons, New York, 1974.

MONTAGU, A. and MATSON, F. *The Human Connection.* McGraw-Hill, New York, 1979.

MORRIS, D. *et al. Gestures.* Jonathan Cape, London, 1979.

ROBINSON, W. P. *Language and Social Behaviour.* Penguin Books, London, 1972.

RUMBAUGH, D. M. *Language Learning by a Chimpanzee.* Academic Press, New York, 1977.

SLOBIN, D. I. *Psycholinguistics.* Scott, Foresman and Company, Glenview, Ill., 1979.

SMITHERMAN, G. *Talkin' and Testifyin': the Language of Black America.* Houghton Mifflin, New York, 1972.

TERRACE, H. S. *Nim: A Chimpanzee Who Learned Sign Language.* Eyre Methuen, London, 1979.

WHITEHURST, G. J. and ZIMMERMAN, B. J. (eds.) *The Functions of Language and Cognition.* Academic Press, London, 1979.

WHITING, J. W. M. *Children of Six Cultures.* Harvard University Press, 1977.

Passionate survivors *(sexuality and aggression)*

ALTNER, G. (ed.) *The Nature of Human Behaviour.* George Allen and Unwin, London, 1976.

ARDREY, R. *The Hunting Hypothesis.* Atheneum, New York, 1976.

AYISI, E. O. *An Introduction to the Study of African Culture.* Heinemann, London, 1979.

BASION, W. and HERSKOVITS, M. (eds.) *Continuity and Change in African Cultures.* University of Chicago Press, 1959.

BOWLBY, J. *Attachment Vol. 1.* Basic Books, New York, 1980.

BRIGGS, D. *In Place of Prison.* Maurice Temple Smith, London, 1975.

CHAGNON, N. A. *Yanamamö, the Fierce People.* Holt, Rinehart and Winston, New York, 1968.

CHALMERS, N. *Social Behaviour in Primates.* Edward Arnold, London, 1979.

COHEN, A. K. *Deviance and Control.* Prentice Hall, Englewood Cliffs, 1966.

COHEN, S. *Folk Devils and Moral Panics.* MacGibbon and Kee, London, 1972.

COOK, J. M. *In Defence of Homo sapiens.* Dell Publishing Company, New York, 1976.

EIBESFELDT, I. E. *The Biology of Peace and War.* Thames and Hudson, London, 1979.

ELLUL, J. *The New Demons.* Seabury Press, New York, 1975.

FOX, R. *Kinship and Marriage.* Penguin Books, London, 1977.

HALL, S. and JEFFERSON, T. (eds.) *Resistance through Ritual.* Hutchinson University Library, London, 1976.

HOCKETT, C. F. *Man's Place in Nature.* McGraw-Hill, New York, 1973.

KEEGAN, J. and DARRACOTT, J. *The Nature of War.* Jonathan Cape, London, 1981.

KEISER, R. L. *The Vice Lords, Warriors of the Streets.* Holt Rinehart and Winston, New York, 1969.

KOCH, K. F. *War and Peace in Jalémó.* Harvard University Press, 1974.

MAIR, L. *African Societies.* Cambridge University Press, 1976.

MARSH, P., ROSSER, E., and HARRE, R. *Rules of Disorder.* Routledge and Kegan Paul, London, 1978.

MEGGITT, M. *Blood is their argument.* Mayfield Publishing Company, Paolo Alto, 1977.

MORRIS, D. *Patterns of Reproductive Behaviour.* Granada, London, 1972.
—— *Intimate Behaviour.* Jonathan Cape, London, 1971.

OFFERBEIN, K. F. *The Evolution of War.* Hraf Press, New Haven, 1970.

ROBERTS, S. *Order and Dispute.* Penguin Books, London, 1979.

ROBINS, P. and COHEN, P. *Knuckle Sandwich.* Penguin Books, London, 1978.

SKINNER, E. P. (ed.) *Peoples and Cultures of Africa.* Doubleday/Natural History Press, New York, 1973.

SPENCER, P. *The Samburu.* Routledge and Kegan Paul, London, 1965.

TAYLOR, J. V. *The Primal Vision.* SCM Press, London, 1963.

TURNBULL, C. M. *Man in Africa.* David and Charles, Newton Abbot, 1976.

WAITLEY, D. *The War Makers.* Robert B. Luce, London, 1971.

WARD, C. *Violence: its Nature, Causes and Remedies.* Penguin Books, London, 1978.

Defiant optimists *(religion and art)*

ALLAND, A. *The Artistic Animal: An Inquiry into the Biological Roots of Art.* Doubleday, New York, 1977.

ALLEGRO, J. *The Sacred Mushroom in the Cross.* Hodder and Stoughton, London, 1970.

ARNHEIM, R. *Art & Visual Perception*. University of California Press, 1974.

CATLIN, G. *North American Indians*. Dover Publications, New York, 1973.

CAWLEY, A. C. (ed.) *Everyman and Medieval Miracle Plays*. Dent, London, 1956.

COVARRUBIAS, M. *Island of Bali*. New York, 1956.

FIRTH, R. *Elements of Social Organisation*. Tavistock Publications, London, 1971.

GEERTZ, C. *The Interpretation of Cultures*. Basic Books, New York, 1973.

GLOCK, C. Y. and BELLAH, R. N. (eds.) *The New Religious Consciousness*. University of California Press, 1976.

GOMBRICH, E. H. *The Story of Art*. Phaidon, Oxford, 1978.

—— *The Sense of Order*. Phaidon, Oxford, 1979.

JUNG, C. G. (ed.) *Man and his Symbols*. Aldus/Jupiter Books, London, 1964.

KELLOGG, R. *Analysing Children's Art*. National Press Books, 1969.

LANCASTER, J. B. *Primate Behaviour and the Emergence of Human Culture*. Holt, Rinehart and Winston, New York, 1975.

LEHNER, E. *Symbols, Signs and Signets*. Dover Pictorial Archives, New York, 1950.

LLOYD, C. *A Picture History of Art: Western Art Through the Ages*. Phaidon, Oxford, 1979.

MARSHACK, A. *The Roots of Civilization*. McGraw-Hill, New York, 1972.

—— *Ice Age Art*. California Academy of Sciences, San Francisco, 1979.

MAY, R. *Power and Innocence*. Souvenir Press, London, 1974.

MAZONOWICZ, D. *Voices from the Stone Age*. George Allen and Unwin, London, 1975.

MORRIS, D. *The Biology of Art*. Methuen, London, 1962.

NEEDLEMAN, J. and BAKER, G. (eds.) *Understanding the New Religions*. Seabury Press, New York, 1978.

OAKLEY, K. P. *Man the tool-maker*. Trustees of the British Museum, London, 1972.

OTTEN, C. (ed.). *Anthropology of Art*. American Source Books in Anthropology.

POPPER, K. R. and ECCLES, J. C. *The Self and its Brain*. Springer International, New York, 1977.

PFEIFFER, J. E. *The Emergence of Man* (rev. ed.). Harper and Row, New York, 1972.

—— *The Emergence of Society*. McGraw-Hill, New York, 1977.

RAMSEYER, U. *The Art and Culture of Bali*. Oxford University Press, 1977.

SIEVEKING, A. *The Cave Artists*. Thames and Hudson, London, 1979.

STEINBAUER, F. *Melanesian Cargo Cults*. George Prior, London, 1979.

SWELLENGREBEL, J. L. *et al*. *Bali, Studies in Life, Thought and Ritual*, The Hague and Bandung, 1960.

TURNBULL, C. *The Forest People*. Pan, London, 1976.

Curious giants (*technology and the future*)

BERRY, A. *The Next Ten Thousand Years*. Jonathan Cape, London, 1974.

BETÉILLE, A. (ed.) *Social Inequality*. Penguin Books, London, 1969.

DUNN, P. D. *Appropriate Technology*. Macmillan Press, London, 1978.

FISHER, J. *Predictions*. Sidgwick and Jackson, London, 1981.

FULLER, B. F. *Critical Path*. St Martins Press, New York, 1980.

GEORGE, S. *How the Other Half Dies* (revised ed.) Penguin Books, London, 1977.

GRIBBEN, J. *Future Worlds*. Abacus, London, 1979.

HARRISON, P. *Inside the Third World*. Penguin Books, London, 1979.

—— *The Third World Tomorrow*. Penguin Books, London, 1980.

HATCH, A. *Buckminster Fuller*. Crown Publishers, New York, 1974.

HEINE, C. *Micronesia at the Crossroads*. The University Press of Hawaii, 1974.

HODA, M. M. (ed.) *Proposal for Development of Appropriate Technology in India*. Appropriate Technology Development Association, Lucknow, 1980.

KLEMM, F. *A History of Western Technology*. George Allen and Unwin, London, 1959.

LAPPÉ, F. M. and COLLINS, J. *Food First: Beyond the Myth of Scarcity*. Ballantine, New York, 1979.

—— *World Hunger – Ten Myths*. Institute for Food and Development Policy, San Francisco, 1979.

LOVELL, B. *In the Centre of Immensities*. Hutchinson, London, 1979.

MCGRAW, E. *Population Today*. Kaye and Ward, London, 1979.

MCHENRY, D. F. *Micronesia: Trust Betrayed*. Carnegie Endowment for International Peace, Washington, 1975.

MADDIN, R., MUHLY, J. D. and WHEELER, T. S. *How the Iron Age Began*. Scientific American, New York, 1977.

MEDAWAR, J. S. and P. B. *The Life Science*. Wildwood House, London, 1979.

MURDOCH, W. W. *The Poverty of Nations*. Johns Hopkins University Press, 1980.

NAKANE, C. *Japanese Society* (revised ed.). Penguin Books, London, 1973.

NEVIN, D. *The American Touch in Micronesia*. W. W. Norton, New York, 1977.

PFEIFFER, J. *The Emergence of Man*. Harper and Row, New York, 1972.

—— *The Emergence of Society*. McGraw-Hill, New York, 1977.

PILBEAM, D. *The Ascent of Man*. Collier MacMillan, New York, 1972.

PYKE, M. *Man and Food*. World University Library, London, 1970.

SASSIN, W. *Energy*. Scientific American, New York, 1980.

SAHLINS, M. *The Use and Abuse of Biology*. Tavistock Publications, London, 1977.

TIGER, L. *Optimism: The Biology of Hope*. Secker and Warburg, London, 1979.

TUDGE, C. *The Famine Business*. Pelican Books, London, 1979.

THRING, M. *Machines – Masters or Slaves of Man*. Peter Peregrinus, Stevenage, 1973.

—— *The Engineer's Conscience*. Northgate Publishing, London, 1980.

UNITED NATIONS. *The State of World Population*. Report from the United Nations Fund for Population Activities, 1981.

WARD, B. *Progress for a Small Planet*. W. W. Norton, New York, 1979.

YOUNG, J. Z. *Introduction to the Study of Man*. Oxford University Press, 1971.

—— *Programs of the Brain*. Oxford University Press, 1978.

Index

Italic numbers refer to illustrations and captions